Networking the Desktop

NetWare®

Networking the Desktop

NetWare®

Deni Connor
Mark Anderson

AP PROFESSIONAL
Boston San Diego New York
London Sydney Tokyo Toronto

AP PROFESSIONAL
An Imprint of ACADEMIC PRESS, INC.
A Division of HARCOURT BRACE & COMPANY

ORDERS (USA and Canada): 1-800-3131-APP or APP@ACAD.COM
AP Professional Orders: 6277 Sea Harbor Dr., Orlando, FL 32821-9816

Europe/Middle East/Africa: 0-11-44 (0) 181-300-3322
Orders: AP Professional, 24–28 Oval Rd., London NW1 7DX

Japan/Korea: 03-3234-3911-5
Orders: Harcourt Brace Japan, Inc., Ichibancho Central Building 22-1, Ichibancho Chiyoda-ku, Tokyo 102

Australia: 02-517-8999
Orders: Harcourt Brace & Co. Australia, Locked Bag 16, Marrickville, NSW 2204, Australia

Other International: (407) 345-3800
AP Professional Orders: 6277 Sea Harbor Dr., Orlando, FL 32821-9816

Editorial: 1300 Boylston St., Chestnut Hill, MA 02167; (617) 232-0500

Web: http://www.apnet.com/

This book is printed on acid-free paper. ∞

United Kingdom Edition published by
ACADEMIC PRESS LIMITED
24–28 Oval Road, London NW1 7DX

Library of Congress Cataloging-in-Publication Data
Connor, Deni.
Networking the desktop : NetWare / Deni Connor, Mark Anderson.
p. cm.
Includes index.
ISBN 0-12-185866-9
1. Local area networks (Computer networks)--Computer programs.
2. NetWare (Computer file) I. Anderson, Mark, 1956– .
TK5105.7.C6758 1996
005.7'136--dc20 96-13743
CIP

Printed in the United States of America
96 97 98 99 CP 9 8 7 6 5 4 3 2 1

CONTENTS

II Connecting to Other Environments

III Troubleshooting

Appendices

INTRODUCTION

Consider your predicament. Novell has said that there will be a billion nodes of NetWare installed by the year 2000, ten times the number of nodes installed today. It may be an optimistic forecast, but it does signify growth—lots of growth. And you and your peers are the ones that will make it happen.

While many of the nodes you'll be installing will be DOS nodes using the Windows environment or, as the year progresses, Windows 95 or NT Workstation nodes, a lot of nodes you'll work with also will use OS/2 or UNIX. We haven't even considered the Macintoshes in the group or talked about letting those nodes communicate with a mainframe, midrange computer or the Internet. What about making TCP/IP connections? Have you brushed up on your IP addressing skills?

That's what this book is about—making connections. We know that you'll be faced with making the connections to other environments and working with other operating systems. We won't explain the inner workings of those operating systems to you (we'll leave that to the operating system documentation), but we will tell you, once you have the OS installed, how to connect the workstation to the network and keep it working.

When we're finished, we'll touch on some of the skills you'll need to make sure those connections are operating correctly, and we'll let you know some troubleshooting tips we've gained from our experience.

How This Book Is Organized

This book is organized in three sections: Configuring Operating Systems, Connecting to Other Environments, and Troubleshooting.

Configuring Operating Systems covers the intricacies of making connections from DOS, Windows, Windows 95, OS/2, Windows for Workgroups, Personal NetWare, and Windows NT to the network. We have also included a chapter on diskless workstations, if you have any of them in your midst.

Connecting to Other Environments includes chapters on the primary connections you'll be making to other networks—IBM mainframe or midrange computer networks, Macintoshes, and TCP/IP-based networks and the Internet. In these chapters you'll find concise tips for communicating in these environments, including information that is often buried deep within IBM documentation and Requests for Comments (RFCs).

Troubleshooting consists of a chapter that gives you a background in snooping out the cause of network problems when they occur, including cabling and communication problems. We've included a chapter of some of the invaluable utilities you can use when such problems occur.

If during reading this book, you have questions, please contact us. We'll be there to help. Send an e-mail to 74227.524@compuserve.com.

Making connections is the name of this game—you're the key player. So here we go.

Deni Connor
Mark Anderson
March 1996

Acknowledgments

From Mark Anderson: This work is dedicated to Belinda, to my sister Patricia, and to my grandmother Virginia for their help and support in writing this book. Also to my son Kevin, who made it a requirement. In addition, I would like to thank Compaq IPG for giving me the education and encouragement I needed to complete the book.

From Deni Connor: To Kathy Mills for keeping me sane at work; to Dena Bockelman for her assistance; to Mike Williams for his patience; and to my husband Terry forever.

About the Authors

Mark Anderson is a systems test engineer for Compaq, a manufacturer of computers, network interface devices, and software. He is a Master CNE and a Microsoft Certified Systems Engineer. Anderson is the co-author of *LAN Survival: A Guerrilla Guide to NetWare* and *Networking the Desktop: Cabling, Configuration, and Communications* by AP PROFESSIONAL. He has written for *NetWare Solutions, LAN Times,* and *LAN Magazine.*

Deni Connor is the editor of *NetWare Solutions* magazine and the director of multimedia services for New Media Productions. Connor is the co-author of the CD HELPdesk Series: Novell Products, published by Charles River Media. She is the co-author of IDG's *NetWare for Dummies,* AP PROFESSIONAL's *LAN Survival: A Guerrilla Guide to NetWare,* and *Networking the Desktop: Cabling, Configuration, and Communications.* Deni is a former *LAN Times* technical editor and has written for *Datamation, PC Today, PC Novice, ComputerWorld,* and *LAN Times.*

part

I

Configuring Operating Systems

In spite of what Microsoft says about Windows 95, you'll still be attaching DOS, DOS with Windows, and OS/2 workstations onto your network long into the future. While you may master installing one operating system, as networks become more heterogeneous and more users are empowered, you'll certainly be faced with installing an operating system you aren't familiar with.

This section details making connections with the existing PC operating systems. We'll discuss Macintosh, UNIX, and attachments to IBM mainframe and midrange environments in Part II.

c h a p t e r

1

DOS and Novell DOS Clients

The heart of any networked or standalone computer is the operating system. It is responsible for setting the basic structures of your computer; it determines how data is read and written to your disk drives and how it attaches to the network. The most commonly used operating system is DOS. It has three versions: Microsoft's MS-DOS, IBM's PC-DOS, and Novell DOS 7. The two most often used DOS operating systems are MS-DOS and PC-DOS; Novell DOS 7 is used by very few people today. The current version of MS-DOS is 6.22. The current version of PC-DOS is 6.3.

Several years ago Novell acquired Digital Research Corporation, the company that produced DR-DOS 5, and revamped and renamed the system Novell DOS 7. DR-DOS had several innovations, including memory management and disk compression. Novell extended these technologies with DOS Protected Mode Services (DPMS) memory management and built-in networking. Novell has since dropped Novell DOS 7 from its product line.

DOS consists of several hidden boot files and a file called COMMAND.COM. The other files associated with DOS are device drivers that run specific parts of the machine, such as the keyboard (KEYBOARD.SYS) or the internal clock (CMOSCLK.SYS), or programs that perform specific functions, such as XCOPY.EXE, which is used to copy files from unlike drive types. Most new DOS systems include the following:

- Memory management
- Disk compression
- Disk defragmentation
- Antivirus software
- Improved utilities for backup and undeleting files
- DOSKEY, an extended command line utility
- QBASIC and a basic editor
- A DOS shell program
- A text editor (EDIT in DR-DOS and MS-DOS, E in PC-DOS)
- A line editor (EDLIN)
- Windows versions of many DOS utilities

Note:

Some versions of MS-DOS and PC-DOS include the program INTERLNK, which lets you connect your laptop to your desktop machine through a null modem cable and use the drives from your laptop as if they were drives on your local machine. The need for this utility is obviated by a network. However, if you do not want to attach your laptop to the network or buy a network adapter for the laptop, this utility can be a useful tool.

Two of the best improvements in more recent versions of DOS are its help system and menu utility. You can receive help on any command by typing HELP followed by the command you want information on. The menu utility lets you to store multiple configurations of your CONFIG.SYS and AUTOEXEC.BAT files. These configurations may include changes in screen color, device drivers, and memory managers for different applications. When the system boots, you will see a menu that allows you to choose the configuration you want or boot the system to the default configuration in a user-definable number of seconds.

Requirements

DOS workstation requirements are minimal. The first and major requirement is that DOS works only on Intel-based systems. While DOS works on any variant from Intel 8086 to Pentium processors, you are better off with an 80286 or above processor, preferably an 80386, 80486, or Pentium-class machine. To run DOS, you will also need a video source, monitor, and keyboard. Unlike most other operating systems, DOS does not require a hard drive. You can boot DOS from a diskette, from the disk drive, or from a boot ROM. The boot ROM installs on the network adapter, brings up the computer, attaches it to the network, and downloads the necessary boot files from the NetWare server. It then runs the boot files from memory and starts the computer.

Note:

Be careful when you purchase a boot ROM for your network adapter. The boot ROM is specific to the version of DOS you are using and the type of network adapter you are using. Some boot ROMs work with older versions of DOS, but not with newer ones.

Tip:

If you are using a diskette to boot the workstation and you have a hard drive attached that uses disk compression, be sure to include the device drivers for the disk compression software on the boot diskette.

DOS and its utilities take a substantial amount of disk space. If you are installing DOS on a hard drive, you should allow approximately seven megabytes of drive space for MS-DOS and PC-DOS versions 6.x and Novell DOS 7. You should also install DOS into a subdirectory off the root directory and create a path statement to it in your AUTOEXEC.BAT file.

DOS File Basics

Several DOS files are used in NetWare workstation configuration. They are the two hidden files and the command interpreter. For MS-DOS, these files are IO.SYS, MS-DOS.SYS, and COMMAND.COM; for PC-DOS, the files are IBMBIO.COM, IBMDOS.COM, and COMMAND.COM.

COMMAND.COM translates DOS commands into actions. For example, when you type DIR to look at a directory of the files in a subdirectory, the command interpreter issues the command to the DOS filing system to display a list of the files in the current subdirectory (Figure 1-1).

Most of the commands you issue will be commands contained in the operating system that are controlled by COMMAND.COM or external programs shipped with DOS, such as XCOPY or DISKCOPY.

The operation of a DOS system is controlled by two files, CONFIG.SYS and AUTOEXEC.BAT. The CONFIG.SYS file governs the configuration of the operating system, such as the number of files and buffers available to the system and the basic memory structure. Device drivers, such as memory managers, run from the CONFIG.SYS file. The AUTOEXEC.BAT file sets how the system looks and runs programs. Within the AUTOEXEC.BAT file, you will set the system path and run programs such as SMARTDRV.EXE, the drive caching program for MS-DOS and PC-DOS. AUTOEXEC.BAT and CONFIG.SYS are ASCII text files that can be edited with a text editor such as EDIT or EDLIN or with the Windows Notepad utility.

```
Volume in drive C is DOS_622
Volume Serial Number is 1ECB-3015
Directory of C:\WINWORD\BKSER\BOOK2\graphics
   <DIR>         03-19-95        10:48p
   <DIR>         03-19-95        10:48p
SET TXT  350     03-19-95 10:49p
MEM TXT  1,861   03-19-95 10:49p
VER TXT  36             03-19-95 10:49p
DIR TXT  0              03-19-95 10:53p
   4 file(s)            2,247 bytes
                 149,307,392 bytes free
```

Figure 1-1. *Files in the root directory and associated structures.*

Installation and Configuration

DOS installation and configuration varies for the different versions and types of DOS. While the various installation processes are similar in many ways for each version of DOS, we are only discussing the latest version of the most popular DOS systems.

MS-DOS Installation

MS-DOS is one of the easiest operating systems to install and use. MS-DOS v6.22 is the latest version. It provides excellent features, including enhanced memory management and new utilities for both DOS and users of the Windows graphical environment.

MS-DOS v6.22 ships as a two-diskette upgrade or a three-diskette series. The majority of users will install DOS 6.22 as an upgrade to their existing versions of DOS.

Note:

The upgrade only works if you have an existing version of MS-DOS on your system. If you have Novell DOS or IBM PC-DOS, you must purchase the three-diskette version.

To install MS-DOS, you may either boot with the first diskette or boot to your existing operating system. From drive A:, type SETUP. SETUP verifies the operating system currently on the computer and makes a backup copy of the existing DOS so you can revert to your existing system if you want. The installation then upgrades your existing boot files, IO.SYS, MS-DOS.SYS, and COMMAND.COM. IO.SYS and MS-DOS.SYS boot the machine and install the DOS File Allocation Table (FAT) file system.

After the boot files are upgraded, the remaining DOS files are replaced with the newer operating system.

Configuration of the MS-DOS Operating System

Configuring a DOS workstation is performed in two files: the CONFIG.SYS and AUTOEXEC.BAT files, which are created during workstation installation. The contents of these files varies depending on the operating environment of the workstation. Following are the contents of these files after DOS installation completes:

```
CONFIG.SYS
   DEVICE=SETVER.EXE
   DEVICE=HIMEM.SYS
   OS=HIGH
   OS=UMB
   FILES=50
   BUFFERS=35
   STACKS=9,256
AUTOEXEC.EAT
   PROMPT $P$G
   PATH=C:\;C:\DOS;C:\WNDOWS
   C:\DOS\SMARTDRV.EXE
```

You should modify these files to add your network client software and take advantage of your machine's capabilities. NetWare ships with a DOS client installation kit that allows you to install the workstation software through a graphical interface. Once your client software has been installed, you should begin to look at tuning your operating system.

PC-DOS Installation

PC-DOS, the IBM version of MS-DOS, installs similarly to MS-DOS. Instead of typing SETUP, you type INSTALL. PC-DOS runs the same setup and configuration routines as MS-DOS to configure your system and copy files to disk. It also creates an Uninstall diskette that allows you to remove the operating system later if necessary. PC-DOS comes in a three-diskette set. While it ships as the standard operating system on many IBM machines, it is also available commercially.

Note:

While many IBM systems ship with PC-DOS, many others ship with MS-DOS. On many high-end systems, you can also get OS/2 or A/IX.

PC-DOS contains unique utilities for power management for IBM laptop systems and PCMCIA devices. These utilities will be of little use to most users, but are essential for IBM hardware. In addition, IBM added compatibility to PC-DOS with OS/2 for dual-boot systems.

Another unique feature of PC-DOS is its inclusion of DOS utilities, such as backup software, disk compression, and Central Point's antivirus software.

Novell DOS 7 Installation

Novell DOS 7 installation is a departure from MS-DOS and PC-DOS. It was designed from the beginning to operate on Intel 80286 or above processors and includes much improved memory management, including the DOS Protected Mode Interface (DPMI) and the DOS Protected Mode Services (DPMS). In DPMS, device drivers and programs can be loaded in protected mode, reducing the conventional memory space they normally take. In addition, Novell DOS 7 includes numerous system security and disk performance commands. The one major difference between MS-DOS, PC-DOS, and Novell DOS 7 is that Novell DOS 7 includes built-in peer-to-peer networking and client support for NetWare networks.

Novell DOS 7's graphical installation utility takes you through the setup of DOS, memory management, and cache options, including installation of the task manager for preemptive multitasking on Intel 80386 or above machines. It also includes task-switching on 80286-based machines, hard drive performance and setup, networking, and DOS environment issues.

The installation for Novell DOS 7 is more comprehensive than MS-DOS or PC-DOS because it includes both preemptive multitasking and built-in network services through the NetWare Client and Personal NetWare Desktop Server installation. As a result, you not only must install the basic structure of your operating system, but also must be concerned with much of the environment, such as the number of logical drives that must be used.

Tip:

Depending upon your installation, the installation utility requires a lot of memory (512KB). It may be necessary to boot from the installation disks or a clean boot diskette.

Upon installation, you are presented with a series of screens that allow you to configure one section of the system at a time. The first screen gives you the choice of installing the operating system or creating a bootable diskette. The second screen allows you to choose between installing the operating system, networking options, and Windows utilities. You will then see a series of screens that allow you to choose the installation options for your operating system.

These screens include memory management screens that allow you to choose the memory manager you want to use, including third-party managers previously installed, 80286 memory managers, and DPMS memory management. The disk management installation includes disk optimization and compression utility installation.

The network section allows you to install and configure the NetWare client software for your network hardware and Novell Personal NetWare and the Desktop Server, which allows operation in a peer-to-peer network.

As the installation proceeds, the installation utility replaces your existing operating system and copies needed files to the appropriate subdirectory on your hard drive. The entire installation takes approximately 12.1 megabytes of disk space, depending on the options chosen.

Novell DOS 7 also comes with an on-line utility, DOSBOOK, that contains the complete documentation. This utility is similar to the UNIX system man, which provides a manual of any function. While helpful, DOSBOOK takes up a lot of disk space. If you are new to the features of Novell DOS 7, we suggest that you allow the system to install DOSBOOK. Once you are familiar with the majority of Novell DOS 7 functions, you can remove it.

NetWare for DOS and Windows Client Installation

Now that you have MS-DOS or PC-DOS installed, you must install the NetWare Client for DOS and Windows. (If you have Novell DOS 7, we've already discussed that installation.) The NetWare CD-ROM installation has a function that allows you to create DOS diskettes for installation or create subdirectories on the server from which you can later create diskettes.

Either method results in six diskettes that install all the NetWare client software and contain the LAN drivers for network adapters Novell has certified. Third-party drivers not contained on the diskette can also be installed through this procedure. To do so, the vendor must provide you with an .INS file in addition to the driver.

Start installation by putting the first diskette in the diskette drive and typing INSTALL. The screen allows you to make changes to the directory structure, install Windows utilities, and select the driver you want to install from the list provided. If you want to install another driver, highlight driver selection option and press the Insert key.

Note:

The default network subdirectory is \NWCLIENT. There is no reason to change this unless you want to maintain a specific structure for all your clients that is different.

During adapter driver installation you will be prompted to enter various options for your adapter driver. These might include interrupt, port address, base memory address, or DMA channel. An Ethernet adapter will often use an interrupt and a port address. Token-ring adapters will use an interrupt, port, and memory address. Some token-ring adapters will also use a DMA setting. ARCnet adapters will use an interrupt, port, and memory address. Depending on your adapter driver, there may be other settings such as packet size you will need to set. Additionally, you will need to set the frame type you plan to use. The available frame types are shown in Table 1-1.

Table 1-1. *Available Frame Types for Different Access Methods*

Access Methods	Frame Types
Ethernet	
ETHERNET_802.2	The default IPX frame type
ETHERNET_802.3	A NetWare IPX frame type used in earlier versions of NetWare
ETHERNET_SNAP	The TCP/IP frame type
ETHERNET_II	The original TCP/IP frame type
Token-ring	
Token-Ring	The default IPX frame type
Token-Ring_SNAP	The TCP/IP frame type
ARCnet	
Novell_RX-NET	The default IPX and TCP/IP frame type

After you choose the installation options and the network adapter driver, highlight the last option to begin installation and press the Enter key. The installation program will prompt you to insert diskettes until you complete the installation.

The installation procedure also installs the drivers and related files. In addition, if you choose to install the Windows utilities, the installation procedure will automatically make changes to the Windows .INI files and copy the appropriate utilities to the disk. The CONFIG.SYS

```
@ECHO OFF
c:
CD \NWCLIENT
SET NWLANGUAGE=ENGLISH
fileinfo
set model=IBM Value Point 486/33
set adapter=TC3045 Rev D
LH LSL
LH TCTOKSH.COM
LH IPXODI
LH netx
rem VLM
f:
login supervisor
```

Figure 1-2. *The STARTNET.BAT file.*

file is modified to set the last drive to Z. The AUTOEXEC.BAT file is modified to include a path to the \NWCLIENT subdirectory and call the STARTNET.BAT file. STARTNET.BAT is located in the \NWCLIENT subdirectory or the directory you specify and loads the NetWare drivers. A typical STARTNET.BAT file appears in Figure 1-2.

After installation is completed, you will need to create the configuration file for NetWare, called NET.CFG, with an ASCII text editor. This file contains the settings for the Open Data-Link Interface (ODI) Link Support Layer (LSL), IPXODI, the adapter driver, and the Virtual Loadable Modules (VLM) or NETX. The VLMs are executable files that can be loaded to provide the necessary network functionality for your workstation. Drivers have a number of settings.

LSL Parameters

Several parameters apply to the LSL (LSL.COM) that affect the configuration of the NetWare workstation. They are specified in the Link Support section of the NET.CFG file. The parameters for LSL.COM are as follows:

BUFFERS *number, size*
MAX BOARDS *number*
MAX STACKS *number*
MEMPOOL *number*

BUFFERS

The BUFFERS statement sets the number of receive buffers the LSL will maintain. The number of communications buffers must be large enough to hold all the media headers and the maximum data size of a frame. The default value for BUFFERS is 0. This parameter is not used for IPX. For IP, we suggest a value of 1,514 for Ethernet and 4,096 for token-ring. The buffer size may also be set with the BUFFERS command. The minimum size is 628 bytes. The total buffer space must fit into approximately 59 kilobytes (KB). The total buffer space is determined by multiplying the number of buffers by the size of the buffer.

MAX BOARDS

The MAX BOARDS statement configures the maximum number of logical boards (adapters) the LSL can handle. Each LAN driver logical board uses one board resource. A logical board is used each time a FRAMETYPE is loaded. An Ethernet driver should support all four logical FRAMETYPEs for a maximum of four logical boards per adapter. The default value is 4 with a range of 1 to 16. For example, you have two adapters in the machine. Board 1 is bound to ETHERNET_802.2, ETHERNET_802.2, and ETHERNET_SNAP. Board 2 is bound to two token-ring frame types. The maximum number of boards will be five, one for each frame type.

MAX STACKS

The MAX STACKS statement configures the maximum number of logical protocol stack IDs the LSL can utilize. Each protocol stack uses one or more stack ID resources. The MAX STACKS statement also controls the amount of resident memory the LSL uses, which is directly proportional to the number of stacks. The amount of memory used by the LSL can be controlled by reducing the MAX STACKS value to the actual number of protocol stack IDs used. The default value is 4 with a range of 1 to 16.

MEMPOOL

MEMPOOL configures the size of the memory pool buffers maintained by the LSL. The IPXODI protocol stack does not use the MEMPOOL buffers. IP does.

Driver Parameters

Each driver also has a specific set of parameters that can be specified in the NET.CFG file. The list of parameters includes:

DMA	INT
MEM	PORT
NODE ADDRESS	SLOT
PCMCIA	FRAME
PROTOCOL	SAPS
LINK STATIONS	ALTERNATE
MAX FRAME SIZE	DOUBLE BUFFER OFF

Not all these parameters are used by every adapter, and each parameter doesn't have the same values for each adapter. You should refer to the documentation supplied with the adapter to determine the parameters the adapter uses and the values available. In brief, these are the definitions of each setting:

DMA	Represents the DMA channel used.
MEM	This parameter is the memory address of the adapter.
NODE ADDRESS	The locally administered node ID of the adapter.
PCMCIA	The type of PCMCIA device.
PROTOCOL	The first protocol used by the adapter.
LINK STATIONS	Setting used by LANSUP.COM to set the link stations.
MAX FRAME SIZE	Represents the largest frame size used by the driver.
INT	The interrupt used by the adapter.
PORT	The port the adapter uses.
SLOT	The slot used for EISA and PCI adapters.
FRAME	The frame type the adapter uses.
SAPS	This setting is used by LANSUP.COM to set the number of Service Access Points.
ALTERNATE	This setting is used to designate a second adapter for token-ring adapters.
DOUBLE BUFFER OFF	Allows double buffers for transmitting and receiving packets.

IPX Parameters

IPXODI is the protocol stack used by Novell to implement the IPX/SPX network transport protocol. It may be configured to your needs with a variety of configuration options:

BIND	IPX SOCKETS
INT64	PBURST WRITE WINDOWS SIZE
INT7a	SPX ABORT TIMEOUT
IPATCH	SPX CONNECTIONS
IPX PACKET SIZE LIMIT	SPX LISTEN TIMEOUT
IPX RETRY COUNT	SPX VERIFY TIMEOUT

BIND

IPXODI binds to the first board it finds in the NET.CFG file. If you want to bind the IPX/SPX protocol to a different board, add the BIND statement to the PROTOCOL IPXODI section of the NET.CFG file, which forces IPXODI to bind to a subsequent logical board. To add the BIND statement to the IPXODI section, simply place the statement BIND [driver] under the heading PROTOCOL IPXODI section. The [driver] represents the name of the adapter driver you are using. For an NE3200 Ethernet adapter, the syntax of the BIND statement is:

```
PROTOCOL IPXODI
BIND NE3200
```

INT6

The INT64 parameter allows applications to use Interrupt 64h to access IPX services. This parameter is used for older applications that do not use INT64.

INT7A

The INT7A parameter allows applications to use Interrupt 7Ah to access IPX services. Only specific applications must use this interrupt.

IPATCH

The IPATCH parameter allows any address in the IPXODI.COM file to be patched with any specified byte offset value. This statement should be used only when an application requires a specific byte offset value.

IPX PACKET SIZE LIMIT

The IPX PACKET SIZE LIMIT parameter reduces the maximum packet size set by each LAN driver. The default setting is the lesser of 4,160 bytes or the size specified by the LAN driver. The range is 576 to 6,500 bytes.

IPX RETRY COUNT

The IPX RETRY COUNT parameter sets the number of times IPX allows the DOS shell and SPX to resend a packet. The default is 20 retries. You may want to increase this parameter when you have a lot of traffic, or if you are sending traffic over a wide-area network.

IPX SOCKETS

The IPX SOCKETS parameter configures the maximum number of sockets IPX can have open at the workstation. IPX-specific programs may require that this number be increased. The default number of sockets is 20. You rarely need more than 20 sockets unless you are running an application on a workstation that is communicating with several other workstations.

MINIMUM SPX RETRIES

The MINIMUM SPX RETRIES parameter determines the number of unacknowledged transmit requests that will be allowed before the connection is assumed to be bad. This parameter should be increased if an application that uses SPX loses its connection. The range for this parameter is 0 to 255.

SPX ABORT TIMEOUT

The SPX ABORT TIMEOUT parameter adjusts the amount of time SPX waits without receiving any response from the other side of the connection. The value for this parameter is the number of clock-ticks (approximately 1/18 second) that SPX waits. The default value is 540 ticks, approximately 30 seconds. It should be used when SPX programs timeout too quickly.

SPX CONNECTIONS

This parameter configures the maximum number of SPX connections a workstation can have open at one time. If you plan to use RPRINTER.EXE to use a local printer on a NetWare v2.x, v3.x, or 4.x network, you will need to increase this parameter to 60.

SPX LISTEN TIMEOUT

This parameter sets the time SPX waits without receiving a packet from the other side of the connection before it requests a packet from the other side to assure the connection. The timeout values is also specified in number of ticks. The default value is 108 ticks. You should change this setting only if you experience time-outs on your SPX link.

SPX VERIFY TIMEOUT

This parameter configures the frequency at which SPX sends a packet to the other side of the connection to indicate that the connection is still alive. SPX sends the alive packet when no other SPX traffic is sent by the session. The value is measured in ticks. The default value is 54 ticks.

Universal Client Parameters

The configuration of the Universal Client is controlled in the NETWARE DOS REQUESTER section of the NET.CFG file. The parameters specified in this file configure the client to the individual user and network options. In most cases, you should use the default settings, unless the application or performance requires changes. The available configuration parameters are:

AUTO LARGE TABLE
AUTO RECONNECT
AUTO RETRY
AVERAGE NAME LENGTH
BIND RECONNECT
CACHE BUFFERS
CACHE BUFFER SIZE
CACHE WRITES
CHECKSUM
CONNECTIONS
DOS NAME
FIRST NETWORK DRIVE
HANDLE NET ERRORS
LARGE INTERNET PACKETS
LOAD CONN TABLE LOW
LOAD LOW CONN
LOAD LOW IPXNCP
LOCAL PRINTERS
LONG MACHINE TYPE
MAX TASKs
MESSAGE LEVEL
MESSAGE TIMEOUT
NAME CONTEXT
NETWARE PROTOCOL
NETWORK PRINTERS
PB BUFFERS
PBURST READ WINDOWS SIZE
PBURST WRITE WINDOWS SIZE
PREFERRED SERVER
PREFERRED TREE
PREFERRED WORKGROUP
PRINT BUFFER SIZE
PRINT HEADER
PRINT TAIL
READ ONLY COMPATIBILITY
SEARCH MODE
SET STATION TIME
SHOW DOTS
SHORT MACHINE TYPE
SIGNATURE LEVEL
TRUE COMMIT
USE DEFAULTS
VLM

AUTO LARGE TABLE

When AUTO LARGE TABLE is enabled, AUTO.VLM allocates a table of 178 bytes per connection for bindery reconnects. The default setting is OFF. When disabled, the setting is 34 bytes per connection. The parameter BIND RECONNECT must also be set to ON.

AUTO RECONNECT

The AUTO RECONNECT parameter sets AUTO.VLM to reconnect a workstation to a NetWare server and rebuild the workstation's environment after a connection loss. If AUTO RECONNECT is set to OFF, reconnection is manual. The default value is ON.

AUTO RETRY

The AUTO RETRY parameter sets the number of seconds AUTO.VLM waits before to attempting a retry after receiving a network error. When you set AUTO RETRY to 0, AUTO.VLM will make no retry attempts. The default time is 0 and the range is between 0 and 3,640.

AVERAGE NAME LENGTH

The AVERAGE NAME LENGTH parameter reserves space for a table of NetWare server names based on the AVERAGE NAME LENGTH and the value of the CONNECTIONS parameter. You may save additional memory by setting the length to a lower value. The default value is 48 characters and the range is from 2 to 4.

BIND RECONNECT

BIND RECONNECT automatically rebuilds the bindery connection and restores drives and printer connections. This parameter also requires that AUTO RECONNECT be set to ON. BIND RECONNECT's default value is OFF.

CACHE BUFFERS

CACHE BUFFERS determines the number of cache buffers the requester allocates for local caching of nonshared, non-transaction-tracked files. This parameter allows the DOS Requester to cache one file. Increasing the number of cache buffers increases the speed of sequential reads and writes and thus, performance, but also increases memory use. The default is five cache blocks and the range is from 0 to 64.

CACHE BUFFER SIZE

The CACHE BUFFER SIZE sets the size of the cache buffer. Increasing the size parameter increases performance, but also increases memory usage. The parameter should never be set to a size larger than the

MAXIMUM PACKET SIZE set for the network adapter driver. The default is 512 bytes and the range is from 64 to 4,096 bytes.

CACHE WRITES

The CACHE WRITES parameter may be set to ON or OFF. If the parameter is set to OFF, performance will decrease, but data integrity will increase. Setting the parameter to ON potentially causes data loss if the server runs out of disk space between writes. The default value is ON.

CHECKSUM

The CHECKSUM parameter forces NCP packet validation. There are various levels of security for this parameter:

Value	Action
0	Disabled
1	Enabled but not preferred
2	Enabled and preferred
3	Required

Setting the parameter to 2 or 3 increases data integrity, but decreases system performance. The default is 1. The ETHERNET_802.3 frame type does not support checksums.

CONNECTIONS

The CONNECTIONS parameter sets the maximum number of connections the requester supports. The range of values is 2 to 50. A value larger than necessary increases memory use without increasing performance. Setting the value to a number larger than 8 can also affect NETX compatibility with older versions of NetWare. The default value is 8.

DOS NAME

DOS NAME sets the name of the operating system the shell uses. The %OS variable in the login script uses this parameter to map search drives to the network's DOS directory. The requester automatically recognizes the name DRDOS and NWDOS without setting the DOS NAME parameter. Setting this variable disables the autorecognition feature. The maximum number of characters is five.

FIRST NETWORK DRIVE

The FIRST NETWORK DRIVE parameter sets the first network drive letter specified when a connection is made. The default is the first available DOS drive found. The range is from A to Z.

HANDLE NET ERRORS

HANDLE NET ERRORS determines the method for handling network errors. A network error is generated whenever the workstation does not receive a response from the server. If HANDLE NET ERRORS is set to ON, INT24h handles network errors. If HANDLE NET ERRORS is set to OFF, a NET_REC_ERROR return is made on a network error. Some applications may not recognize NET_REC_ERROR returns.

LARGE INTERNET PACKETS

LARGE INTERNET PACKETS determines the size of packets used when crossing bridges and routers. Previously NetWare set the MAXIMUM PACKET SIZE to 576. When set to ON, the maximum packet size is negotiated between the destination NetWare server and the workstation when crossing bridges and routers. The access method used determines the maximum packet size.

LOAD CONN TABLE LOW

The LOAD CONN TABLE LOW parameter is used with the initial release of NetWare 4.0 utilities. When set to ON, the connection table loads in low memory, increasing memory usage. The default setting of OFF loads the table in upper memory.

LOAD LOW CONN

The LOAD LOW CONN parameter set to OFF loads the CONN.VLM into upper memory, saving memory but decreasing performance. The default is ON, which loads the VLM into conventional memory.

LOAD LOW IPXNCP

The LOAD LOW IPXNCP parameter designates where the IPXNCP.VLM is loaded in memory. Set to ON, the VLM loads into conventional memory. Set to OFF, the VLM loads in upper memory, increasing conventional memory space and decreasing performance.

LOCAL PRINTERS

LOCAL PRINTERS overrides the number of local printers determined by the system BIOS. Normally the BIOS allocates the local printers to one for each parallel port. The default is 3 with the range from 0 to 9.

LONG MACHINE TYPE

The LONG MACHINE TYPE tells the requester the type of machine used when the %MACHINE variable is accessed. This variable sets the machine's search path to the correct version of DOS on the server. The default is IBM_PC.

MAX TASKS

MAX TASKS configures the maximum number of active tasks. The default is 31 tasks; the range is from 20 to 128 tasks.

MESSAGE LEVEL

The MESSAGE LEVEL sets the amount of information displayed with load time messages. Each message level implies the previous level's message. The default is 1. The values are as follows:

Value	Action
0	Always display copyright message and critical errors
1	Display warning messages
2	Display program load information for VLMs
3	Display configuration information
4	Display diagnostic information

MESSAGE TIMEOUT

MESSAGE TIMEOUT sets the timeout in ticks before broadcast messages are cleared from the screen without user intervention. The default 0 requires you to clear the message. The range is from 0 to 10,000 ticks.

NAME CONTEXT

The NAME CONTEXT parameter allows you to set the current position in the NetWare Directory Services tree structure and applies only to NetWare 4.x networks. The default NAME CONTEXT is the root directory. Quotation marks must enclose the directory name. The complete syntax is:

```
NAME CONTEXT = "name context"
```

NETWARE PROTOCOL

NETWARE PROTOCOL sets the network protocols that will be bound at the workstation. Available protocols are listed below:

Value	Protocol
DS	NetWare Directory Services
BIND	NetWare bindery for NetWare v2.x and v3.x
PNW	Personal NetWare

NETWORK PRINTERS

The NETWORK PRINTERS parameter sets the number of LPT ports the NetWare DOS Requester can capture. The range is from 0 to 9 with a default of 3. Setting the value to 0 specifies that the PRINT.VLM does not load.

PB BUFFERS

PB BUFFERS sets the number of packet burst protocol buffers. Packet burst is automatically enabled in the requester. Setting the value to 0 disables packet burst. The default is 3 with a range from 0 to 10. Setting the number to a higher value increases memory usage. Setting the value to 0 decreases memory usage and in some cases may decrease performance.

PREFERRED SERVER

PREFERRED SERVER sets the NetWare v2.x or v3.x server to first attach if the server has a connection available. If both the PREFERRED SERVER and PREFERRED TREE parameters are specified, the first protocol to successfully build an attachment is used.

PREFERRED TREE

PREFERRED TREE sets the tree to connect to in a NetWare 4.0 network environment if the tree specified has a server with a free connection. If both the PREFERRED SERVER and PREFERRED TREE parameters are specified, the first protocol to successfully build an attachment is used.

PREFERRED WORKGROUP

PREFERRED WORKGROUP sets the name of the workgroup for Personal NetWare to search and attach to.

PRINT BUFFER SIZE

The PRINT BUFFER SIZE determines the print buffer size in bytes. The default is 64 bytes and the range is from 0 to 256 bytes. Increasing this value increases printing output and memory usage.

PRINT HEADER

PRINT HEADER sets the size of the buffer that holds the information used to initialize a printer for each print job. This parameter should be used if print jobs with many instructions, such as forms, are used. The default is 64 bytes and the range is from 0 to 1,024 bytes.

PRINT TAIL

PRINT TAIL sets the size of the buffer that holds the information used to reset the printer after print jobs. The default is 16 bytes and the range is from 0 to 1,024 bytes. You should only need to change this if the printer does not reset properly.

READ ONLY COMPATIBILITY

READ ONLY COMPATIBILITY determines if a file marked Read Only (RO) can be opened with a read/write access call. Prior to NetWare v2.1, a program could open a Read Only file with write access without an error. To maintain compatibility with DOS, NetWare v2.1 and above do not allow a Read Only file to be opened for write access. Setting the parameter forces the shell to allow the open request to succeed. The default is OFF. You should only need to reset this if you are using an older version of DOS.

SEARCH MODE

SEARCH MODE changes the way the NetWare Requester searches for .EXE and .COM files that are not in the current directory. Valid search modes are 0–7. In previous versions of NetWare, the default drive had to be a network drive. The DOS Requester will search all drives regardless of the current drive.

SET STATION TIME

SET STATION TIME synchronizes the workstation date and time with the NetWare server that the workstation initially attaches to. The default is ON; setting the parameter to OFF disables synchronization.

SHOW DOTS

SHOW DOTS shows the DOS directory entries for . and .. This setting is used with Windows 3.x to show the DOS dots for directory searches.

SHORT MACHINE TYPE

The SHORT MACHINE TYPE parameter is used with the %MACHINE variable in the login script. The SHORT MACHINE TYPE is used specifically with overlay (.OVL) files. The default SHORT MACHINE TYPE is IBM and is limited to four letters.

SIGNATURE LEVEL

SIGNATURE LEVEL sets the level of enhanced security support. The available values are

Value	Action
0	Disabled
1	Enabled, but not preferred
2	Preferred
3	Required

Setting the option to 2 or 3 increases the level of security but decreases performance.

TRUE COMMIT

The TRUE COMMIT variable selects whether the commit NetWare Core Protocol (NCP) is sent on DOS commit requests. The option should be set to ON to guarantee integrity when processing critical data. This variable also sacrifices performance over integrity. The default value is OFF.

USE DEFAULTS

USE DEFAULTS overrides the default VLMs that VLM.EXE loads. If USE DEFAULTS is set in the NET.CFG file, then the DOS Requester installs VLMs to control NetWare services. The default VLMs are

CONN.VLM
TRAN.VLM
NDS.VLM
NWP.VLM
GENERAL.VLM
PRINT.VLM
IPXNCP.VLM
SECURITY.VLM
BIND.VLM
FIO.VLM
REDIR.VLM
NETX.VLM

If this parameter is set to ON and the default VLMs are specified in the NET.CFG file, they will attempt to load twice, generating an error during the load. The default value is ON.

VLM

This parameter specifies the VLMs that the VLM.EXE should load. This allows VLMs not listed in the default for VLM.EXE to be added. The syntax for the parameter is

```
VLM = [path]\*.VLM
```

The .VLM extension must be used. A maximum of 50 VLMs can be loaded.

DOS Command Summary

As we discussed, the commands you will use for DOS are divided between those contained in the base operating system, COMMAND.COM, and utilities that are provided with DOS. Table 1-2 is a list of some of the most commonly used DOS commands.

Table 1.2 *Common DOS Commands*

Command	Action
APPEND	Allows programs to open data files in specified directories as if they were in the current directory
ASSIGN	Redirects requests for disk operations on one drive to a different drive
ATTRIB	Displays or changes file attributes
BREAK	Sets or clears extended CTRL-C checking

Table 1.2 *Common DOS Commands, continued*

Command	Action
CALL	Calls one batch program from another
CD	Displays the name of, or changes, the current directory
CHCP	Displays or sets the active code page number
CHDIR	Displays the name of, or changes, the current directory
CHKDSK	Checks a disk and displays a status report
CHOICE	Waits for you to choose one of a set of choices
CLS	Clears the screen
COMMAND	Starts a new instance of the MS-DOS or IBM PC-DOS command interpreter
COMP	Compares the contents of two files or sets of files
COPY	Copies one or more files to another location
CPBACKUP	Backs up one or more files from one disk to another
CPBDIR	Gives a report on backup directories
CPSCHED	Schedules unattended program execution at specific periods
CTTY	Changes the terminal device used to control your system
DATAMON	Guards against data loss on your computer
DATE	Displays or sets the date
DEBUG	Starts DEBUG, a program testing and editing tool
DEFRAG	Reorganizes files on disks for optimal performance
DEL	Deletes one or more files
DELOLDDOS	Deletes the OLD_DOS.— directory and the files it contains
DELTREE	Deletes a directory and all the files and subdirectories in it
DIR	Displays a list of files and subdirectories in a directory
DISKCOMP	Compares the contents of two floppy disks
DISKCOPY	Copies the contents of one floppy disk to another
DOSKEY	Edits command lines, recalls MS-DOS commands, and creates macros
DOSSHELL	Starts the MS-DOS or IBM PC-DOS shell
DRVLOCK	Locks the drive so that media cannot be removed
E	Starts the IBM PC-DOS Editor, which creates and changes ASCII files
ECHO	Displays messages, or turns command echoing ON or OFF
EDIT	Starts the MS-DOS Editor, which creates and changes ASCII files
EDLIN	Starts EDLIN, a line-oriented text editor
EJECT	Ejects the media from a drive
EMM386	Enables or disables EMM386 expanded memory support
ERASE	Deletes one or more files
EXE2BIN	Converts .EXE (executable) files to binary format

Table 1.2 *Common DOS Commands, continued*

Command	Action
EXIT	Quits the COMMAND.COM program (command interpreter)
EXPAND	Decompresses one or more compressed files
FASTHELP	Provides summary help information for MS-DOS commands
FASTOPEN	Decreases the amount of time needed to open frequently used files and directories
FC	Compares two files or sets of files, and displays the differences between them
FDISK	Configures a hard disk for use with MS-DOS
FIND	Searches for a text string in a file or files
FOR	Runs a specified command for each file in a set of files
FORMAT	Formats a disk for use with MS-DOS
GOTO	Directs IBM DOS to a labeled line in a batch program
GRAPHICS	Loads a program that can print graphics
HELP	Provides complete, interactive help information for MS-DOS and IBM PC-DOS commands
IBMAVD	Detects and removes viruses from a system
IBMAVSP	Interactive, standalone antivirus program for recovery from catastrophic virus damage
IF	Performs conditional processing in batch programs
INTERLNK	Connects two computers via their parallel or serial ports
INTERLNK	Displays status of INTERLNK-INTERSVR redirected drives
INTERSVR	Starts the INTERLNK server
INTERSVR	Provides serial or parallel file transfer and printing capabilities via redirected drives
JOIN	Joins a disk drive to a directory on another drive
KEYB	Configures a keyboard for a specific language
LABEL	Creates, changes, or deletes the volume label of a disk
LH	Loads a program into the upper memory area
LOADFIX	Loads a program above the first 64KB of memory, and runs the program
LOADHIGH	Loads a program into the upper memory area
MD	Creates a directory
MEM	Displays the amount of used and free memory in a system
MEMMAKER	Starts the MEMMAKER program, which optimizes a computer's memory
MKDIR	Creates a directory
MODE	Configures a system device

Table 1.2 *Common DOS Commands, continued*

Command	Action
MORE	Displays output one screen at a time
MOUSE	Provides mouse pointer device support
MOVE	Moves one or more files. Also renames files and directories
MSAV	Scans your computer for known viruses
MSBACKUP	Backs up or restores one or more files from one disk to another
MSD	Provides detailed technical information about your computer
NLSFUNC	Loads country-specific information
PATH	Displays or sets a search path for executable files
PAUSE	Suspends processing of a batch file and displays a message
POWER	Turns power management on and off
PRINT	Prints a text file while you are using other MS-DOS commands
PROMPT	Changes the MS-DOS command prompt
QBASIC	Starts the MS-DOS QBasic programming environment
QCONFIG	Assists IBM support personnel in obtaining detailed technical information about your computer
RAMSETUP	Installs RAMBOOST, which optimizes your computer's memory
RD	Removes a directory
RECOVER	Recovers readable information from a bad or defective disk
REM	Records comments (remarks) in batch files or CONFIG.SYS files
REN	Renames a file or files
RENAME	Renames a file or files
REPLACE	Replaces files
RESTORE	Restores files that were backed up by using the BACKUP command
RMDIR	Removes a directory
SCHEDULE	Schedules unattended program execution at specific periods
SET	Displays, sets, or removes MS-DOS environment variables
SETVER	Sets the version number that MS-DOS or IBM PC-DOS reports to a program
SHARE	Installs file-sharing and locking capabilities on your hard disk
SHIFT	Shifts the position of replaceable parameters in batch files
SMARTDRV	Installs and configures the SmartDrive (SMARTDRV) disk-caching utility
SORT	Sorts input
SUBST	Associates a path with a drive letter
SYS	Copies the MS-DOS system files and command interpreter to a disk you specify
TIME	Displays or sets the system time

Table 1.2 *Common DOS Commands, continued*

Command	Action
TREE	Graphically displays the directory structure of a drive or path
TYPE	Displays the contents of a text file to the screen
UNDELETE	Restores files previously deleted with the DEL command
UNFORMAT	Restores a disk erased by the FORMAT command or restructured by the RECOVER command
VER	Displays the MS-DOS version
VERIFY	Directs MS-DOS or IBM PC-DOS to verify that files are written correctly to a disk
VOL	Displays a disk volume label and serial number
VSAFE	Continuously monitors a computer for viruses
XCOPY	Copies files (except hidden and system files) and directory trees

Configuration and Installation

In Novell DOS 7, all configuration should be done through the configuration utility. However, in the case of MS-DOS or PC-DOS, installation is only the beginning.

The CONFIG.SYS File

The configuration of your machine is maintained by the CONFIG.SYS file. It contains your device drivers and memory managers. The commands available for CONFIG.SYS files are as follows:

BREAK

Specifies whether DOS should check for a CTRL-C or CTRL-Break from the keyboard

BUFFERS

Specifies the amount of memory DOS reserves for transferring information from disks

COUNTRY

Sets the language for a system

DEVICE

Loads a device driver

DEVICEHIGH
Loads a device driver into upper memory

DOS
Specifies whether DOS will use the high memory area and whether it will provide access to upper memory blocks (DOS=HIGH and DOS=UMB)

DRIVPARM
Sets the characteristics of a disk drive, such as the drive letter or type

FCBS
Specifies the number of file control blocks (FCBs) DOS can have open at the same time

FILES
Specifies the number of files that can be open at any time

INSTALL
Loads a memory resident program

LASTDRIVE
Sets the number of valid drive letters; this parameter can be especially important in setting network drive options

NUMLOCK
Sets whether the NUMLOCK key is initially ON or OFF when the computer is booted

REM
Indicates that following information is nonexecutable text; used for remarks and documentation

SET
Sets an environment variable for a system; also available in AUTOEXEC.BAT

SHELL
Configures the environment for COMMAND.COM or specifies the location of another command interpreter

STACKS
Specifies the amount of memory available for processing hardware interrupts

SWITCHES
Specifies special options for DOS

Memory Management

There are various forms of memory a computer can use:

Conventional Memory
: Up to the first 640KB of memory on a computer. This is where programs actually run. You do not need a memory manager to use this memory.

Upper Memory
: This the next 384KB above your system's initial conventional or 640KB of RAM. This memory is used by system hardware, such as display or network adapters. Unused parts of this memory are called upper memory blocks (UMBs) and can be used to run device drivers or terminate-and-stay-resident programs.

Extended Memory
: The area above the conventional and upper memory areas. This is the area above one megabyte on a 286 or above processor-based computer. This area requires an extended memory manager like HIMEM.SYS.

High Memory Area
: The first 64KB of extended memory. On computers with extended memory, DOS is installed in this area.

Virtual Memory
: Space on a hard drive that Windows uses as if it were actual system memory.

Expanded Memory
: In addition to conventional memory, you can also use expanded memory. To configure and use this memory, you must have an expanded memory manager. EMM386 can simulate expanded memory. Programs that can take advantage of expanded memory use 64KB blocks by paging the memory in and out of an area called the EMS page frame. Because the memory must be paged in and out of this page frame, it is slower than using extended memory.

DOS installation adds the HIMEM.SYS command file to the CONFIG.SYS file. HIMEM.SYS is the extended memory manager. Both MS-DOS and PC-DOS also come with EMM386.EXE, which is the protected mode memory manager. This command file allows you to configure all or some of the memory as expanded or extended depending upon your needs. To maximize memory, you should run a program called MEMMAKER.EXE that ships with DOS. This program evaluates a system and determines the most effective memory scheme. It attempts to load as many programs into upper memory as possible to provide you with as much free memory in the lower 640KB for running programs. MEMMAKER.EXE will also configure expanded and extended memory to your specifications.

Commercial memory managers are also available, such as Quarterdeck's QEMM or Qualitas 386MAX. All commercial memory managers operate in a manner similar to EMM386.EXE. However, they often contain better installation and configuration utilities and are in some cases faster than the utilities that ship with DOS.

Disk Compression

If you have limited disk space and money, you can use one of the disk compression utilities that come with DOS or a disk compression utility such as STACKER. These utilities operate by creating a small host drive and then compressing the files into a single very large file. The compression utility then reads from its table of files and expands the file currently requested. The uncompressed section of the hard drive is called the Host file and is shown as drive H. The actual DOS boot file and File Allocation Table are maintained on the uncompressed portion of a bootable compressed drive. The compressed file is relocated and acts as drive C.

The amount of disk space you will recover with disk compression utilities depends on a number of factors including the types of files you have on the system and the compression ratio you request. The general rule of thumb is that you will receive about a 2 to 1 ratio. Any less than that and you are not gaining enough to make using a disk compression utility worthwhile. You may also risk data corruption.

Note:

If you want to maintain a permanent swap file for Windows or other programs, you should leave additional space equal to the size of the swap file uncompressed. Windows will not create a permanent swap file to a compressed drive. If you want to use a temporary swap file, you can have it on the compressed drive.

Menu Systems

The menu systems available in PC-DOS and MS-DOS are almost identical. The menu system for Novell DOS 7 is marginally different. In either case, menus are a means of running multiple configurations from a standard menu provided by DOS or for simply building menus for users to choose applications from. This would allow you to have one configuration for running the system standalone, one for attaching to the network, and one for playing games that require additional or expanded memory. The menu system affects your CONFIG.SYS and AUTOEXEC.BAT files.

While there are many ways of configuring your menu system, a typical one would appear as follows:

```
CONFIG.SYS
   [menu]
   menuitem=Windows, Use WFW v3.11
   menuitem=Games, Play games
   menuitem=CDGames, CD ROM Games
   menuitem=Program, DOS Workstation
   menuitem=Programcd, DOS Workstation_CD
   menudefault=Windows,20

[Windows]
DEVICE=C:\DOS\SMARTDRV.EXE/DOUBLE_BUFFER\
DEVICE=C:\DOS\HIMEM.SYS
DEVICE=C:\DOS\EMM386.EXE NOEMS X=D000-D1FF
FILES=40
BUFFERS=10,0
DOS=UMB
LASTDRIVE=Z
FCBS=16,0
DOS=HIGH
DEVICE=C:\DOS\DBLSPACE.SYS /MOVE
SHELL=C:\DOS\COMMAND.COM C:\DOS\ /e:1024 /p
STACKS=9,256
DEVICE=\DOS\MTMCDE.SYS /D:MSCD001 /P:300 /A:0 /M:20 /T:6 /I:10
DEVICEHIGH /L:1,4560 =C:\WINDOWS\IFSHLP.SYS

[Games]
DEVICE=C:\DOS\SMARTDRV.EXE /DOUBLE_BUFFER
DEVICE=C:\DOS\HIMEM.SYS
DEVICE=C:\DOS\EMM386.EXE RAM
BUFFERS=10,0
FILES=40
DOS=UMB
LASTDRIVE=Z
FCBS=16,0
DOS=HIGH
DEVICE=C:\DOS\DBLSPACE.SYS /MOVE
SHELL=C:\DOS\COMMAND.COM C:\DOS\ /e:1024 /p
STACKS=9,256

[CDGames]
DEVICE=C:\DOS\SMARTDRV.EXE /DOUBLE_BUFFER
DEVICE=C:\DOS\HIMEM.SYS
DEVICE=C:\DOS\EMM386.EXE RAM X=D000-D1FF
BUFFERS=10,0
```

```
FILES=40
DOS=UMB
LASTDRIVE=Z
FCBS=16,0
DOS=HIGH
DEVICE=C:\DOS\DBLSPACE.SYS /MOVE
SHELL=C:\DOS\COMMAND.COM C:\DOS\ /e:1024 /p
STACKS=9,256
DEVICE=\DOS\MTMCDE.SYS /D:MSCD001 /P:300 /A:0 /M:20 /T:6 /I:10

[Program]
DEVICE=C:\DOS\SMARTDRV.EXE /DOUBLE_BUFFER
DEVICE=C:\DOS\HIMEM.SYS
DEVICE=C:\DOS\EMM386.EXE NOEMS X=D000-D1FF
BUFFERS=10,0
FILES=40
DOS=UMB
LASTDRIVE=Z
FCBS=16,0
DOS=HIGH
DEVICEHIGH /L:2,39488 =C:\DOS\DBLSPACE.SYS /MOVE
SHELL=C:\DOS\COMMAND.COM C:\DOS\ /e:1024 /p
STACKS=9,256
DEVICEHIGH /L:2,12048 =C:\DOS\SETVER.EXE

[Programcd]
DEVICE=C:\DOS\SMARTDRV.EXE /DOUBLE_BUFFER
DEVICE=C:\DOS\HIMEM.SYS
DEVICE=C:\DOS\EMM386.EXE NOEMS X=D000-D1FF
BUFFERS=10,0
FILES=40
DOS=UMB
LASTDRIVE=Z
FCBS=16,0
DOS=HIGH
DEVICE=C:\DOS\DBLSPACE.SYS /MOVE
SHELL=C:\DOS\COMMAND.COM C:\DOS\ /e:1024 /p
STACKS=9,256
DEVICE=\DOS\MTMCDE.SYS /D:MSCD001 /P:300 /A:0 /M:20 /T:6 /I:10
DEVICEHIGH /L:1,12048 =C:\DOS\SETVER.EXE

[COMMON]
REM *****SOUND BLASTER NEW DOS DRIVERS **************
REM DEVICE=C:\SB16\DRV\CTMMSYS.SYS
REM DEVICE=C:\SB16\DRV\CTSB16.SYS /UNIT=0 /BLASTER=A:220 I:5 D:1 H:5
```

The block MENU in the CONFIG.SYS file tells DOS to start the menu system. The statement *menuitem* specifies the menu item displayed. The listing after the = is the subroutine in the CONFIG.SYS file to go to. The text after the comma is the displayed menu item. The item *menudefault* is the default menu to use, and the number after the default is the number of seconds DOS waits before automatically choosing the item. The COMMON subroutine is run for all menu items. You can also specify the color of the displayed menu by adding *menucolor* as a statement.

A typical AUTOEXEC.BAT file would appear as follows:

```
REM *******Configuration Block***************************
IF "%CONFIG%" == "Windows" goto WFW
IF "%CONFIG%" == "Games" goto REG_Games
IF "%CONFIG%" == "CDGames" goto CD_Games
IF "%CONFIG%" == "Program" goto Pgram
IF "%CONFIG% == "Programcd" goto pgramcd
goto end
REM ****************************************************

REM ***********WINDOWS*********************************
:WFW
LH /L:0;1,12880 /S C:\WINDOWS\net start
LH /L:1,16944 C:\DOS\SHARE /L:500 /F:2048
@ECHO OFF
LH /L:0 C:\DOS\SMARTDRV.EXE 2048 128
PROMPT $P$G
path c:\dos;c:\qtw;c:\windows;c:\excel;c:\winword;c:\;c:\util;c:\monologw
set bpath=;c:\util\macros
set bhelp=c:\util\help
set bbackup=\util\backup
set bflags=-i120r -mMKA
set btmp=util
SET MSINPUT=C:\MSINPUT
C:\MSINPUT\KEYBOARD\KBDCPL.EXE /S
SET TEMP=C:\WINDOWS\TEMP
SET NSE_DOWNLOAD=e:\DOWNLOAD
set mouse=C:\DOS
C:\DOS\mouse.exe /Q
LH /L:2,36544 C:\DOS\MSCDEX.EXE /S /d:mscd001 /m:10 /s
REM ****** Sound Blaster Statements ********************
SET BLASTER=A220 I5 D1 H5 P330 T6
SET SOUND=C:\SB16
SET MIDI=SYNTH:1 MAP:E
SET SOUND=C:\SB16
C:\SB16\SB16SET /M:220 /VOC:220 /CD:220 /MIDI:220 /LINE:0 /TREBLE:0
C:\SB16\SBCONFIG.EXE /S
REM *****************End Sound Blaster Statements
WIN
GOTO END2
REM ****************************************************

REM *****************Regular GAMES**********************
:REG_Games
LH /L:1,16944 C:\DOS\SHARE /L:500 /F:2048
@ECHO OFF
LH /L:0 C:\DOS\SMARTDRV.EXE 2048 128
```

```
PROMPT $P$G
path c:\dos;c:\qtw;c:\windows;c:\excel;c:\winword;c:\;c:\util;c:\monologw
set bpath=;c:\util\macros
set bhelp=c:\util\help
set bbackup=\util\backup
set bflags=-i120r -mMKA
set btmp=util
SET TEMP=C:\WINDOWS\TEMP
SET NSE_DOWNLOAD=e:\DOWNLOAD
set mouse=C:\DOS
C:\DOS\mouse.exe /Q
REM ****** Sound Blaster Statements *********************
SET BLASTER=A220 I5 D1 H5 P330 T6
SET SOUND=C:\SB16
SET MIDI=SYNTH:1 MAP:E
SET SOUND=C:\SB16
C:\SB16\SB16SET /M:220 /VOC:220 /CD:220 /MIDI:220 /LINE:0 /TREBLE:0
C:\SB16\SBCONFIG.EXE /S
REM *****************End Sound Blaster Statements
GOTO END2
REM ****************************************************

REM ***************CD GAMES*****************************
:CD_games
LH /L:1,16944 C:\DOS\SHARE /L:500 /F:2048
@ECHO OFF
LH /L:0 C:\DOS\SMARTDRV.EXE 2048 128
PROMPT $P$G
path c:\dos;c:\qtw;c:\windows;c:\excel;c:\winword;c:\;c:\util;c:\monologw
set bpath=;c:\util\macros
set bhelp=c:\util\help
set bbackup=\util\backup
set bflags=-i120r -mMKA
set btmp=util
SET TEMP=C:\WINDOWS\TEMP
SET NSE_DOWNLOAD=e:\DOWNLOAD
set mouse=C:\DOS
C:\DOS\mouse.exe /Q
LH /L:2,36544 C:\DOS\MSCDEX.EXE /S /d:mscd001 /m:10
REM ****** Sound Blaster Statements *********************
SET BLASTER=A220 I5 D1 H5 P330 T6
SET SOUND=C:\SB16
SET MIDI=SYNTH:1 MAP:E
SET SOUND=C:\SB16
C:\SB16\SB16SET /M:220 /VOC:220 /CD:220 /MIDI:220 /LINE:0 /TREBLE:0
C:\SB16\SBCONFIG.EXE /S
goto END2
REM *****************************************************

REM *************Programmer Section*********************
:Pgram
LH /L:1,16944 C:\DOS\SHARE /L:500 /F:2048
@ECHO OFF
LH /L:0 C:\DOS\SMARTDRV.EXE 2048 128
```

```
PROMPT $P$G
path c:\dos;c:\qtw;c:\windows;c:\excel;c:\winword;c:\;c:\util;c:\monologw
set bpath=;c:\util\macros
set bhelp=c:\util\help
set bbackup=\util\backup
set bflags=-i120r -mMKA
set btmp=util
SET TEMP=C:\WINDOWS\TEMP
SET NSE_DOWNLOAD=e:\DOWNLOAD
set mouse=C:\DOS
C:\DOS\mouse.exe /Q
LH /L:1,6384 C:\DOS\DOSKEY
REM ****** Sound Blaster Statements ********************
SET BLASTER=A220 I5 D1 H5 P330 T6
SET SOUND=C:\SB16
SET MIDI=SYNTH:1 MAP:E
SET SOUND=C:\SB16
C:\SB16\SB16SET /M:220 /VOC:220 /CD:220 /MIDI:220 /LINE:0 /TREBLE:0
C:\SB16\SBCONFIG.EXE /S
REM *****************End Sound Blaster Statements
goto END2
REM *****************************************************

REM *************PROGRAMER_CD***************************
:Pgramcd
LH /L:1,16944 C:\DOS\SHARE /L:500 /F:2048
@ECHO OFF
LH /L:0 C:\DOS\SMARTDRV.EXE 2048 128
PROMPT $P$G
path c:\qtw\bin;c:\dos;c:\tempra;c:\windows;
  c:\excel;c:\winword;c:\;c:\util;c:\monologw
set bpath=;c:\util\macros
set bhelp=c:\util\help
set bbackup=\util\backup
set bflags=-i120r -mMKA
set btmp=util
SET TEMP=C:\WINDOWS\TEMP
SET NSE_DOWNLOAD=e:\DOWNLOAD
set mouse=C:\DOS
C:\DOS\mouse.exe /Q
LH /L:2,36544 C:\DOS\MSCDEX.EXE /S /d:mscd001 /m:10
LH /L:1,6384 C:\DOS\DOSKEY
REM ****** Sound Blaster Statements ********************
SET BLASTER=A220 I5 D1 H5 P330 T6
SET SOUND=C:\SB16
SET MIDI=SYNTH:1 MAP:E
C:\SB16\SB16SET /M:220 /VOC:220 /CD:220 /MIDI:220 /LINE:0 /TREBLE:0
C:\SB16\SBCONFIG.EXE /S
REM *****************End Sound Blaster Statements
goto END2
REM *****************************************************
:end
:END2
```

TROUBLESHOOTING

Troubleshooting the newer versions of DOS is a simple matter. With previous versions, to see what was wrong, you had to be quick pressing a CTRL-C combination or boot from a floppy. While that may still be true for some DOS problems, the easiest way to isolate a DOS problem is to use the options available in DOS itself.

By using the F8 key when the "starting MS-DOS or PC-DOS" statement is displayed, you can individually choose which lines in your CONFIG.SYS and AUTOEXEC.BAT files to run. This allows you to ferret out errant device drivers or other commands that aren't working as they should. If you really have a problem, you can bypass CONFIG.SYS and AUTOEXEC.BAT file by using the F5 key at the same place in the boot sequence.

If you suspect you have a problem with one of your disk drives, use the CHKDSK or SCANDISK utilities. CHKDSK is a command line utility that verifies the File Allocation Table and files. If you use CHKDSK with the /F switch, it will fix any problems it finds. SCANDISK is a graphical utility that verifies the entire hard drive and performs surface scans. If you suspect your hard drive is faulty, you might want to verify its status using FDISK. This utility shows the low-level status of the drive. If you use the /MBR switch, you will recreate your master boot record.

Tip:

Do not use CHKDSK with compressed drives. Only use SCANDISK.

Tip:

A lot of problems perceived as disk problems are caused by viruses. If after using all the other utilities you still have a problem, scan your disk and diskette drives for viruses.

Problems with insufficient memory can often be solved with MEMMAKER. If you want to see your current memory configuration, use the MEM command. With the /C switch, MEM allows you to view all the memory including upper and extended memory as well as the programs loaded into it.

A utility for users of MS-DOS or Windows is MSD.EXE, which shows you most of the system and configuration files, and also displays a memory map of the system it is run on. MSD can be useful in determining interrupt and address conflicts within your system. It also contains an editor to allow you to edit your configuration files, including the CONFIG.SYS, AUTOEXEC.BAT, and Windows .INI files.

Workstation Problems

On the workstation, most problems are related to software or hardware conflicts. LAN adapters use one or more of the following:

Base I/O port
Interrupt
Shared RAM address
DMA channel

A conflict can occur with any of these characteristics. However, the most likely causes of conflicts are interrupts, shared RAM address, or the DMA channel. Interrupt conflicts are most likely to occur with modems and video adapters. A program designed to poll the machine for devices and used ports will be helpful in isolating the problem.

One of the most common conflicts involves interrupt channels. Most adapters in a computer will generate an interrupt. ISA machines cannot share interrupts, so each one must be unique. Many Micro Channel and EISA devices are designed to share interrupts at least with like devices. This makes a lot of the problems easier to work with. Table 1-3 lists the most common interrupt conflicts with ISA machines.

Table 1-3. *Common Interrupt Conflicts with ISA Bus Machines*

Interrupt 2/9	Video adapters, other LAN adapters, mouse
Interrupt 3	COM2
Interrupt 4	COM1
Interrupt 5	LPT2, mouse
Interrupt 6	Floppy controller
Interrupt 7	LPT1
Interrupt 10	Hard drive controller, PS/2 mouse
Interrupt 11	Hard drive controller
Interrupt 12	Hard drive controller

Shared RAM addresses can also conflict with the machine or other devices in the machine. Many machines shadow the BIOS and video into RAM. This shadowing can conflict with the RAM address space of the network adapter. Also, VGA controllers often use the address space from C000 to C7FF.

Tip:

Another problem may occur between VGA controllers and 16-bit shared RAM adapters that involves the way adapters send information along the bus. Data is sent in blocks. Sixteen-bit adapters that occupy the same 128KB memory segment (i.e., from D000 to DFFF) must decode the information in the same way. The available sizes are 16KB and 128KB. If the sizes are different, only one of the adapters will work. The majority of video adapters and shared RAM adapters allow you to adjust this size to allow them to match.

Another source of problems with shared RAM adapters is memory managers. You must exclude the area of memory the adapter will be using. If the adapter is using memory segment from C800 to CBFF, you must exclude this area of memory. The exclusion statements for memory managers are different, but must include a statement of exactly how much memory to exclude.

Tip:

WINDOWS users may also have to exclude the area of memory for shared RAM adapters in the SYSTEM.INI file. To do this, place the following statement in the [386enh] section of the SYSTEM.INI file:

```
EMMEXCLUDE=XXXX-YYYY
```

in which X is the beginning of the shared RAM address and Y is the end.

Tip:

For ARCnet workstations, most vendors require a 16KB address space for shared RAM. However, only the first 8KB is critical. The last 8KB is reserved for a boot ROM. If you are not going to remote boot, only exclude the first 8KB. This can be a bit of a help if you are truly subject to RAM cram.

DMA conflicts occur with other ISA devices using DMA. The other adapters that use this space include SCSI device controllers. An additional problem can occur with bus-mastering devices. The problem revolves around bus access with multiple bus-mastering devices. Bus-mastering devices hold the bus until they have completed the DMA data transfer or until the next video refresh cycle. However, when multiple bus-mastering adapters are in place they must give up the bus more often. The criteria for doing this are based on the priority of the DMA channel and an algorithm called fairness. Most of the drivers for bus-mastering adapters invoke fairness; however, some do not. For those that do not invoke fairness, you can sometimes manipulate the device's time on the bus.

Another alternative is to place the device that is not operating properly at a higher-priority DMA channel. To do this, place the device at a channel with a lower number than the device that will not invoke fairness.

Another problem related to DMA bus-mastering in ISA machines is that some machines on the market will not support ISA bus-mastering. In that case, you must disable bus-mastering. The majority of these problems do not appear with EISA machines or with EISA bus-mastering adapters. With Micro Channel machines, you must set an arbitration level. The arbitration level automatically sets bus priority between multiple bus-mastering adapters.

NET.CFG Problems

The NET.CFG file controls the configuration files for the NetWare workstation components. The values placed in NET.CFG are designed to override the default configuration. Most of the time, the default configuration works well. However, if you change the adapter from the default settings you must record the changes in the NET.CFG file. The settings you place here must match the settings on the adapter. They will override the default settings built into the driver. If the settings do not match, the driver will fail to load. The applicable NET.CFG settings are placed under the LINK DRIVER statement. The options include:

DMA number
: This option is used to configure the DMA channel for the adapter.

INT number
: This option is used to configure the interrupt.

MEM number

This option specifies the beginning memory address range for shared RAM adapters.

PORT address

This option is used to configure the starting port address for adapters using a port address.

FRAME type

This option is used to override the default FRAMETYPE. The driver will load if this option is incorrect; however, unless it matches the option set at the file server, you will not be able to find the file server.

chapter 2

The NetWare Requester for OS/2

OS/2 is designed as a true multitasking operating system that allows increased productivity by allowing users to run more than one application at a time. For users, OS/2 is a vast improvement over the way they worked on their computers before. For the network administrator, OS/2 is an operating system that must work compatibly with the network operating system. As a result, it has its own set of utilities and carries with it its own attendant problems. Because OS/2 is a multitasking operating system, the user can run multiple NetWare sessions at the same time. OS/2 eliminates the 640 kilobyte (KB) barrier of its predecessor, DOS. Programs designed for OS/2 use all the memory available on the computer to complete their tasks. Programs can load in any area of memory and each program is protected from the operations of the others. Thus, if one program crashes, it will not in most cases bring down the entire system.

Note:

While OS/2 is designed as a protected environment in which most program operations are not affected by others running simultaneously on the system, misbehaved programs occasionally will bring down the system. The obvious solution is to buy programs that have been written correctly.

OS/2 started as a combined effort of IBM and Microsoft. These companies were looking to provide a multitasking environment for PC users who needed the additional power that DOS could not provide. IBM and Microsoft also saw OS/2 as the core operating system for their network offerings, LAN Manager and OS/2 LAN Server. Early versions of OS/2, however, were not welcomed in the marketplace. Eventually Microsoft dropped development of OS/2 in favor of Windows NT and the Windows operating environment for DOS. However, IBM began a complete rework of OS/2 and eventually developed OS/2 v2.0, which was a full graphical user environment that solved many of the problems of the earlier versions. OS/2 v2.0 boasted a 32-bit operating system and enhanced user features. It also provided a facility to operate Windows programs and included a copy of Windows. However, OS/2 still presented problems with the amount of memory it required and the speed of the operating system required to run it. Answering these problems, IBM introduced OS/2 Warp (v3.0).

With the advent of NetWare 4.x, Novell introduced NetWare for OS/2, which allowed a NetWare server to run as a protected mode application on an OS/2-based machine.

Tip:

If you are running NetWare for OS/2, you should have a minimum of 20 megabytes (MB) of RAM and enough disk space for a NetWare partition. The minimum requirement for a NetWare SYS volume under OS/2 is 50MB.

The far more popular use of OS/2 is as a client to a NetWare server. In this chapter, we will discuss client configuration exclusively.

Requirements

The workstation requirements for OS/2 are substantial. OS/2 no longer can run on Intel 8086/8088 or 80286 machines. The minimum workstation is a 386 25MHz machine with four megabytes of RAM. If you intend to run the NetWare Requester for OS/2, you should have at least 8MB of workstation RAM. You will also want to be sure that you have a minimum of 4MB of disk space.

Some additional requirements are made at the NetWare server prior to successful OS/2 connection. First, the OS/2 support utilities must be installed at the server. These utilities include the additional OS/2 version 2.x versions of standard DOS utilities. If you have NetWare v3.12

or 4.x, these utilities are automatically copied to the server during installation and reside in the \LOGIN\OS2 directory.

If you plan to support OS/2's High Performance File System (HPFS) extended file names, you must also add the OS/2 name space to the server for each volume OS/2 clients will use. Name space support takes the original DOS file name and creates a separate entry in the file allocation table (FAT) to support OS/2 extended names.

Installation and Configuration

The NetWare Requester for OS/2 installation program, which allows you to install OS/2 from its distribution diskettes, is located on the NetWare CD-ROM. If you choose to install from diskettes, a batch file allows you to create five diskettes and a boot diskette for the Virtual Loadable Modules (VLMs) OS/2 uses.

To install the NetWare Requester for OS/2, open an OS/2 window or full-screen session on the workstation. Insert the WSOS2_1 diskette and type INSTALL. You will see a screen with basic instructions and a series of menus at the top. (See Figure 2-1.)

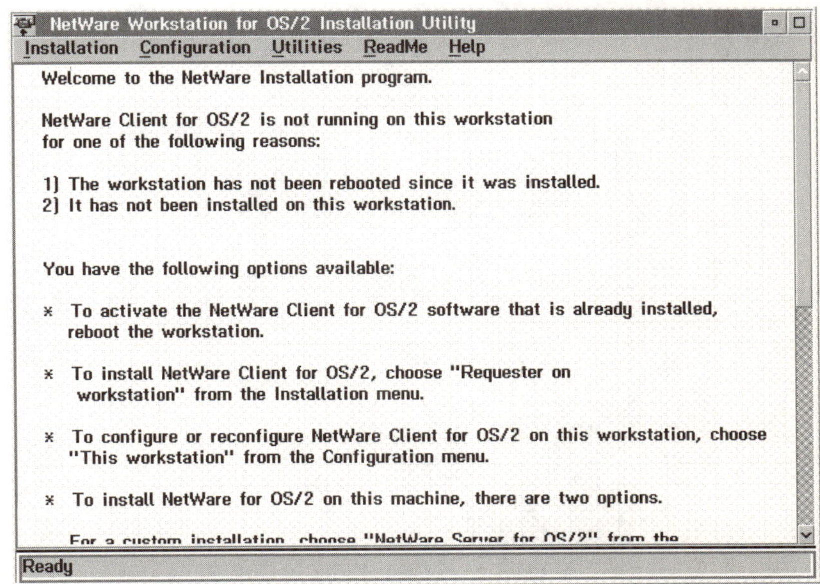

Figure 2-1 *The OS/2 Installation screen.*

From the Installation menu, select the option Requester on Workstation. The installation process will ask you to select a target directory and a source drive for the OS/2 Requester files. The default target directory is \NETWARE; drive A is the source drive. (See Figure 2-2.)

After you select the directory and drive, you must select the operations you want to perform. (See Figure 2-3.) If this is the first time you

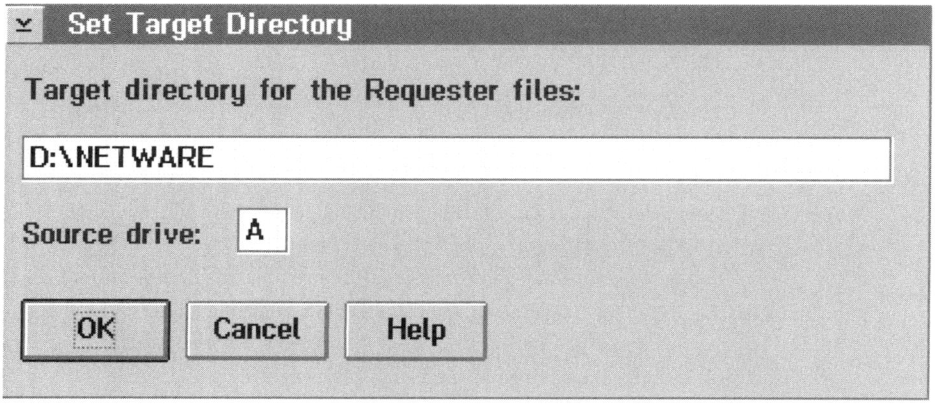

Figure 2-2. *OS/2 target directory and source drive selections.*

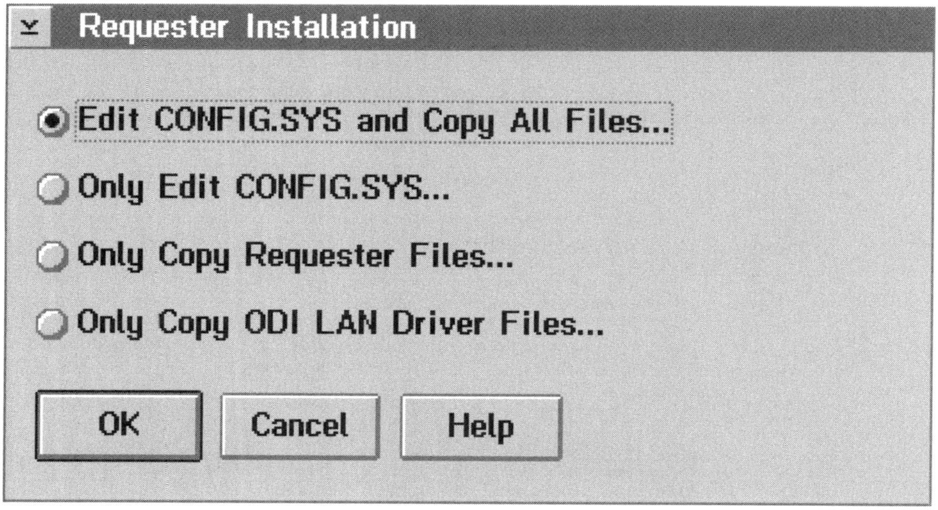

Figure 2-3. *Installation options.*

have installed the OS/2 Requester, accept the default option Edit CONFIG.SYS and Copy All Files. If you are modifying a workstation configuration, choose the installation choice that matches the actions you need to perform. These options are:

- Only Edit CONFIG.SYS
- Only Copy Requester Files
- Only Copy ODI LAN Driver Files

If you have previously installed a LAN driver and only want to modify the options, select Edit CONFIG.SYS. If you are upgrading your copy of the OS/2 Requester, select Only Copy Requester Files. If you are upgrading your Open Data-Link Interface (ODI) drivers, select Only Copy ODI LAN Driver Files.

Driver Support

The next step in NetWare Requester for OS/2 installation is to select the ODI driver you want to install. You may type the name of the driver or select from a list. (See Figure 2-4.) If you select from the list of available drivers, you will be prompted to insert the diskette labeled

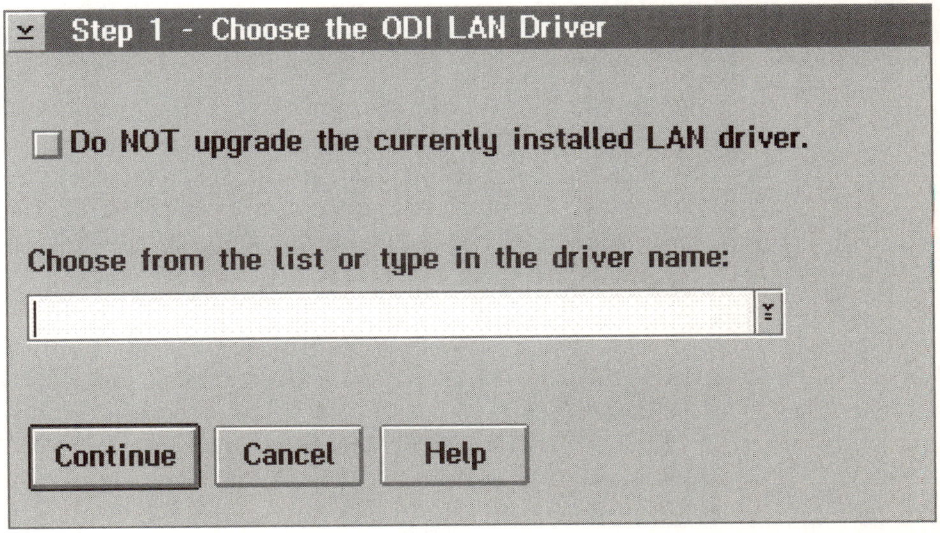

Figure 2-4. *Driver options.*

Step 1 - Choose the ODI LAN Driver

Do NOT upgrade the currently installed LAN driver.

Choose from the list or type in the driver name:

E21ODI.SYS
PIOS2ODI.SYS
PMOS2ODI.SYS
SMC8000.SYS
SMC8100.SYS
SMC8232.SYS

Figure 2-5. *Driver list.*

WSDRV_1. This diskette provides a list of drivers. OS/2 Requester drivers have a SYS extension and load from the CONFIG.SYS file. (See Figure 2-5.)

Note:

At this point, we should remind you that when you create the boot diskettes you should label them according to the electronic diskette label. If you fail to do this, you may become confused. The installation program calls the diskettes by their electronic label. The installation batch file tells you which labels to use.

Once you choose the driver, you are asked to choose NetWare Support for DOS and Windows Applications. (See Figure 2-6.) This option determines how DOS and Windows sessions are supported under OS/2. If you choose Private Support, each DOS or Windows session has a separate login to NetWare and represents a new NetWare session. You may have multiple logins under NetWare or multiple user names. This convention can be useful if your DOS or Windows sessions

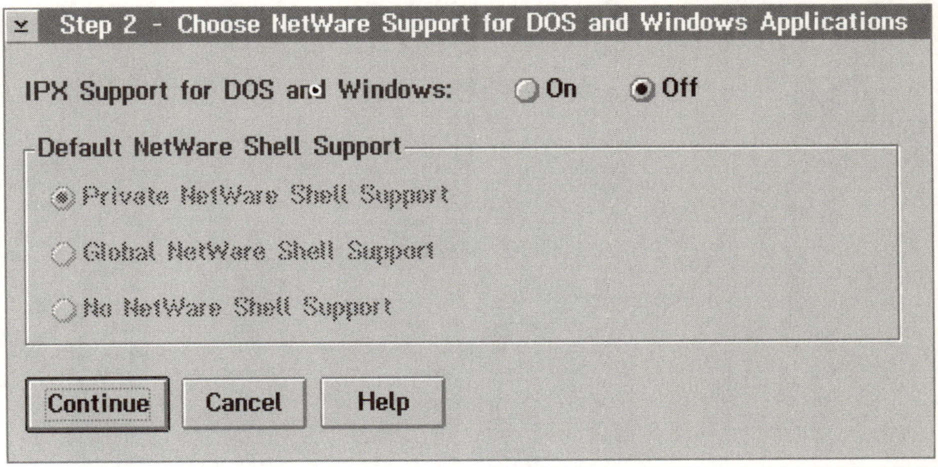

Step 2 - Choose NetWare Support for DOS and Windows Applications

IPX Support for DOS and Windows: On Off

Default NetWare Shell Support

Private NetWare Shell Support

Global NetWare Shell Support

No NetWare Shell Support

Continue Cancel Help

Figure 2-6. *NetWare client support for DOS and Windows.*

require a different set of drive mappings or if you need to login as a different user for accounting purposes. For example, if you have NetWare accounting enabled, you could login as different users for different chargeable purposes.

If you select Private NetWare Shells, the installation process creates an AUTOEXEC.BAT file in the root directory of the workstation's OS/2 partition. This file runs each time you use a DOS window or full-screen DOS session and each time you run a Windows session. After selecting this option, you will need to verify or make some configuration changes. To do this, select Settings by clicking the right mouse button on the DOS icon. Select the Session, then tab and click on the DOS Settings radio button. (See Figure 2-7.)

The DOS Settings dialog box lets you make various changes in a CONFIG.SYS file and other settings for each DOS session. If you have multiple icons, each representing a different DOS session, you will need to make the changes in each one. Verify that the following settings are enabled:

DOS_LASTDRIVE	Z
DOS_FILES	214 (This setting is used for Private sessions only)
VIPX_ENABLED	Set to ON for both Private and Global sessions
DOS_DEVICE	path\OS2\MDOS\LPTDD.SYS

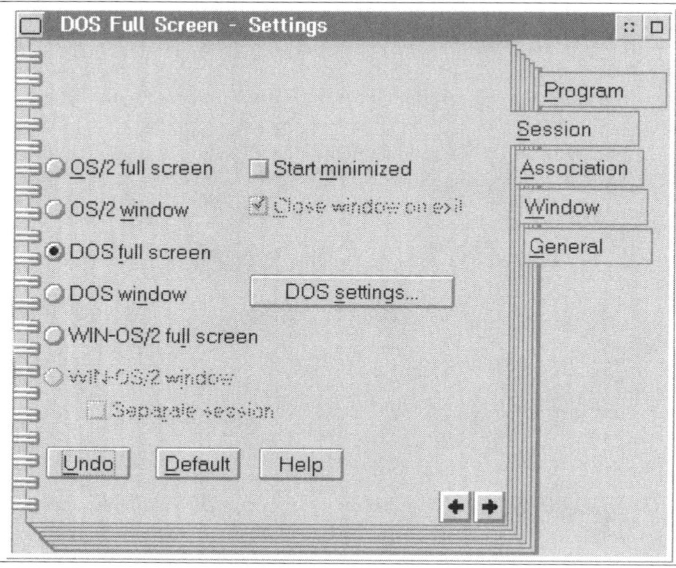

Figure 2-7. *Settings session.*

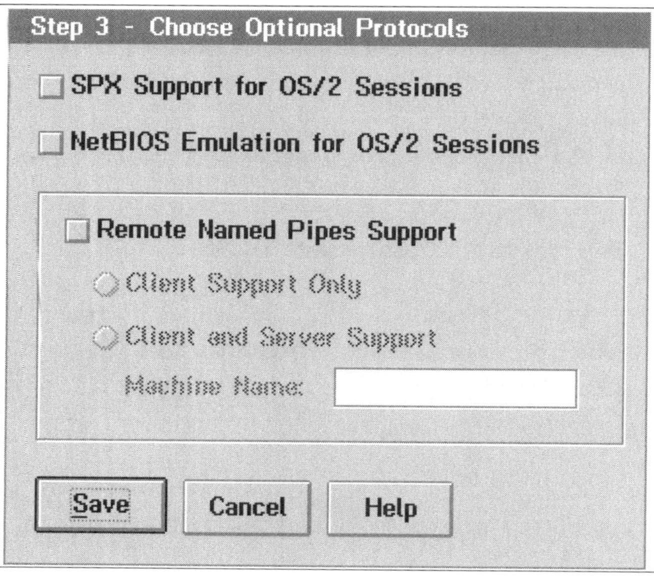

Step 3 - Choose Optional Protocols

SPX Support for OS/2 Sessions

NetBIOS Emulation for OS/2 Sessions

Remote Named Pipes Support

Client Support Only

Client and Server Support

Machine Name:

Save Cancel Help

Figure 2-8. *Additional protocol support.*

For sessions in which a Windows program operates under OS/2, called WIN OS/2, set the following as a DOS_DEVICE:

```
path\os2\mdos\winos2\system\tbm12.com
```

Note:

If you experience a problem with WIN OS/2 sessions, add the following to your DOS settings:

```
INT_DURING_IO WIN-OS/2 - OFF
```

Use this command in the NET.CFG file if applications fail to launch during a Windows OS/2 session.

If you choose a Global NetWare shell, the NetWare Support for DOS and Windows sessions operate through the original OS/2 login. You cannot change the attributes for individual sessions to use a single user login. For most OS/2 users, this login will be sufficient.

Additional Protocol Support

The next step after choosing the shell you will use is to choose additional protocols OS/2 sessions need to support. (See Figure 2-8.) You may add support for the Sequenced Packet Exchange (SPX) protocol, NetBIOS, and Named Pipes. If you choose support for Named Pipes, you must also choose the type of support—whether Client Support Only or Client and Server Support. You must also choose a machine name. For most purposes, this additional support is not necessary and can greatly diminish the speed of your machine on the network. Once you have chosen the support you need, choose the Save option.

The installation program then records changes to the CONFIG.SYS file. After the changes are made to the CONFIG.SYS file, the NetWare files are copied to the directory you selected. During the copy process you have the option to copy all the adapter drivers shipped with the OS/2 client kit or only the driver you selected. Unless you plan to change drivers frequently, you should only copy the driver you plan to use. (See Figure 2-9.)

Once the files are copied, the installation program returns you to the original installation screen. You should then select the Configuration Menu option to verify the contents of the workstation's NET.CFG file

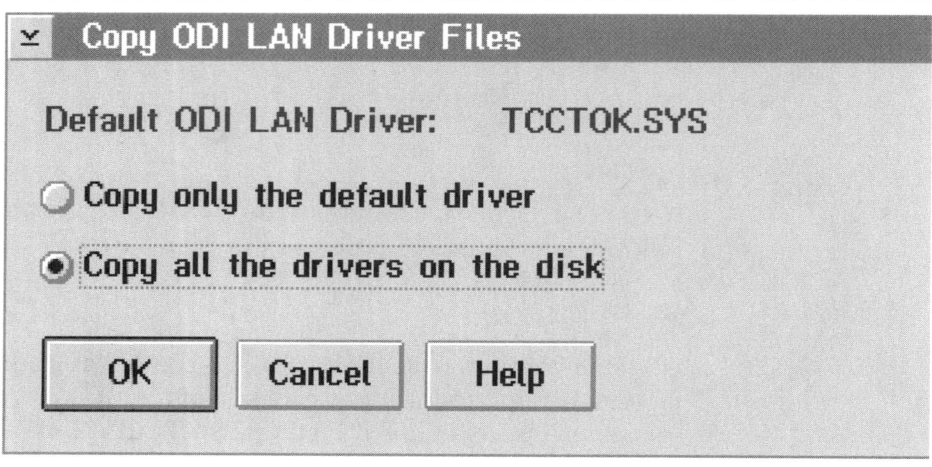

Figure 2-9. *Copy ODI driver.*

contained in the root directory of the OS/2 partition. The location of this file differs from the DOS location. Be sure that it is located in the root directory and that it contains the information you require. The options for the NET.CFG are as follows:

- DAEMON CONFIGURATION
  - MESSAGE TIMEOUT
- LINK DRIVER
  - DMA
  - FRAME
  - INT
  - MEM
  - NODE ADDRESS
  - PORT
  - PROTOCOL
  - SLOT
- LINK SUPPORT
  - BUFFERS
- NAMED PIPES
  - ADVERTISE BOARD

    CLIENT SESSIONS
    MACHINE NAMES
    SERVER SESSIONS
NETWARE NETBIOS
    ABORT TIMEOUT
    BIND
    BROADCAST COUNT
    BROADCAST DELAY
    COMMANDS
    INTERNET
    LISTEN TIMEOUT
    NAMES
    RETRY COUNT
    RETRY DELAY
    SESSIONS
    VERIFY TIMEOUT
NETWARE REQUESTER
    CACHE BUFFERS
    DEFAULT LOGIN DRIVE (Default is first NetWare drive)
    DISPLAY HARD ERRORS
    LARGE INTERNET PACKETS
    NAME CONTEXT
    PACKET BURST OFF
    PREFERRED SERVER
    PREFERRED TREE
    REQUEST RETRIES
    SESSIONS
    SIGNATURE LEVEL
    PROTOCOL ODINSUP
    BIND
PROTOCOL STACK IPX
    BIND
    ROUTER MEM
    SOCKETS
PROTOCOL STACK SPX
    ABORT TIMEOUT
    LISTEN TIMEOUT
    VERIFY TIMEOUT
    RETRY COUNT
    SEND TIMEOUT
    SESSIONS
TOKEN RING SOURCE ROUTING

DEF
GBR
MBR
NODES
BOARD
VIRTUAL MLID FOR LAN SHARING
VIRTUAL BOARD SIZE

The definitions of each of these settings are in the *NetWare Requester for OS/2* manual that ships with NetWare.

Configuration changes to the NET.CFG file can be made with any ASCII text editor, but should be made from the Configuration Menu option. (See Figure 2-10.)

Additional Configuration Options

The NetWare Requester for OS/2 has additional configuration options. If you are using Network Driver Interface Specification (NDIS) as well as ODI drivers, you must configure a shim that allows an ODI driver to operate within the NDIS protocol stack. This is accomplished through

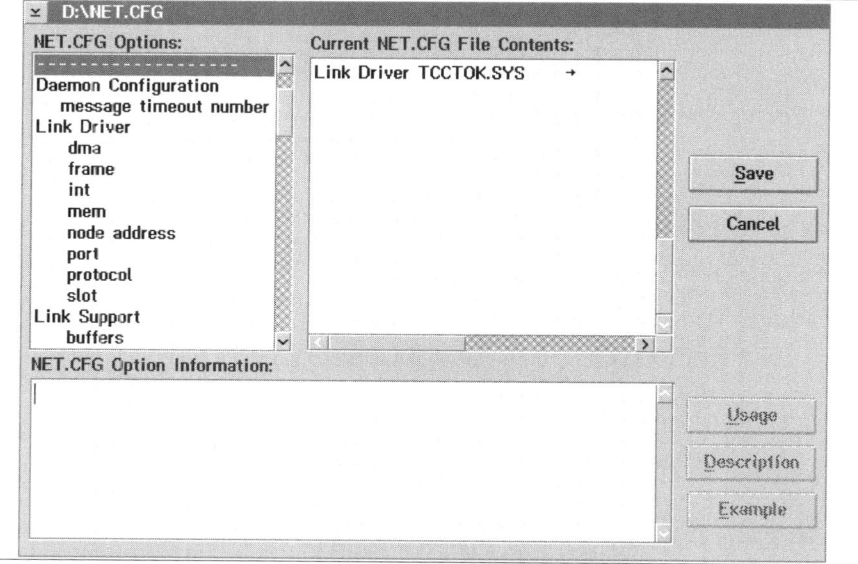

Figure 2-10. *The NET.CFG configuration screen.*

Figure 2-11. *Novell icons.*

the ODINSUP shim. To configure ODINSUP, select ODINSUP from the main Installation menu.

If you have installed everything properly, when you reboot you should have a Novell folder on your desktop. The Novell folder contains the NetWare tools and other utilities for printing and help. (See Figure 2-11.)

The CONFIG.SYS is modified to include your NetWare file in LIBPATH, SET PATH, and SET DPATH. In addition, the following additional changes are made to the CONFIG.SYS file.

```
REM — NetWare Requester statements BEGIN --
SET NWLANGUAGE=ENGLISH
DEVICE=D:\NETWARE\LSL.SYS
RUN=D:\NETWARE\DDAEMON.EXE
REM — ODI-Driver Files BEGIN —
DEVICE=D:\NETWARE\TCCTOK.SYS
REM — ODI-Driver Files END —
REM DEVICE=D:\NETWARE\ROUTE.SYS
DEVICE=D:\NETWARE\IPX.SYS
REM DEVICE=D:\NETWARE\SPX.SYS
REM RUN=D:\NETWARE\SPDAEMON.EXE
REM DEVICE=D:\NETWARE\NMPIPE.SYS
REM DEVICE=D:\NETWARE\NPSERVER.SYS
REM RUN=D:\NETWARE\NPDAEMON.EXE
DEVICE=D:\NETWARE\NWREQ.SYS
IFS=D:\NETWARE\NWIFS.IFS
RUN=D:\NETWARE\NWDAEMON.EXE
REM DEVICE=D:\NETWARE\NETBIOS.SYS
REM RUN=D:\NETWARE\NBDAEMON.EXE
REM DEVICE=D:\OS2\MDOS\LPTDD.SYS
REM -- NetWare Requester statements END --
```

Tip:

Do not remove the REM statements. These are used by the installation utility to locate the Novell file and ODI driver statements when they are modified by the installation utility.

Note:

In NetWare Requester for OS/2, drive mappings appear as branches from the root of the NetWare volume. In Global DOS sessions, drives mapped in the OS/2 session appear as root drives. However, if a drive is mapped in the Global DOS session, it appears as a normal branched drive in the OS/2 session. Private DOS sessions do not show the drive mappings from the OS/2 session and vice versa. In addition, search drives are not required in OS/2 sessions.

Troubleshooting the NetWare Requester for OS/2

The NetWare Requester for OS/2 presents some major troubleshooting challenges. All required files load in the CONFIG.SYS file, so if something crashes there is no way to repair it and move on or stop a device from loading except to remove the line referring to it and try again. However, if the device fails to load, you will be presented with an error message and the boot process will halt until you press a key to continue. The final problem may be apparent when NetWare cannot get a connection ID. The system will attempt to establish a connection until that error message appears, causing the system to slow considerably.

Much of the troubleshooting for DOS sessions applies to OS/2 itself. These are some tips to try to resolve DOS session problems.

1. Be sure that everything is installed and contains the correct path statements or is in the right place. Remember, the NET.CFG file must be in the root directory.
2. Verify that there are no IRQ conflicts in the system.
3. Watch each LOAD statement to be sure it contains the information you think you entered. LAN drivers will attempt to load at defaults if they cannot find an appropriate statement in the NET.CFG file. If the driver appears to load at the wrong settings

or fails to load the settings should be reflected in the messages the driver displays.

4. Verify your cable connections. For example, most token-ring drivers will not load unless the adapter can enter the ring. This process requires that a cable be attached. If it is not, the driver will fail to load and will generate an error message.

Performance

Performance under OS/2 is generally slower than under DOS for any given adapter. The overhead associated with the NetWare Requester for OS/2 slows the connection considerably. However, there is some performance tuning that can be done.

First, be sure that packet burst is installed properly. Its default setting is ON, but can be turned OFF with a keyword in the NET.CFG file. Also, the performance under packet burst can be altered by adjusting the number of buffers available. The buffer size is a function of the packet size you are using. For Ethernet, the correct packet size is 1,514–1,522 bytes depending upon the adapter chipset in use. (Refer to the documentation with the adapter for the correct packet size.) For token-ring, the correct packet size is 1KB to 17KB. Increasing the number of buffers will generally increase performance.

Second, VLMs generally improve performance. Use the VLM boot diskette if performance under the NETX redirector is an issue. The VLM boot option ships with the latest version of the NWCLIENT for OS/2 installation.

Third, use Global as opposed to Private sessions for DOS utilities. This option eliminates some overhead from the redirector and lets the redirector operate more efficiently.

chapter 3

Windows and Windows for Workgroups

Windows was designed by Microsoft Corp. as a front-end environment for DOS. It replaced the cryptic C:\ prompt with a series of user-friendly applications that allowed both novice and experienced PC users to more fully exploit their machines. It went through several reiterations of software that attempted to use the features of the chip for which it was designed. Windows 1.0 offered a mostly text-based series of additional programs. Windows 286 took advantage of increased memory and protected-mode capabilities. It was only with the advent of the Intel 8386 chip that Microsoft developed a winner with Windows v3.1 and its later version, Windows v3.11. This icon-based operating environment sat on top of DOS and functioned like a shell. However, it took over most of the functions of DOS, leading to a revitalization of the computer market, particularly for home use.

With the explosion of Windows also came an onslaught of PC-based networks. Users who would not touch a computer before Windows now found themselves in a quandary. They had learned to use the various features of Windows and had gotten used to an icon-based computing environment, as well as many of the extension programs such as File Manager that made the routine DOS functions much easier to manage.

In response, Microsoft made several changes to Windows in v3.11 that made it extremely friendly to networks, particularly those running NetWare. First, you could install a common version of Windows on a

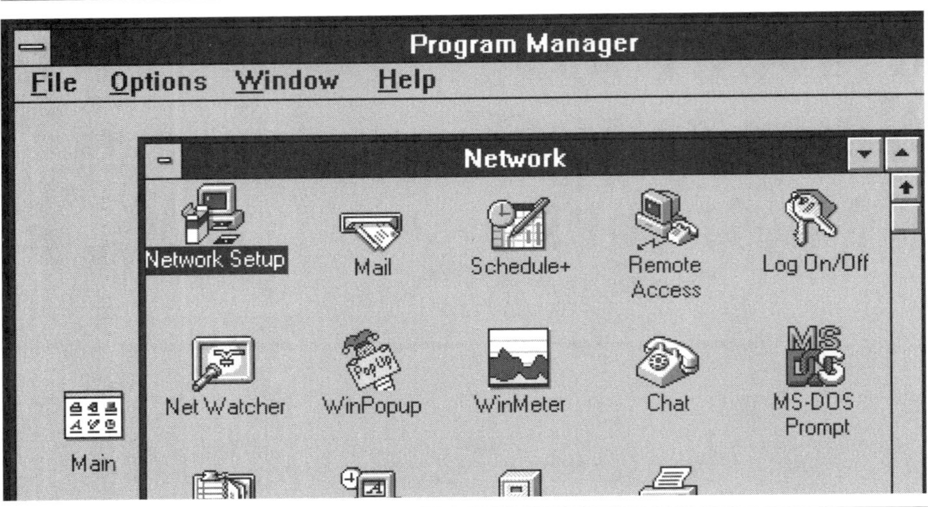

Figure 3-1. *The NetWare Program Group on Windows v3.11.*

network and have each user run Windows from the network environment. File Manager, Print Manager, and other programs were redesigned to allow you to work with mapped network drives and to map drives and printers from these utilities (see Figure 3-1). With the addition of the NETWARE.DRV, NWUSER.EXE, and related dynamic link libraries (DLLs), you could perform many of the functions performed by DOS-based programs or command line options. In particular, you could change the drive and printer mappings, run USERLIST, and send broadcast messages.

Note:

One of the annoying aspects of broadcast messages was that sometimes they could lock Windows. The ability to not accept any broadcast messages while in Windows was a big boost to the network use of Windows.

Now users who were comfortable in the Windows environment could use Windows and Windows programs over the network; added functionality for NetWare allowed them to more easily perform their jobs. This added functionality led to a wild expansion of Windows on the network. The only thing that held back the use of Windows on the network was the general decrease in its speed.

The addition of Windows for Workgroups on the network alleviated some of the speed problems and allowed users to include an added dimension to their network environment: the workgroup. A workgroup is a series of computers arranged together as a group for the purpose of sharing files and printers from the users' individual machines.

Windows Setup and Configuration

In Windows v3.1 and 3.11, Microsoft introduced NetWare-specific configuration options and additional driver and application support.

Tip:
The applications and drivers are available from Novell on the CompuServe NetWire forum, from Novell's Web site WWW.NOVELL.COM, or from Novell's FTP server, FTP.NOVELL.COM. Additionally, these applications and drivers now come with the DOS Client Kit that ships with NetWare v3.12 and 4.x.

Windows Network Setup

Windows has several setup options designed for network use, which speed installation time and simplify its use. The first option, SETUP /A, allows the network administrator to set up a common version of Windows on the network. This is not a usable version, but it contains the files necessary for the user to set up his or her version of Windows on a local drive or hard drive. After the files have been transferred to the network drive using SETUP /A, the network administrator must make this drive available to all users, with shareable, read-only access.

Tip:
Failure to set the access to shareable read-only could allow a user to delete files that must be available to all users, save confidential information to the common drive, or set up his or her

own version of Windows over the common version. All these options, to varying degrees, are undesirable.

The second option, SETUP /N, allows the network administrator to set up a networked version of Windows in the user's home directory on the network or local hard drive. The user's individual .INI and other setup files will be stored in his or her home directory, along with the user's individual WIN.COM file. However, all the applications will be stored in the common directory with access available to all users. This saves precious network drive space. This setup method works for Windows v3.1, 3.11, and Windows for Workgroups.

Tip:

If you allow users to run Windows from the network, you will need to make some allowance for users to set up swap files. Swap files are created through the 386 Enhanced icon in the Control Panel. They allow Windows to create virtual memory from available hard disk space. The swap file can hold up to several megabytes of data and can be maintained on the network or on a local hard drive. Putting the swap files on the network will take up valuable disk space and create additional network traffic as the users' Windows applications swap memory out to the network. Many network managers provide small local hard drives for Windows swap files.

Windows v3.1 Installation for NetWare

NetWare files are easily installed and integrated with Windows v3.1. First, select the Network section from the main setup menu. Then, select Novell NetWare v3.1x or above as the Network option (see Figure 3-2).

Windows will copy the following files to the Windows subdirectory:

NETX.COM
IPXODI.COM
TBM12.COM
IPX.OBJ
LSL.COM

Change System Settings

Display: VGA

Keyboard: Enhanced 101 or 102 key US and Non US keyboards

Mouse: Microsoft, or IBM PS/2

Network: No Network Installed

No Network Installed
Novell NetWare (shell versions 3.21 and above)
Novell NetWare (shell versions 3.26 and above)
Novell NetWare (shell versions below 3.01)

Figure 3-2. *Windows v3.1 network setup.*

The Windows installation program assumes you are using an ODI shell. If the versions of LSL.COM, IPXODI.COM, and NETX.COM are older than those included with Windows, use the ones supplied with Windows. If they are newer, continue to use the newer versions. The IPX.OBJ file is provided for older linkable NetWare shells. If you are using these shells, you must relink the shells with the IPX.OBJ file included with Windows.

Note:

At this point you should be using ODI-compliant client software. If you are not, this is a good time to upgrade. Most adapter vendors will supply you with ODI-compliant drivers, making the switch relatively painless. Not only will the Windows installation run better, you will gain the additional benefits that come with using the latest driver specification. These benefits include compatibility with most of Novell's new products.

Once NetWare support is installed, the SYSTEM.INI file should appear as in Figure 3-3.

```
[boot]
shell=progman.exe
mouse.drv=mouse.drv
network.drv=NMETWARE.DRV
language.dll=
sound.drv=mmsound.drv
comm.drv=comm.drv
keyboard.drv=keyboard.drv
system.drv=system.drv
386grabber=vga.3gr
oemfonts.fon=vgaoem.fon
286grabber=vgacolor.2gr
fixedfon.fon=vgafix.fon
fonts.fon=vgasys.fon
display.drv=vga.drv
drivers=mmsystem.dll

[keyboard]
subtype=
type=4
keyboard.dll=
oemansi.bin=

[boot.description]
keyboard.typ=Enhanced 101 or 102 key US & Non US keyboards
mouse.drv=Microsoft, or IBM PS/2
network.drv=Novell NetWare (shell versions 3.26 and above)
language.dll=English (American)
system.drv=MS-DOS System
codepage=437
woafont.fon=English (437)
aspect=100,96,96
display.drv=VGA

[386Enh]
32BitDiskAccess=OFF
device=*int13
device=*wdctrl
mouse=*vmd
network=*vnetbios, vnetware.386, vipx.386
ebios=*ebios
woafont=dosapp.fon
display=*vddvga
EGA80WOA.FON=EGA80WOA.FON
EGA40WOA.FON=EGA40WOA.FON
CGA80WOA.FON=CGA80WOA.FON
CGA40WOA.FON=CGA40WOA.FON
```

Figure 3-3. *The Windows v3.1 SYSTEM.INI file.*

```
keyboard=*vkd
device=vtdapi.386
device=*vpicd
device=*vtd
device=*reboot
device=*vdmad
device=*vsd
device=*v86mmgr
device=*pageswap
device=*dosmgr
device=*vmpoll
device=*wshell
device=*BLOCKDEV
device=*PAGEFILE
device=*vfd
device=*parity
device=*biosxlat
device=*vcd
device=*vmcpd
device=combuff
device=*cdpscsi
local=CON
FilSysChange=off
PagingFile=D:\WIN386.SWP
MaxPagingFileSize=12288
OverlappedIO=off

[standard]

[NonWindowsApp]
localtsrs=dosedit,ced

[mci]
WaveAudio=mciwave.drv
Sequencer=mciseq.drv
CDAudio=mcicda.drv

[drivers]
timer=timer.drv
midimapper=midimap.drv
```

Figure 3-3. *The Windows v3.1 SYSTEM.INI file, continued*

When you have completed the installation you will need to exit Windows and restart the system. When you restart the system, NWPOPUP will automatically run, providing you with access to NetWare broadcast messages during the Windows session.

Tip:

It is a good idea to turn off broadcast messages during a Windows session. First, broadcast messages are similar to certified mail: Nothing good is ever delivered. Second, a broadcast message may lock the Windows session, forcing you to reboot.

When Windows reloads, the NetWare drivers will allow you to see the network drives under File Manager and to add network printers with Print Manager (see Figure 3-4).

In addition, you will be able to log into the NetWare server as Windows loads. If you have logged into the NetWare network from a batch file, the NetWare login screen is omitted.

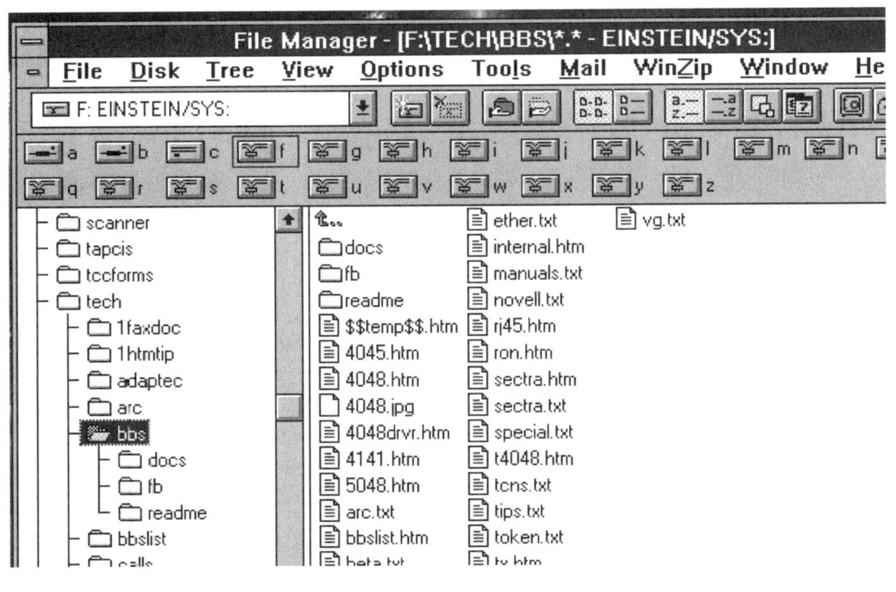

Figure 3-4. *File Manager screen.*

Tip:

Logging in from within a DOS prompt in Windows will yield unpredictable results. Also, you will not be able to use the drive mappings from within any other DOS prompt or from Windows applications. The reverse is also true. Never log out from within a Windows DOS prompt in Windows v3.1, Window 3.11, or Windows for Workgroups.

By installing Windows v3.1, you combine two sets of applications to provide an effective and useful interface. Many applications that were designed for Windows use, such as Word for Windows, WordPerfect, and Excel, have special operational capabilities on a network. In addition, the majority of applications designed for network analysis have Windows-compatible versions, such as LANalyzer for Windows and Novell and Intel's ManageWise.

Windows for Workgroups

Windows for Workgroups (WFW) includes many network and NetWare support enhancements for disk access, file access, and improved caching. Although enhancements to the base operating environment alone provide sufficient reason to change environments, the inclusion of peer-to-peer networking offers additional possibilities. The combination of NetWare and Windows for Workgroup's peer services provides you with an easy-to-use and powerful set of network services.

Network Setup

The installation of Windows for Workgroups on a network is the same as for Windows. The SETUP /A command allows the network administrator to set up a common version of Windows on the network. This is not a usable version, but it contains the files necessary for the user to set up his or her own version of Windows in a local drive or hard drive. After the files have been transferred to the network drive using SETUP /A, the network administrator must make this drive available to all users, with shareable, read-only access.

The user, or better yet, the network administrator, will then use the SETUP /N command to set up a networked version of Windows in the user's home directory on the network or on his or her local hard drive. The user's individual .INI and other setup files will be stored in the user's home directory along with his or her individual WIN.COM file. However, all of the applications will be stored in the common directory with access to all users. This saves precious network drive space.

During the setup of individual Windows for Workgroups sessions you may install the Windows peer-to-peer network functionality, client software for a variety of other network operating systems including NetWare, or both. If you install the Windows peer network, you may also elect to have files and printers shared over the peer network (see Figure 3-5).

Note:

If you load Windows for Workgroups from the NetWare server, you will only have the peer services of Windows for Workgroups when you are attached to the NetWare server. Most installations of Windows for Workgroups will load from a local hard drive.

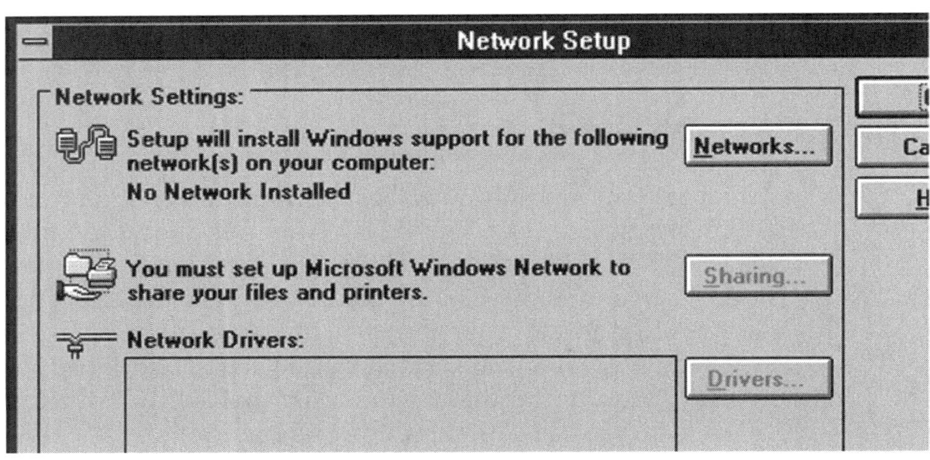

Figure 3-5. *Windows for Workgroups network installation.*

Tip:

If you allow users to run Windows from the network, you will need to make some allowance for the users to set up swap files. Swap files are set up through the 386 Enhanced icon in the Control Panel. They allow Windows to create virtual memory from available hard disk space. The swap file can hold up to several megabytes and can be maintained on the network or a local hard drive. Putting the swap files on the network will take up valuable disk space and create additional network traffic as the users' Windows applications swap memory out to the network. Many network managers provide small local hard drives for Windows swap files.

Enhancements for WFW

Several enhancements to Windows have been made in Windows for Workgroups. Among them are changes to the File Manager and Print Manager.

The Windows File Manager has been updated in Windows for Workgroups to allow users to connect network drives by pressing the Connect Network Drive icon or selecting it from the Drives menu bar. You will then be presented with a screen for selecting a network drive (see Figure 3-6). This screen is normally used to attach shared drives under WFW's peer services. You will notice a radio button marked NetWare. Select this button and then select the network drive you want to use. You will be taken to a NWUSER.EXE screen; select the network drive to map and a list of available drives (see Figure 3-7). You can elect to make this drive mapping permanent. If you do, the next time you run Windows this drive connection will be made for you.

The Print Manager and the Printers icon in the Control Panel work in a similar manner. To select a network printer in Print Manager, select Connect Network Printer, click on the NetWare radio button, and make the printer selection (see Figure 3-8). To install a printer using the Printers icon in the Control Panel, select the Printer icon. Then select the network radio button (see Figure 3-9). You will notice a NetWare radio button; select it and install the printer normally (see Figure 3-10). You will need to know the location of the printer driver for the printer you are selecting. Windows for Workgroups must have a copy of the printer driver in either the shared version of NetWare on the network or in the local Windows drive.

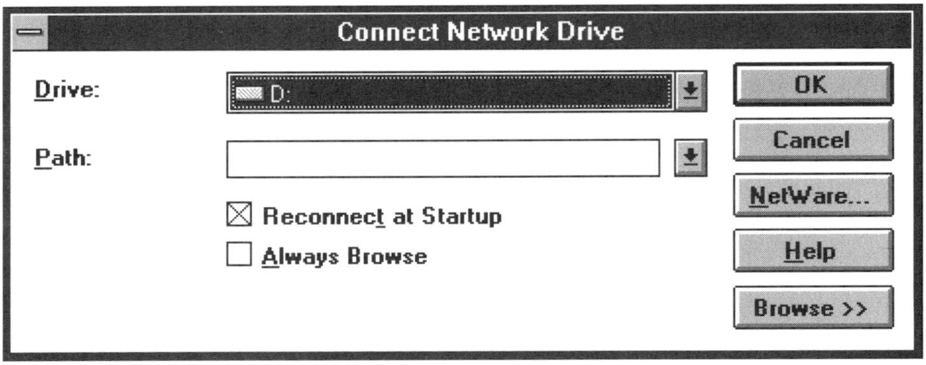

Figure 3-6. *Drive selection screen.*

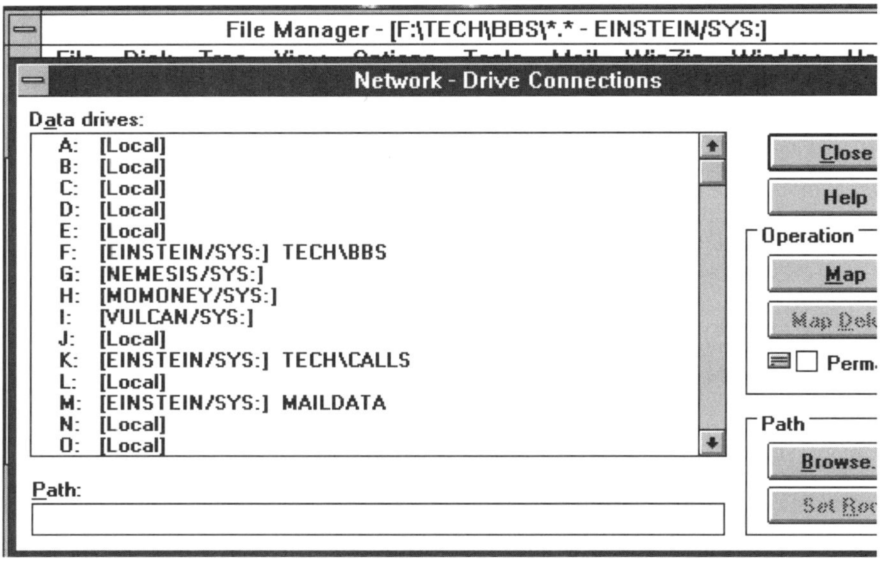

Figure 3-7. *NetWare mapping screen.*

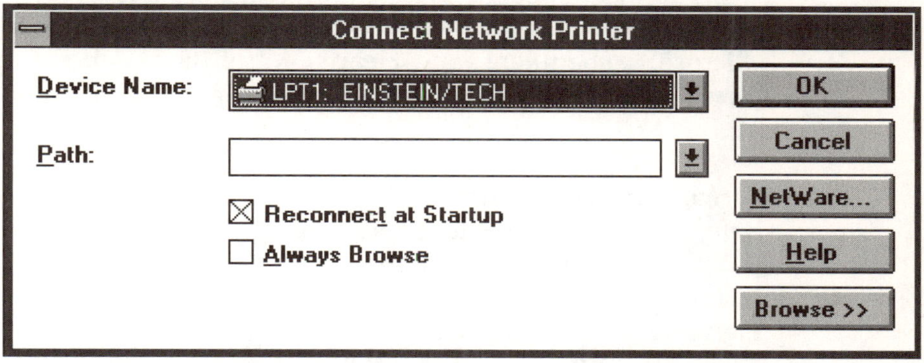

Figure 3-8. *Print Manager printer selection.*

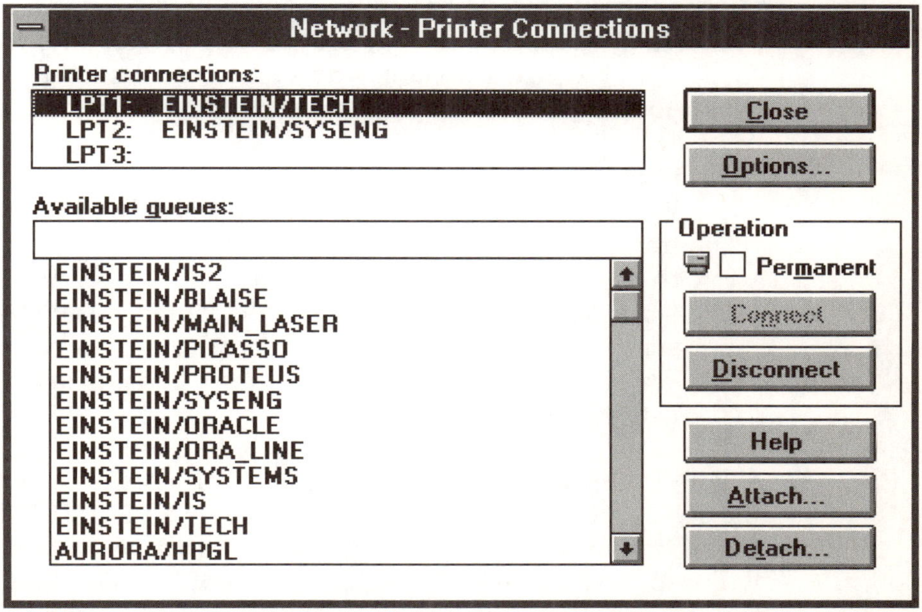

Figure 3.9. *Printer installation screen.*

If you install peer services along with the standard NetWare services you will have additional programs, including Microsoft Mail, Chat, Microsoft Scheduler+, and Hearts. All of these depend upon network services and require some additional setup.

Installing the Client Software

Before installing the client software on Windows for Workgroups, you must make several decisions. First, determine whether you will be installing only the NetWare client, or whether you will be installing the NetWare client along with peer service. If you install only the NetWare client, you must use either ODI drivers or a linked IPX.COM. During the installation of Windows for Workgroups you will be presented with the network option screens described earlier. Choose the network support you require. In the main installation screen you will be presented with a radio button for installing drivers (see Figure 3-10).

After selecting the radio button you will be taken to the Drivers installation screen. Select Add Adapter (see Figure 3-11).

The Add Adapter button will provide you with a list of driver options. You only need to be concerned with the ones labeled ODI support for ARCnet, Ethernet, or token-ring networks. Select the driver support appropriate for the access method you are using. Windows for Workgroups uses a shim to hook the ODI drivers into its NDIS interface, which allows the ODI drivers to be used in Windows for Workgroups peer networking, as well as in NetWare.

Note:

With WFW, Microsoft abandoned NetBEUI as its network transport protocol. It now uses a Microsoft version of IPX/SPX that is fully compatible with NetWare. Windows for Workgroups peer services can be routed through a NetWare server or Novell's MultiProtocol Router to connect workgroups that use different access methods or are on different network segments.

WFW will install the driver support for a standard interface using the access method chosen. It will then create a PROTOCOL.INI file and modify an existing NET.CFG file, or create a new file if necessary. It will also modify the WIN.INI and SYSTEM.INI file. When the installation is complete, the installation files should appear as shown in Figures 3-12 through 3-16.

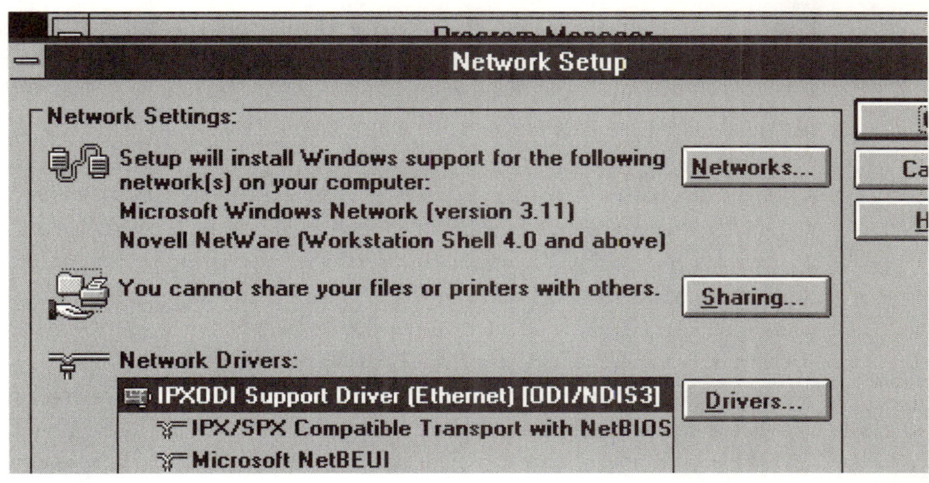

Figure 3-10. *Main network installation screen.*

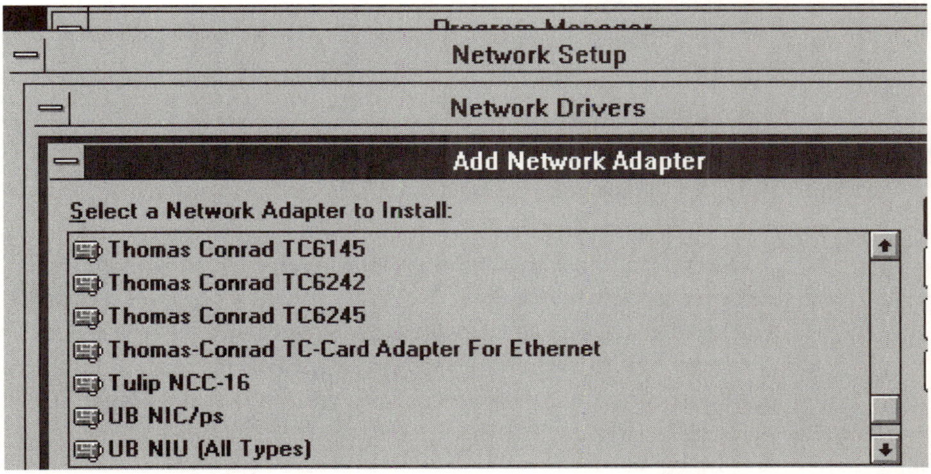

Figure 3-11. *Drivers installation screen.*

Note:

If the Windows for Workgroups installation finds an existing driver, the modifications will include the name of the driver in the appropriate sections of the NET.CFG and PROTOCOL.INI files. If it does not, it uses XXXX as a placeholder. If this happens during the installation, you must manually edit the files using a standard text editor. In addition, the Windows for Workgroups installation procedure will sometimes place the ODIHLP.EXE file out of place. It must appear after the ODI driver loads.

If you are installing the NetWare client software, you can install additional functionality and updated drivers by obtaining the latest client diskettes from either a newer version of NetWare, NetWire on CompuServe, Novell's FTP site (FTP.NOVELL.COM), or its Web site (WWW.NOVELL.COM). The NetWare client diskettes will install files to the WINDOWS subdirectory, make the necessary changes to the .INI files and to added drivers, and create a NWUSER.EXE.

The following files are contained on the NetWare client diskettes:

NETWARE.DRV	NWUSER.EXE
NETWARE.HLP	PNW.DLL
NWCALLS.DLL	TASKID.COM
NWGDI.DLL	TBM12.COM
DWIPXSPX.DLL	TLI_SPX.DLL
NWLOCALE.DLL	TLI_TCP.DLL
NWNET.DLL	TLI_WIN.DLL
NWPOPUP.EXE	VIPX.386
NWPSRV.DLL	VNETWARE.386

These files are the drivers, dynamic link libraries (DLLs), and applications necessary to link NetWare with Windows applications. Two of the applications are present as programs: NWPOPUP.EXE provides support for NetWare messages, and NWUSER.EXE lets you map drives and printers and use some of the more common NetWare utilities, such as USERLIST.

The drivers VIPX.386 and VNETWARE.386 allow for virtual sessions in 386 Enhanced mode, allowing you to use the interface in 386 Enhanced mode for virtual network services.

```
DEVICE= C:\DOS\HIMEM.SYS
DOS=HIGH
DEVICE=C:\DOS\SETVER.EXE
DEVICE=C:\WIN31\EMM386.EXE NOEMS X=B000-BFFF X=C800-D1FF
DEVICEhigh=C:\DOS\POWER.EXE
FILES=30
BUFFERS=30
DOS=HIGH,umb
DEVICEhigh=C:\thinkpad\IBMDSS01.SYS /S0=2
DEVICEhigh=C:\thinkpad\IBMDOSCS.SYS
DEVICEhigh=C:\thinkpad\DICRMU01.SYS /MA=C800-CFFF
DEVICEhigh=C:\thinkpad\$ICPMDOS.SYS
DEVICEhigh=C:\AUDIODD\TPAUDDD.SYS
lastdrive=z
STACKS=9,256
remDEVICE=C:\IBMAUDIO\DIAG\AUDTEST.SYS /
  F=C:\IBMAUDIO\DIAG\AUDTEST.OUT /V=10DE
DEVICE=C:\WINDOWS\IFSHLP.SYS
```

Figure 3-12. *Windows for Workgroups CONFIG.SYS file.*

```
C:\WINDOWS\net start
C:\WINDOWS\odihlp.exe
@echo off
rem lh C:\AUTOINST\MODACTIV /c2 /sA /PD000
@ECHO OFF
PROMPT $p$g
PATH C:\WIN31;C:\DOS;c:\windows;c:\nwclient
SET TEMP=C:\DOS
lh c:\thinkpad\fueldos
lh doskey
```

Figure 3-13. *Windows for Workgroups AUTOEXEC.BAT file.*

```
Link Driver PCMDMCS
  Frame Ethernet_802.3
  Frame Ethernet_II
  Frame Ethernet+802.2
  Frame Ethernet_SNAP
  PCMCIA

link driver token
      data rate 16
      pcmcia
```

Figure 3-14. *Windows for Workgroups NET.CFG file.*

```
[boot]
shell=program.exe
network.drv=wfwnet.drv
mouse.drv=mouse.drv
;comm.drv=comm.drv
comm.drv=C:\AUTOINST\WIN\SSCOMM.DRV
atm.system.drv=system.drv
386grabber=vga.3gr
oemfonts.fon=wgaoem.fon
fixedfon.fon=vgafix.fon
fonts.fon=vgasys.fon
display.drv=vga.drv
keyboard.drv=keyboard.drv
system.drv=atmsys.drv
286grabbe=vgacolor.2gr
MAVDMApps=
os2mouse.drv=mouse.drv
useos2shield=1
os2shield=winshield.exe
os2fonts.fon=vgasys.fon
fdisplay.drv=vga.drv
sdisplay.drv=vga.drv
secondnet.drv=netware.drv
drivers=mmsystem.dll
SCRNSAVE.EXE=C:\WINDOWS\SSFLYWIN.SCR

[keyboard]
keyboard.dll=kbdus.dll
oemansi.bin=
subtype=
type4=

[boot.description]
mouse.drv=Microsoft, or IBM PS/2
language.dll=English (American)
system.drv=MS-DOS System
codepage=437
woafont.fon=English (437)
aspect=100,96,96
display.drv=VGA
keyboard.typ=Enhanced 101 or 102 key US & Non US keyboards
network.drv=Microsoft Windows Network (version 3.11)
fdisplay.drv=VGA
secondnet.drv=Novell NetWare (Workstation Shell 4.0 and
   above)
[386Enh]
EMMExclude=D000-DFFF
;
REM===================PCMCIA DRIVERS====================
device=C:\AUTOINST/WIN/SSVRDD.386
device=C:\AUTOINST/WIN/SSVCD.386
```

Figure 3-15. *The Windows for Workgroups SYSTEM.INI file.*

```
COM1Base=3F8
Com1Irq=4
COM2Base=02F8
COM2Irq=3
COM3Base=3E8
COM3Irq=4
COM4Base=2E8
COM4Irq=4
TimerCriticalSection=10000

device=*vpd
mouse=*vmd
woafont=dosapp.fon
display=*vddvga
EGA80WOA.FON=EGA80WOA.FON
EGA40WOA.FON=EGA40WOA.FON
CGA80WOA.FON=CGA80WOA.FON
CGA40WOA.FON=CGA40WOA.FON
device=vpmtd.386
device=lpt.386
device=serial.386
device=vcomm.386
device=vtdapi.386
device=vshare.386
device=vcache.386
device=ifsmgr.386
device=C:\BH\DRIVERS/BHSUPP.386
device=C:\BH\DRIVERS/VBH.386
device=C:\WINDOWS\SYSTEM\WIN32S\W32S.386
DEVICE=CS48BA11.386
32BitDiskAccess=OFF
device=*int13
device=*wdctrl
network=*vnetbios,*vwc,vnetsup.386,vredir.386,vserver.386
ebios=*ebios
keyboard=*vkd
device=*vpicd
device=*vtd
device=*reboot
device=*vdmad
device=*vsd
device=*v86mmgr
device=*pageswap
device=*dosmgr
device=*vmpoll
device=*wshell
device=*BLOCKDEV
device=*PAGEFILE
device=*vfd
device=*parity
device=*biosxlat
```

Figure 3-15. *The Windows for Workgroups SYSTEM.INI file, continued*

```
;device=*vcd
device=*vmcpd
device=*combuff
device=*cdpscsi
local=CON
FileSysChange=off
netheapsize=20
InDOSPolling=FALSE
secondnet=vnetware.386
OverlappedIO=off
netmisc=ndis.386,msodisup.386
transport=nwlink.386,nwnblink.386,netbeui.386
PagingFile=C:\WINDOWS\WIN386.SWP
MaxPagingFileSize=5233
ReflectDOSInt2=TRUE
UniqueDOSPSP=TRUE
PSPIncrement=5

[standard]

[NonWindowsApp]
localtsrs=dosedit,ced

[mci]
CDAudio=mcicda.drv
Sequencer=mciseq.drv
WaveAudio=mciwave.drv

[drivers]
midimapper=midimap.drv
WAVE=CS48BA21.DRV
timer=timer.drv

[vcache]
minfilecache=512

[Network]
FileSharing=No
PrintSharing=No
LogonDisconnected=yes
EnableSharing=No
winnet=wfwnet/00025100
multinet=netware4
UserName=user3
Workgroup=ENTERPRISE
ComputerName=THINKPAD_750
Comment=Mark Anderson
logonvalidated=no
PreferredRedir=FULL
```

Figure 3-15. *The Windows for Workgroups SYSTEM.INI file, continued*

```
[DDEShares]
CHAT$=winchat,chat,,31,,0,,0,0,0
SCHAT$=winchat,chat,,31,,0,,0,0,0
CLPBK$=clipsrv,system,,31,,0,,0,0,0
HEARTS$=mshearts,hearts,,15,,0,,0,0,0

[NetWare]
NWShareHandles=TRUE
RetoreDrives=TRUE

[network drivers]
devdir=C:\WINDOWS
LoadRMDrivers=No
netcard=
transport=

[Password Lists]
*Shares=C:\WINDOWS\Share000.PWL
MARKANDE=C:\WINDOWS\MARKANDE.PWL
USER3=C:\WINDOWS\USER3.PWL

;=============================================

[NWNBLINK]
LANABASE=0
```

Figure 3-15. *The Windows for Workgroups SYSTEM.INI file, continued*

The files provided in the NetWare DOS client kit provide additional functionality for File Manager, Print Manager, and the new NWUSER.EXE utility.

To install the new client software, follow the procedures outlined in the Windows 3.1 documentation. The installation utility will update the files as needed. Be sure to select the line that will install the Windows drivers and utilities.

If you chose to install Windows support, the installation utility will make changes to the WIN.INI, SYSTEM.INI, and group files. You will now have a NetWare group and several NetWare utilities. When installing the new Windows utilities, you will find that many of the files and libraries depend on the NetWare shell or VLMs. If you are using VLMs, additional functionality is provided.

Note:

Many of the standard NetWare utilities, such as NETADMIN, have Windows-based components; if you install and use

```
[network.setup]
version=0x3110
netcard=ms$odimac,1,MS$ODIMAC,4
transport=ms$nwlinknb,NWLINK
transport=MS$netbeui,NETBEUI
lana0=ms$odimac,1,ms$nwlinknb
lana1=ms$odimac,1,ms$netbeui

[Link Driver PCMDMCS]
data=Frame Ethernet_SNAP
data=Frame Ethernet_802.2
data=Frame Ethernet_II
data=Frame Ethernet_802.3
data=Link Driver PCMDMCS

[net.cfg]
PATH=C:\WINDOWS\net.cfg


[MS$ODIMAC]


[NWLINK]
BINDINGS=PCMDMCS

[NETBEUI]
BINDINGS=PCMDMCS
LANABASE=1
SESSIONS=10
NCBS=12
```

Figure 3-16. *The Windows for Workgroups PROTOCOL.INI file.*

VLMs with NetWare 4.x, you will be able to use those NetWare utilities in a familiar Windows format.

Remember that the login for NetWare must occur prior to loading WFW. You should include the login statements in either the AUTOEXEC.BAT file or some other batch file called from the AUTOEXEC.BAT that executes prior to loading WFW. If you load Windows for Workgroups from the network, this will not be a problem.

chapter

4

Windows NT and Windows 95

With the failure of OS/2 v1.3, Microsoft broke away from IBM and went on a development path that led to Windows NT. Designed around the Digital VMS operating system, Windows NT promised to be the multiplatform operating system of the future. Windows NT v3.1 was released in 1993 and became a marginal success. Microsoft released an upgraded version of Windows NT in 1994, v3.5. This version has become the platform of choice for many high-powered workstations. It works not only on the Intel platform, but on MIPS and ALPHA as well. It provides true 32-bit multiuser, multithreaded, preemptive multitasking and does so with the familiar look and feel of existing Windows products. It also provides LAN manager style domain-based networking as well as peer services. Windows NT comes in two flavors, server and workstation. The server product has all the features of LAN Manager, and a few others, including peer services, built into the base operating system. Both versions provide excellent access to NetWare also built into the base operating system.

In April 1995, Microsoft decided that the new Intel-based operating system, code-named Chicago and now named Windows 95, would be introduced in August 1995 (hence the name). To complete this time schedule, Microsoft introduced a pay-for-beta scheme, wherein many Windows users were able to obtain beta copies and provide Microsoft with valuable feedback to complete its project. Windows 95 is the true multitasking replacement for DOS and Windows. Like Windows NT, it is a true 32-bit multitasking operating system. Unlike Windows NT, it retains enough Windows 3.1 16-bit code to provide compatibility with existing legacy products and to work with almost all of the existing Windows products. It also retains the peer networking services of Windows for Workgroups (v3.11) and has many built-in features for compatibility with NetWare and other network operating systems.

Windows 95

Windows 95 has made great strides toward integrating Windows, NetWare, and Microsoft networking products into a single 32-bit network client package. In addition, it maintains compatibility with existing NetWare products and applications that require a 16-bit interface by allowing the user to use the NetWare redirector (NETX.EXE or VLMs) and existing NetWare drivers (NETWARE.DRV), and DLLs (NWNET.DLL and NWCALLS.DLL). This is especially important for current Windows-based NetWare-aware applications that require existing DLLs, such as NWADMIN, or older products that require the NetWare Redirector, such as RCONSOLE.

Overview of Windows 95 Networking

If you are unfamiliar with Windows 95, you will notice many things have changed from the traditional desktop available with Windows, Windows for Workgroups, or Windows NT. A true desktop now exists where you can place icons. Networking capabilities appear on the desktop in the form of the Network Neighborhood, an icon that displays the network objects, server, directories, and other devices as icons that you simply click on with your mouse to install or use. The Program Manager has been replaced by the Start menu, a menu bar that can be placed along any outer edge of the monitor. We prefer to leave it at the top edge and force it to disappear when not in use. The menu bar presents the available programs as a series of small icons in pull-down menus. It takes some getting used to, but you will find it much easier to work with than Program Manager. (However, if you find you can't exist without the Program Manager, you can replace the Start menu bar with the Program Manager.) You will also notice that you now actually have something to do with the right mouse button. In fact, it is very important for selecting options and changing settings for the various components. For network operations, the right mouse button is used to share drives for Microsoft networking and to map network drives.

The network services of Windows 95 use the Network Driver Interface Specification (NDIS) version 3.0. This 32-bit driver standard works nicely with the rest of Windows 95's 32-bit operating system. If you have the appropriate .INF file, you can use an NDIS 2.0 driver (a slower 16-bit driver that reduces the overall speed of the network). The .INF files (NETxxx.INF) are text files that provide driver settings and binding information used by the Windows 95 operating system to install the driver. You can also use your 16-bit NetWare ODI driver. These, however, will also reduce your overall network speed.

Available Drivers for Windows 95

NDIS v3.0	A 32-bit Network Driver Interface Specification driver
NDIS v2.0	A 16-bit Network Driver Interface Specification driver
ODI	A 16-bit Open Data-Link Interface driver

Windows 95 provides its own networking in the form of Microsoft peer networking services. This provides workgroup peer file- and print-sharing services compatible with Windows NT peer services and Windows for Workgroups networking services. However, they are more tightly integrated into the base operating system and provide a full 32-bit networking subsystem for peak performance. In addition, Microsoft provides full support for NetWare in its integrated graphical network logon. The logon function includes pass-through security that provides a single login to your Microsoft network and NetWare login. It also provides full support for NetWare login Scripts. NetWare 4.x support is provided if the servers are running bindery emulation. NetWare Directory Services support is supposed to be available from Microsoft, but will more than likely require Novell to come out with its own 32-bit client kit that will provide the support necessary.

Note:

One of the things you will find you like best about the full 32-bit network services using NDIS 3.0 drivers and the Microsoft NetWare Client is that it is incredibly fast. This is by far the recommended use of the network services under Windows 95.

Finally the standard peer services can be configured to integrate and accept user security through the NetWare bindery. Thus, you can control peer access to machines based on Windows 95 share-level security or maintain access in the NetWare bindery. You will then select the NetWare users that may access their hard drives by granting read or full access to specific users. User rights can be maintained by the NetWare administrator without a secondary database. You must only select which of the NetWare users you will allow to access the system. Windows 95 does not yet support NDS, so the database uses the bindery and will not pick up NDS objects. You can then select the NetWare file- and print-sharing services and use workgroup networking with NetWare. This provides the complete integration with NetWare that many users have been looking for. The Windows 95 machine will appear as another server that shares its drives with the rest of the Novell network based upon the NetWare bindery security model.

NetWare Client Support

NetWare servers are accessed through the same network services used to provide access to Microsoft network services. NetWare servers may be accessed by using the Network Neighborhood icon. The Network Neighborhood is an icon on the desktop used to list NetWare servers, LAN Manager, or Windows NT domains and peer workgroups as icons. NetWare print queues can be accessed for installation through the Printer folder available in the Control Panel, or through the Network Neighborhood. To attach a NetWare printer simply open the Network Neighborhood icon. Select the appropriate NetWare server. You will then see the available directories and print queues as icons. Select the appropriate queue, click the right mouse button and select Attach Network Printer. You will be presented with the Printer Wizard, which helps you set up your NetWare print queues. At this point you may need the Windows 95 CD to obtain the correct printer driver. When you have completed the installation through the Printer Wizard, print a test page, and the installation is complete.

Note:

Be advised that NetWare printing is currently problematic. The NetWare print queues have a nasty habit of disappearing just as you are ready to print, and the drag and drop printing function still does not work properly. Many of the NetWare problems that existed in the Pay for Beta (M8) version have been solved in later test versions, but printing is still not foolproof.

While you no longer have the use of NWUSER.EXE, the integration within the base operating system more than makes up for the loss. Even standard command line utilities such as WHOAMI are integrated into the base system. To access WHOAMI, simply click the right mouse button on the Network Neighborhood icon. (Remember, we told you that the right mouse button finally had a purpose in life.) This type of integration is unprecedented and makes the network experience truly enjoyable for the user.

As we discussed previously, NetWare support under Windows 95 has two facets. The first is the built-in Microsoft NetWare support, which is made possible by Microsoft's switch from NetBEUI as its primary protocol to an IPX/SPX-compatible protocol. This provides Microsoft not only with a routable protocol, but with default compatibility with Novell-style networking. The second facet is the support provided by Novell with its latest NETWARE.DRV, the driver used to support NetWare services on a Windows-based client. NETWARE.DRV allows Windows users to use File and Print Manager programs within Windows to attach and use Novell drives and print queues. Also, Novell's latest client kit (now shipping with NetWare v4.1) recognizes the existence of Windows 95 and integrates with the Universal Client.

Installation of NetWare Support

The installation of network services and NetWare support is as easy as using the rest of Windows 95. It is initially configured, as is everything else in Windows 95, through the Installation Wizard. (A Wizard is Microsoft's scripted installation [or other setup] utility.) If your adapter is a plug-and-play adapter, it will be automatically detected and the driver installed. If your adapter is not plug-and-play, Windows 95 will attempt to detect your network adapter. If the network adapter has a driver in its base operating system, Windows 95 will more than likely detect your operating system. However, this is not foolproof and it can cause problems; you may be better off selecting your adapter manually. If your adapter's driver is not available on the base operating system, check to see if your adapter has available an NDIS v2.0 or v3.0 driver and .INF file. If it does, simply select a new or updated driver and install it from a diskette drive. You may also decide to use an existing ODI driver as your network driver. This will require that you install LSL.COM and the ODI driver from the AUTOEXEC.BAT or STARTNET.BAT files. Complete the installation according to the Installation Wizard. To change your settings, simply select the Control Panel and the Network icon. (See Figure 4-1.)

Windows 95 installs the Microsoft network client and the Microsoft NetWare client by default. The default protocols are IPX/SPX (NWLINK) and NetBEUI. TCP/IP is also built-in with TELNET and PING utilities. For those addicted to the Internet, a Web browser has been planned, but not yet implemented. Other clients are available for most of the popular network operating systems, including SUN OS, Banyan VINES, Artisoft's LANtastic, and of course Novell's NetWare.

If you want to change your network settings or to add networking features at a later date, it is done manually through the Control Panel. You can get to the Control Panel through the Start menu by selecting Start and Settings off the first menu bar or by selecting the My Computer icon (hopefully, you have changed the name of this icon to something reasonable, like Fred) and selecting the Control Panel folder. When the Control Panel folder is displayed, select Network. This will present you with a panel with the existing loaded configuration and an

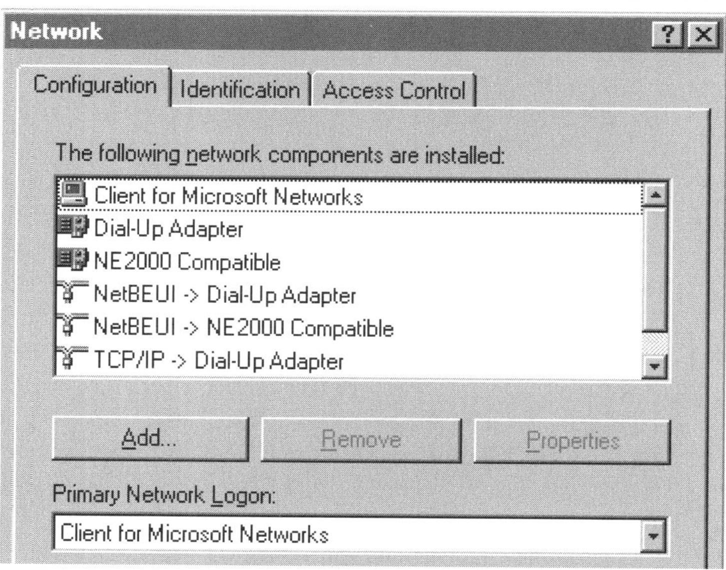

Figure 4-1. *Networking installation dialog box.*

option to set the primary login. When you select Add you will be presented with a list of four options: Client, Adapter, Protocol, and Service.

The Client represents the network operating system you will be connected to (see Figure 4-2). As shown previously, the default clients are Microsoft Network Client and Microsoft NetWare client. You may add a client of your own, including Novell, Banyan, Artisoft, etc. The only real issue here is whether to use Microsoft's NetWare client or Novell's. Versions of Windows 95 prior to beta build 484 would not work properly if Microsoft's NetWare client was selected with ODI drivers. If you choose to use Microsoft's client, the Setup Wizard will automatically remove the IPXODI and Shell statements from your batch file. Microsoft's IPX/SPX (NWLINK) compatible protocol and 32-bit redirector will handle these functions. All things considered, you should probably select the Microsoft NetWare client; it is actually much faster and is a little more integrated with the rest of Windows 95. If, however, you have a special need, such as the fact that you run Novell utilities that require VLMs, you should select the appropriate NetWare v3.x or

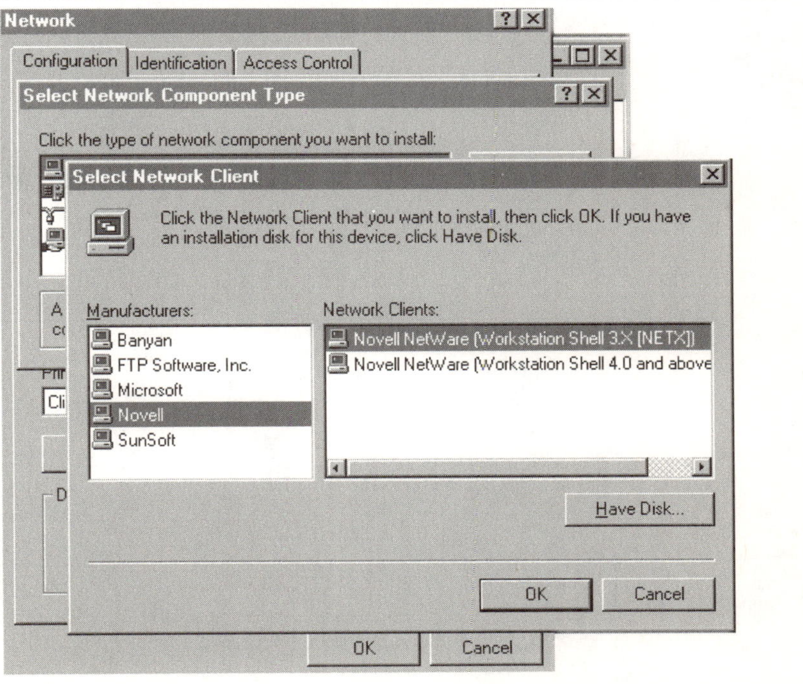

Figure 4-2. *Available clients.*

4.x client. A 16-bit redirector will then be installed to integrate with Novell utilities. Be sure you have your NetWare Client Kit handy. For the NetWare v3.x shell, you will need the NETWARE.DRV file; for the NetWare 4.x client you will need to install the NetWare Client Kit according to instructions.

The adapter section allows you to install the appropriate adapter for your computer. A large number of adapters are built into the base system (see Figure 4-3). If yours is not shown, be sure you have an appropriate NET???.INF file from your vendor. To install the driver, simply click the Have Disk radio button. Depending on your version of Windows 95 (beta or released) you may need to copy this file into the WINROOT\INF subdirectory and reboot the machine to rebuild the database. (This, like several others, is hidden. Don't worry if you can't find it; just copy it there.) Your real choice at this point is which driver standard to use. Windows 95 supports NDIS 3.x, NDIS 2.x, or ODI. Unless you have a specific need, we recommend NDIS 3. It will provide you with a full 32-bit networking interface and greatly enhance your overall system speed. NDIS 2.x is presented only as an

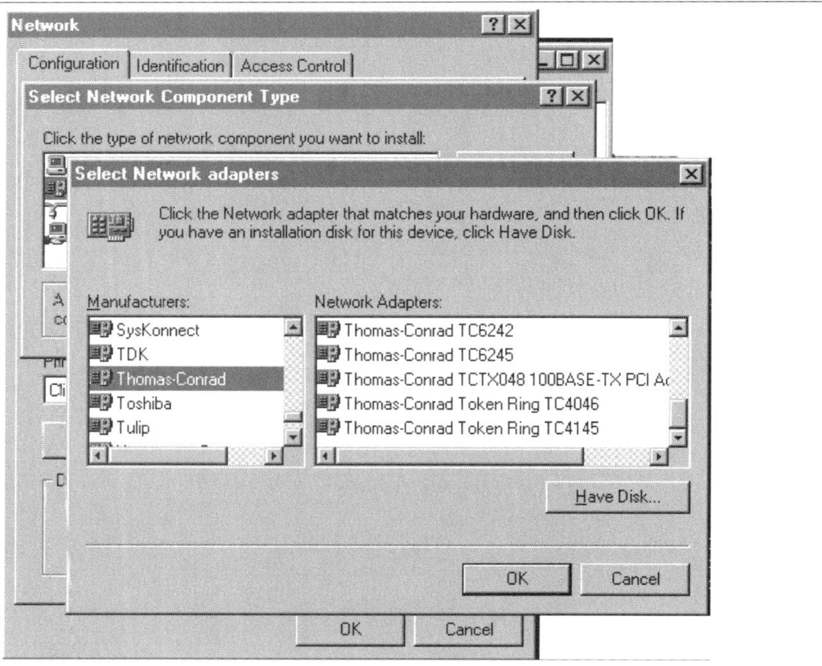

Figure 4-3. *Available adapters.*

option, if it is the only type of driver you have available. ODI drivers should only be used out of necessity. If you are using NetWare-specific applications that require strict Novell protocols, you must use ODI drivers. For ARCnet/TCNS users, ODI drivers are the only choice. The tighter integration of ODI support give you excellent functionality, and the only sacrifice is an overall reduction in network performance.

Note:

NDIS compliance, like ODI, allows multiple protocols to be simultaneously bound to the same driver. This allows you to use IPX/SPX (NWLink), Novell IPX, TCP/IP, and NetBEUI at the same time. Thus, you can have simultaneous connectivity to multiple network operating systems. (See Figure 4-4.)

Protocol support is also an important issue to consider. The default protocol is IPX/SPX (NWLINK). NETBEUI, Novell IPX/SPX, TCP/IP, and specific support for other network operating systems is also available. The importance of IPX/SPX (NWLINK) support as the primary network protocol is the you have a consistent base protocol support with Windows NT and NetWare. Also, IPX/SPX (NWLINK), unlike NETBEUI, is a routable protocol. If you integrate Microsoft Workgroup networking into a Novell network with multiple access methods, you can use the NetWare servers as routers and maintain. Typically the user should maintain the default setting (NWLINK). If you are using a specific application that requires Novell IPX/SPX, you should then select that option. This will require that you also select the NetWare 3.x or 4.x client and have IPX/SPX, as well as NETX or VLM, loaded in your startup batch file. (See Figure 4-5.)

The Service option is also important for NetWare users. File and print sharing, as well as backup and printer administration services, are chosen here. If you are planning on using peer services, you must carefully consider your options. Microsoft file and print sharing allow you to set up workgroups of users that can share files and printers directly that will not be shared with the rest of the NetWare users. This option requires planning and the expectation that overall system speed could suffer if you have a large number accessing the network. (See Figure 4-6.)

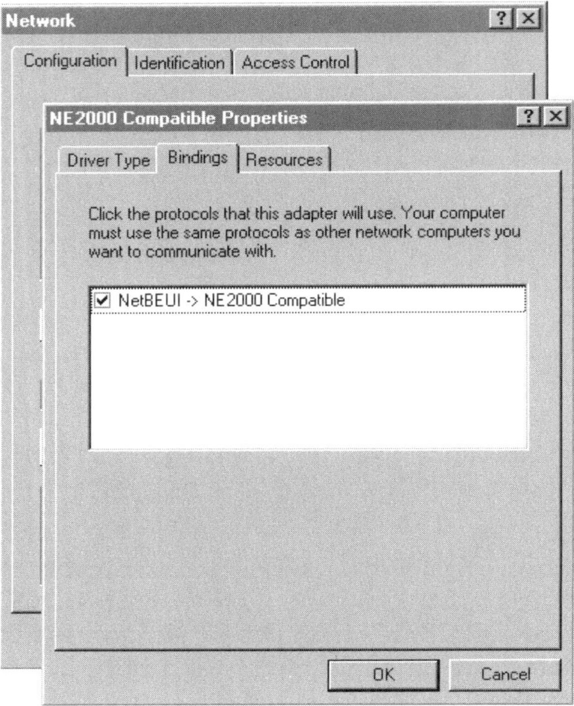

Figure 4-4. *Typical Protocol Bindings screen.*

Security also is important here. As noted previously, security on the Microsoft network is limited to share-level security. This means that you can choose to password protect your shared resources. A user attempting to use your drives must be running network software compatible with Microsoft networking (Windows 95, Windows NT, Windows for Workgroups, LAN Manager, or LAN Server clients) and must know the password. Share-level is not strict security. To diminish this you can select to have your system attach to a Windows NT domain or a NetWare server and obtain a list of users from that system. You can then select which users may use your system from the list provided by the server. Security is enhanced and you don't have to attempt to maintain user security options. If you select NetWare file and print sharing, you will be able to share your files and printers with all NetWare users on the network. (See Figure 4-7.)

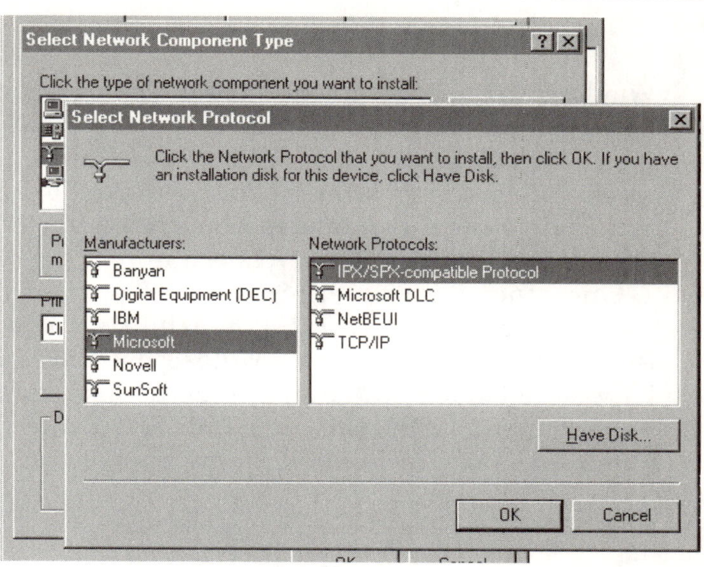

Figure 4-5. *Available protocols.*

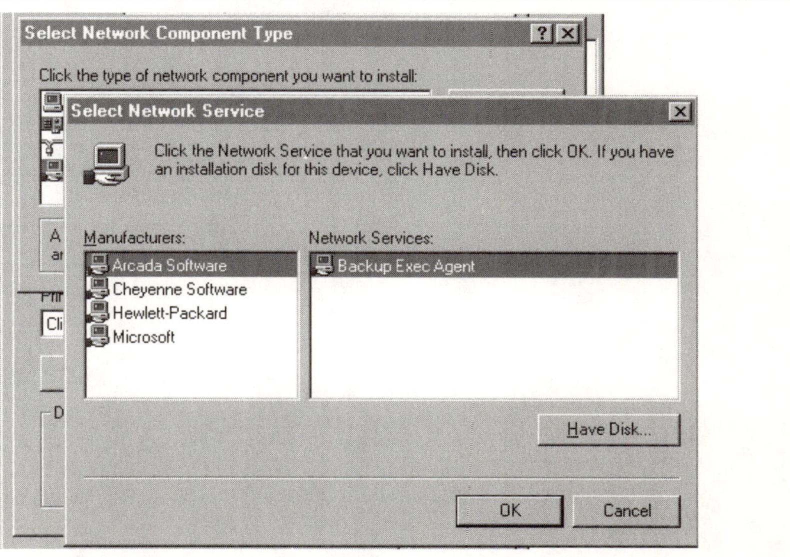

Figure 4-6. *Available client services.*

Windows NT

Windows NT was designed as the operating system of the future for a variety of platforms. No longer would the user be stuck with DOS or high-powered systems such as UNIX. He or she now has the choice of an operating system with the look and feel of Windows v3.1 that can turn his or her existing Intel machine into a powerful multitasking tool. Windows NT is a scaleable architecture.

One other item determined to be of primary importance was credible built-in networking capability. The paramount idea was that all machines, especially those used for business (unless you happen to be extreme computer geeks, like us), would be or should be connected. With this in mind, Microsoft took LAN Manager, which was lying around not doing a whole lot, and updated it to fit

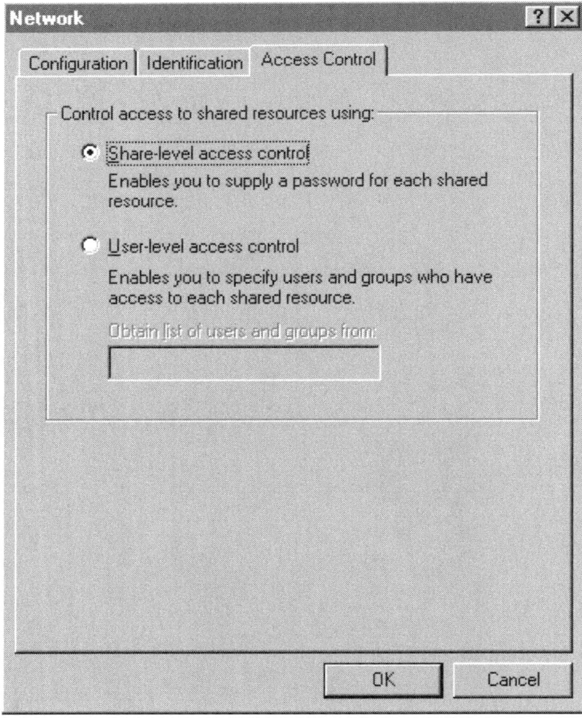

Figure 4-7. *Security Options screen.*

into the scheme it had designed for NT. The company also added peer services that would integrate nicely into a larger heterogeneous networking environment or operate as a small standalone network for those wishing to share files and printers on an irregular basis.

The developments in Windows for Workgroups led Microsoft to finally sound the death knell for NetBEUI as the primary network protocol and replace it with IPX/SPX (NWLINK). As with Windows 95, the decision was based on the fact that IPX/SPX is an easily routable protocol and is already the base protocol for the large majority of medium to large network installations.

Note:

While IPX/SPX (NWLINK) is a routable protocol, a Windows NT machine does not act as a router. Windows NT still requires an external router to perform this task.

In addition to IPX/SPX (NWLINK), Microsoft retained NetBEUI for legacy systems and programs and added TCP/IP as a protocol in its base system. In addition, the company also added Simple Network Management Protocol (SNMP) management. This provides Windows NT with easy entry into a large market of network operating systems.

An offshoot of the decision to use IPX/SPX (NWLINK) as the base protocol was that the integration with NetWare was now incredibly easy. With that in mind, Microsoft designed a simple integration path with NetWare, which comes in the base operating system. In addition, Novell has developed a Windows NT client that uses existing LAN drivers as the adapter drivers for Windows NT.

Windows NT NetWare Basics

Above all else, Windows NT was designed to operate as a full 32-bit multiuser, multitasking operating system. Thirty-two–bit networking requires a new approach for network drivers—in particular, NetWare drivers. Microsoft had been one of the founders of the Network Driver Interface Specification (NDIS). NDIS 2.x is a 16-bit standard and not suited for a true 32-bit system. The goal was speed, and a 16-bit bottleneck at the network was unacceptable.

Note:

Many NetWare users have a bias against NDIS-based protocols, most of which revolve around the fact that NDIS is perceived as slower. Much of this suspicion is correct, not from any flaw in the NDIS design, but from the general lack of good NDIS drivers. A well-written NDIS 2.x driver will perform on a par with the best ODI drivers in the same operating environment.

To solve the problem, Microsoft introduced the NDIS 3.0 standard, which called for a full 32-bit driver. There are two types of NDIS drivers: full Media Access Control (MAC) and Miniport. The full MAC driver covers a wider section of the Open Systems Interconnect (OSI) model and requires more buffer management to perform its operations. A Miniport driver relies on a tighter integration with Microsoft code and a wrapper that handles a lot of the operations contained in the full MAC version. As a result, you have a smaller, faster driver. Many of the drivers written for Windows NT are Miniport, but the difference is great enough that you should check into it before you decide on an adapter.

Microsoft Support for NetWare

From its inception, Windows NT was designed around the need to interoperate with existing network operating systems, such as NetWare. The decision to use IPX/SPX (NWLink), NetWare's default protocol, as the default transport protocol in Windows NT was a major step in the development of NT as an interoperable system.

Note:

NWLink supports the following:

Remote Procedure Calls (RPC)
Windows Sockets
Novell NetBIOS
NWLink NetBIOS

Since NWLink is also NDIS-compliant, you may link simultaneous protocols to the same driver as well as access multiple network operating systems simultaneously.

Microsoft supports access to NetWare through two separate suites. The first is Client Services for NetWare, available on both Windows NT Client and Gateway Services for NetWare, which is only available on Windows NT Servers. The second, file system support, is provided through the Microsoft's multiple provider router (MPR). MPR allows simultaneous access to most file systems, including the following:

FAT	File Allocation Table	DOS
NTFS	Windows NT File System	Windows NT
HPFS	High Performance File System	OS/2
NFS	Network File System	UNIX
NFS	NetWare File System	NetWare

Client Services for NetWare

Microsoft wanted to provide seamless interconnectivity with multiple operating systems in Windows NT. This was accomplished, at least for NetWare, with Client Services for NetWare, which provides a single universal login with authentication by the Windows NT workstation. Client Services for NetWare can be installed as part of the base operating system. Simply enter the Control Panel and select the Network icon. (See Figure 4-8.) Use the Add Program button to add Client Services for NetWare as a network icon. (See Figure 4-9.) Then by using the Configure button, you can indicate the user name and password you want to use for the login to the NetWare server. You also need to set the preferred server you want to use. Remember, the Windows NT user name and the NetWare user name do not need to be the same. Windows NT retains this logon information and when you log in to the Windows NT workstation, it automatically logs you into the NetWare server.

Note:

As with Windows 95, Windows NT does not currently support directory services. If you are going to be using Windows NT services, be sure that your 4.x servers also have bindery emulation enabled.

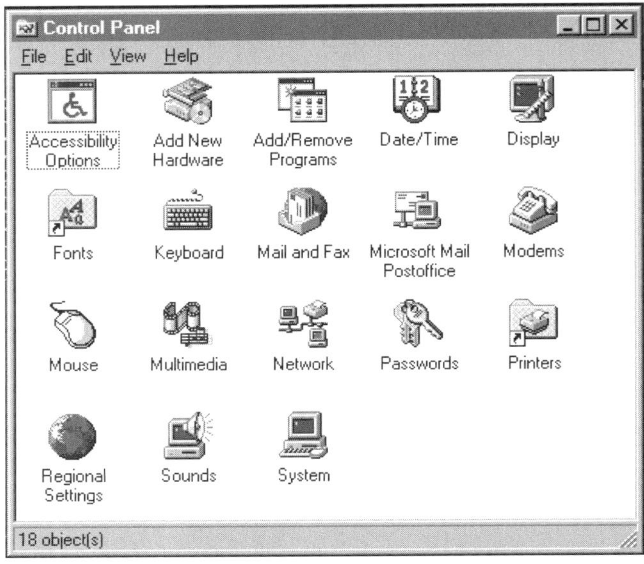

Figure 4-8. *Control Panel folder.*

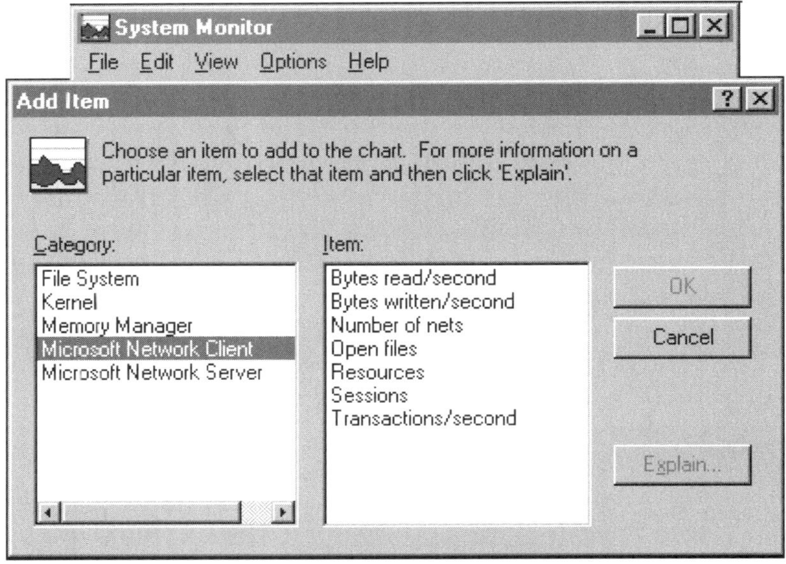

Figure 4-9. *Networks dialog box.*

Note:

If you have your NetWare passwords set to specific expiration dates, you will need to change them using SETPASS. When NetWare returns the password expiration warning, you will need to log in normally and then go to a DOS prompt. Use SETPASS to change your password. The next time you log in, Windows NT will not be able to authenticate you with the old password. You will then be able to change the NetWare password on Windows NT and continue normally until the next time.

Attaching NetWare Drives under NT

NetWare servers appear under the File Manager as connected network drives. To add a network drive, simply use the Attach Network Drive icon in File Manager and a dialog box will appear that lists the various networks you are attached to. It will list the NetWare network separately from the Microsoft network or any others you are attached to. Simply click on the NetWare network to display a list of servers. Click on the server you want to attach a drive from. (See Figure 4-10.) If you are not connected to that server, a dialog box will be displayed that allows you to attach to that server. If you are attached to the server, a list of available volumes will be displayed. Select the appropriate volume and the appropriate directory. Then double-click the directory or select the radio button to connect the drive.

Attaching NetWare Print Queues under NT

Attaching a printer is the same as it is under Windows for Workgroups or Windows. Printer connections are made from the Printer icon in Control Panel. Click on the Printer icon and select the Connect Printer radio button. Select the printer you want to attach; be sure to have the Windows NT CD handy to obtain the appropriate printer driver. (See Figure 4-11.) Then select the Connect radio button and select the appropriate NetWare queue to attach to. You may also find it helpful to select a printer port to print to. It will be rerouted to the appropriate queue by Print Manager and will allow you to print from DOS programs that are network-aware. It will also allow you to use the Novell NPRINT utility.

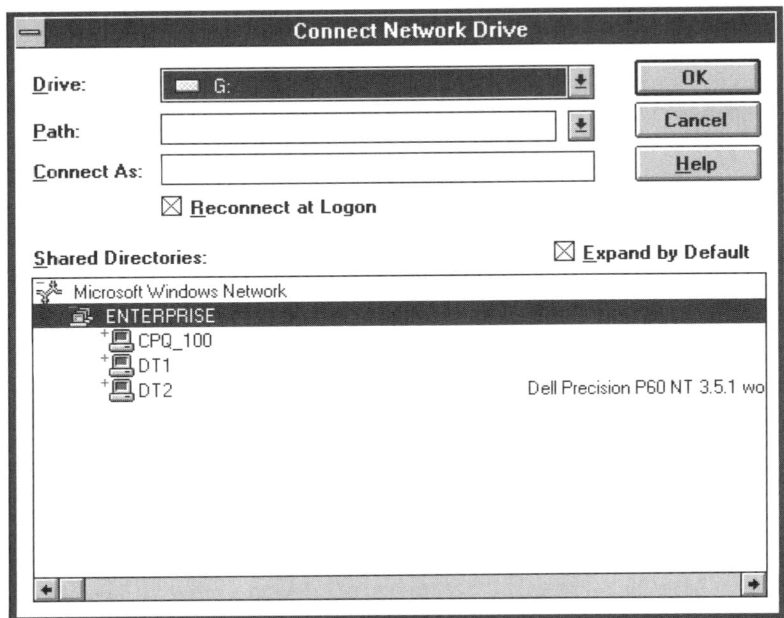

Figure 4-10. *Connect Network Drive dialog box.*

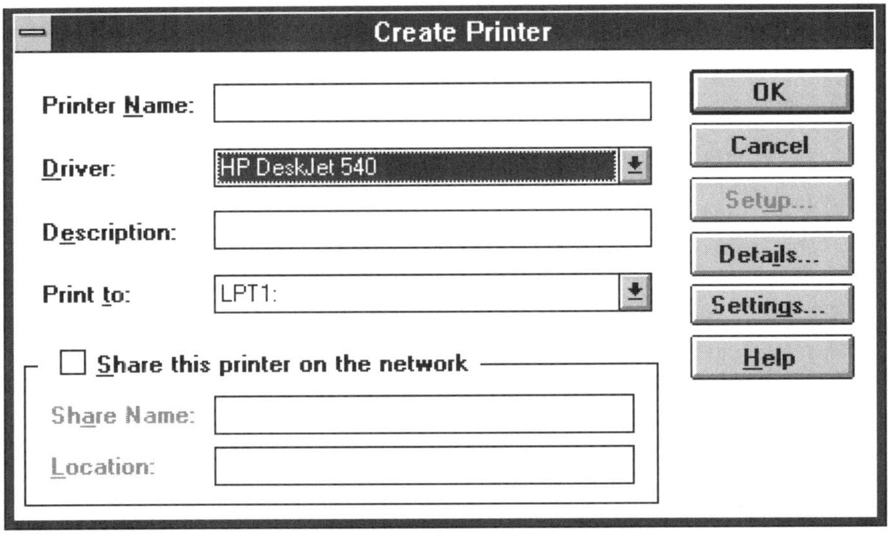

Figure 4-11. *Printers dialog box with selected printer.*

Gateway Services for NetWare

Gateway Services for NetWare is a unique and especially useful feature of the Windows NT system for NT Server. Windows NT Server is distinct from Windows NT Workstation in that it can be used primarily as a server and become a primary or backup domain controller for a Windows NT domain. Gateway Services for NetWare allows non-NetWare Windows NT Workstation clients, Windows for Workgroups workstations, or DOS clients running Windows NT workstation services to access NetWare drives that have been shared by the server. These clients must be able to attach to the Windows NT server through a Windows NT domain or peer services. Once connected, they can access NetWare drives the Windows NT server is attached to.

Note:

Normally in a Windows NT domain or peer network you cannot share the drives that you have attached from another machine. However, Gateway Services provides this as a mechanism for non-NetWare clients to attach to NetWare Services. Security is maintained by the Windows NT authentication process. Each user must be logged in to the Windows NT domain or peer machine and have sufficient rights to use shared NetWare drives.

Gateway Services Installation and Use

Gateway Services are installed in the same manner as Client Services. Select the Network icon from the Control Panel, and in the Network dialog box, select Add Program. Select Gateway Services for NetWare from the list. (See Figure 4-12.) Be sure you have your Windows NT CD handy. You will see Gateway Services for NetWare appear in the list of programs. When the installation is complete, you must reboot the Windows NT machine.

Gateway Services for NetWare will now appear as an icon in the Control Panel. Click on the icon to bring up the Setup dialog box. You will need to enter your preferred server and username. This connection to the server must have sufficient rights to access the volumes and print services you want to share. You will also need to select the volumes and printing resources you want to add to the Gateway Share list. Remember, this will be the only connection the NetWare server

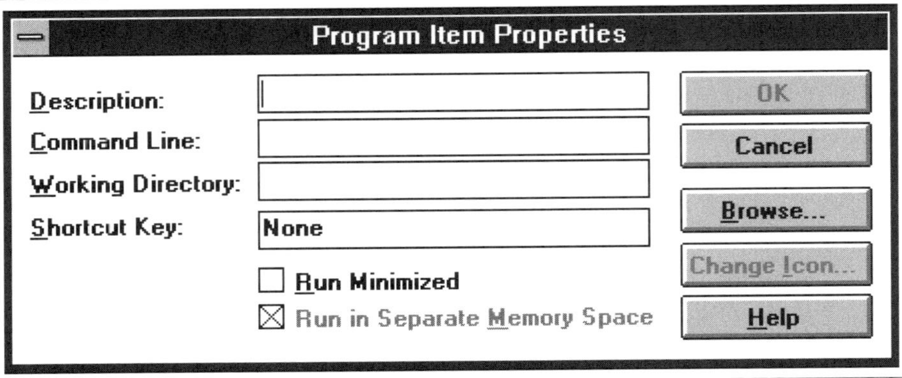

Figure 4-12. *Add Programs dialog box.*

sees. The Windows NT machine acts as a true gateway to allow the Microsoft network client users to see this machine.

It is a good idea to create a group of Microsoft network users who have access rights to NetWare's shared resources. This acts as an easy means to maintain security for shared NetWare resources. You may also want to create a similar group on the NetWare server. This allows you to have several Windows NT machines acting as gateways and maintain additional security at the NetWare servers.

Note:

Remember that all gateway printing services are managed through the Print Manager.

Those users who have been granted access to shared resources will then be able to connect through the Windows NT gateway to access the NetWare resources. The Windows NT redirector will take the request from the client machine and redirect it through the gateway to the NetWare server. The server will respond to the Windows NT Server, which will then send the completed request to the client workstation.

Thoughts

The NetWare services provided by Microsoft in Windows NT are an excellent example of integration between two disparate network operating systems. These services only became usable in Windows NT v3.5. With the advent of Windows NT 3.5.1, the services have become even more stable.

Novell Support for Windows NT

As of this writing, the Novell Client for Windows NT is still in beta. The client interface is available on Novell's NetWire forums on CompuServe or directly from your Novell reseller. Be warned, however, that because the Novell Client for NT is a beta product, you may encounter problems, particularly with heavy use across the link.

The Novell client uses existing ODI LAN drivers and shims them into the NDIS 3.0 Windows NT interface. This provides a 32-bit Novell driver for the Windows NT machine. Also, remember that using the Novell Client for NT is an all-or-nothing proposition. If you use this interface, you will not be able to use the Microsoft Client or Gateway Services for NetWare. Novell learned quite a bit about writing interfaces in Windows 3.1 and Windows for Workgroups. Therefore, you will notice many similarities between those interfaces and the Novell Client for NT.

Novell Client Installation

As is true with the Microsoft clients, the Novell client is installed through the Network icon from Control Panel. The Novell client ships on two diskettes; you will need to have them handy. Select the Add Programs radio button and select Other. (See Figure 4-13.) When prompted, place the diskette in the appropriate drive. When the installation is completed, it will appear in the list of available programs. Also, two icons are placed in the Control Panel. They are a NetWare Client icon and a DOS icon.

The NetWare icon is used to select the preferred server and user name. You do not need to have the same user name for your NetWare and Windows NT logins. The Novell client does not take advantage of the Windows NT login procedure and creates its own login dialog box. You must enter your password each time you log in to the Novell network.

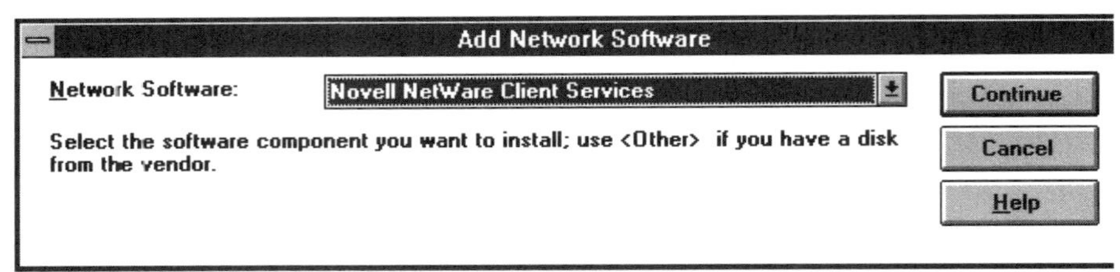

Figure 4-13. *Novell client installation.*

NetWare volumes and directories are accessed through the Windows NT File Manager. When you select the Connect Network Drive icon, the subsequent dialog box has a Network icon from which NetWare drives are selected. This procedure is not as integrated as the Microsoft client, but is similar to existing clients for Windows and Windows for Workgroups.

NetWare printers are attached through the Printer icon in Control Panel. As with the file access method, printer attachment is exactly as it was in previous versions of NetWare clients. Use the Connect button to select the printer; be sure to have the Windows NT CD handy. Then use the Network radio button to select the Novell print queue. Printing tasks may be managed through the Windows NT Print Manager, although it is not necessary. By using the Print Manager, you queue the print job at the Windows NT machine and send it to the network printer. This frees the machine to perform other tasks while the job is sent to the NetWare queue.

The additional DOS prompt box is provide to maintain compatibility for NetWare DOS utilities. Novell noticed a problem with some of its utilities such as SYSCON and RCONSOLE. This DOS prompt provides the ability to use these utilities.

part

Connecting to Other Environments

II

As much as we try to forget the host/terminal environment, there are still legacy applications our users need to use. Often this means making a connection between the NetWare LAN and an IBM host, midrange, or minicomputer. Wading through the IBM documentation to learn to use the IBM LAN Support Program isn't easy. This section tells you how to make that connection.

In addition, as the popularity of the Internet grows and as application-specific UNIX machines make their way into NetWare LANs, it's essential to know the workings of the protocol suite they use—TCP/IP. Finally, let's not forget Macintoshes—we'll talk about those connections too.

In a perfect world, every client workstation would be the same—but you're not so lucky. Making all these clients and hosts cooperate is part of the fun, and part of your job.

chapter 5

NetWare for Macintosh

The ability to interoperate means more than being able to connect to various network access methods or the ability to connect to a mainframe computer. It means being able to connect to a wide variety of operating systems and soon to everything from the mainframe to the toaster. The need for interoperability between competing desktop operating systems began when Apple Computer Corporation developed the Macintosh. This was the first of the Apple computers to gain acceptance in the business world. With its introduction, the need for a way to connect it to the existing corporate network began. As a result Novell introduced NetWare for Macintosh.

Requirements

The requirements for NetWare for Macintosh v4.0 are extensive. Before you begin you must make sure all the requirements are met.

- Macintosh Operating System 6.0.5 or later. (System 7.x is recommended.)
- For System 6.0.5: Finder version 6.1 or later and Chooser version 3.3 or later. AppleShare version 7.1. This version of AppleShare ships with NetWare for Macintosh. Your available network connections are LocalTalk, EtherTalk, TokenTalk, or ARCnet (which uses EtherTalk).

- For System 7.0: Finder and Chooser versions that are compatible with System 7. AppleShare version 7.1. The available network connections are LocalTalk, EtherTalk, TokenTalk, or ARCnet using EtherTalk.
- For printing: For a LaserWriter you will need version 7.0 of the LaserWriter software installed in the System folder. If you are using System 7 be sure that the printer drivers are installed in the Extensions folder. Previous versions of the operating system required that it be in the System folder.
- To use the NetWare Tools: 640KB of free memory and 4MB of installed memory available if you are using System 7 or 2.5MB if you are using System 6.0.5.

Note:

As with the printer drivers, if you are using System 7, your network connection software—LocalTalk, EtherTalk, TokenTalk or ARCnet—must also be located in the Extensions folder located in the System folder. Prior versions of the software placed these programs in the System folder only.

Installation and Configuration

Prior to installing NetWare for Macintosh you must be sure that you have a valid network connection. First install the network adapter in your Macintosh. If you will be using LocalTalk you will not need to install a network adapter. LocalTalk is built into all Macintoshes. After your network adapter is installed you should install the network software according to the manufactures instructions into the proper folder. For System 6.0.5 it is the System folder. For System 7 it is the Extensions folder. When the network software is installed you will then need to enter the Control Panel. You can do this by clicking on the folder or choosing it from the menu. The Control Panel will show a series of icons. Click on the Network icon. This will bring up the Network folder. You should then see the Network folder with the LocalTalk icon. If you are using Ethernet, token-ring, or ARCnet you will also see the appropriate icon for that connection. Click on the appropriate icon to select it.

NetWare for Macintosh is installed using the Installer on the Macintosh disk. The installer must be run on the machine that you are installing NetWare for Macintosh to. However, the installer does not necessarily have to be on the machine. This means that the NetWare for Macintosh software can reside on a server and be installed across the network. There are two installation procedures, the ADMIN installation and the user installation. The ADMIN installation installs all the NetWare tools software and allows unlimited access. The user installation copies all software except the tools application to the local Macintosh machine.

Note:

As administrator you can adapt the installer script to allow the users to install their own NetWare for Macintosh and still restrict access to the tools application. This will make it easier for users to maintain their own machines. You can then create a diskette or folder by moving the User install script to the same folder or disk as the Installer program, and removing the ADMIN Install Script.

To install the software, place the NetWare for Macintosh diskette into the drive or select the folder containing the software from the server. Double-click the Installer icon. A secondary dialog box will appear that will allow you to perform an easy installation or a custom installation. Clicking the Customize button will allow you to selectively install components of the software. You can install the following options:

- AppleShare system software
- NetWare Notify
- NetWare User Authentication Method (UAM)
- Extension Mapper (NetWare 4.x requirement)
- NetWare Tools

When you have finished identifying the components you want to install, click on the Install button to complete the installation. Macintosh system components will complete the installation for you.

Note:

If you will not be connecting to a NetWare 4.x server you will not need to install the Extension Mapper.

Configuration

The AppleShare system software allows you to install the latest version of AppleShare required for NetWare support. Use this if your version of AppleShare is not at least 7.1. If you use the Customize option this can be installed without installing the rest of the software.

Two varieties of password authentication are allowed on NetWare servers. If SET ALLOW UNENCRYPTED PASSWORDS = ON is set on the NetWare server it will allow Apple clear-text passwords. If this NetWare set command is not set to ON then you must use the NetWare encrypted passwords.

To log on to a NetWare server, select the Chooser menu option. Select the AppleShare icon and an AppleTalk Zone and file server. Then choose OK. You will be presented with a dialog box allowing you to select between two password authentication methods:

- Apple Standard UAM
- Encrypted NetWare Authentication

If you want to use the AppleShare clear text method, select Apple Standard UAM. If you need to send a NetWare encrypted password, use the Encrypted NetWare Authentication. Don't worry if you choose the wrong password option; you can always attempt the login again using the other method.

Printing from a NetWare queue is also easy using NetWare for Macintosh. First you must select a print queue. You will use the same method for selecting a print queue as you did for selecting a file server. Open the Chooser. Instead of choosing AppleShare, choose a printer. Then select the zone and the queue from those presented. From this point you can print from any program using the NetWare print queue.

The NetWare tools application allows you to administer a NetWare v3.x or 4.x server from a Macintosh server. To start the application, double-click the NetWare Tools icon. Remember that NetWare for Macintosh does not directly support NDS (NetWare Directory Services) under NetWare 4.x. It will use bindery emulation. Bindery emulation must be installed before you can use the NetWare tools. NetWare for Macintosh accesses directory objects as objects in a bindery context.

Quick List

Installing NetWare for Macintosh workstations takes 10 steps:

1. Install the network adapters.
2. Install the adapter software.
3. Select the appropriate software in the Network folder.
4. Open Chooser, select the Access Method, Zone, and File server.
5. Login using the appropriate User Authentication Method.
6. Insert the NetWare Macintosh disk.
7. Select the Installer and run the appropriate installation script.
8. Select Install or Custom.
9. If Custom is selected, install the software you need.
10. Reboot the Macintosh.

TROUBLESHOOTING

Troubleshooting on a Macintosh will require a modicum of knowledge about the Macintosh and NetWare. First verify that the software for your network adapter is installed in the correct folder. Many installer scripts were written for System 6. If you are using System 7, the script will install to the wrong folder. If it installs to the System folder, simply move it to the Extensions folder.

If your software is installed properly but you still cannot find a file server in Chooser, look first to the obvious cable problems. You can verify the cable connections by seeing first if the Macintosh can see other AppleTalk services. If you can access other AppleTalk file services then use the Echo Test in ATCON, a utility for NetWare for Macintosh at the file server. If the server can see the Macintosh, but the Macintosh cannot see the file server, then verify that you have the latest software on your Macintosh.

If you can find a server, but see no volumes after you log in, verify that the Macintosh name space has been added and that the MAC.NLM has been loaded. It is extremely easy to load the MAC.NLM and not have added the NAMESPACE, or vice versa. The NAMESPACE need only be added once, but the MAC.NLM must be loaded each time the server is booted.

Note:

Make sure that if you run VREPAIR, you remember to run the VREPAIR for MAC NAMESPACE. If it is not correctly repaired, you can wipe out the MAC NAMESPACE and not know it.

It is also possible to have date and file times incorrect on the server. The Macintosh cannot synchronize date and time with the server. Therefore, it is essential to verify the date and time on the Macintosh.

PERFORMANCE

Performance on a Macintosh running NetWare for Macintosh should be comparable with DOS clients on the network, unless you are connecting using AppleTalk. However, if you are using the Macintosh to administer a NetWare server, you can have a performance problem. The Print Queue utility continuously updates the information about print jobs on visible print queues. This is the case even if the print queue window is not active.

If you notice a performance problem under these circumstances, you can select the Preferences option from the Edit menu and deselect the item labeled Update Print Queue in Background. This will mean that the queue is only updated when it is the active window, but it will stop a lot of unnecessary traffic between the Macintosh and the server and restore performance.

chapter

6

The Peer-to-Peer Workstation

Many users of NetWare have always thought there was something missing in the NetWare version of client/server computing. In a pure DOS world it makes a great deal of sense to have machines with dedicated roles. A 286 machine wasn't able to share files and still do its job as a client workstation. (We thought we proved this point with nondedicated NetWare/286.) However, as desktop computers became more powerful and operating systems required that the user have a hard drive, workstations began to be able to take on greater and greater roles.

Note:

Yes, we know that you can still remote boot a workstation and pull Windows for Workgroups and Windows 95 from the server. As a practical matter, unless there is a specific need for this type of security, it is not the best solution. First, you take up a lot of disk space on the server both for Windows files and user swap files. Second, even though Windows on the server works well, it is still the slowest way to run Windows for Workgroups.

NetWare began to have remote printing from workstations that actually worked with the introduction of RPRINTER. Many users wanted the ability to group themselves and share files between the individual workstations without interfering with the company network. Network operating systems such as Artisoft's LANtastic and Performance Technology's PowerLAN began to interoperate well with NetWare. Users soon discovered that there were aspects of the peer-to-peer workstation concept that worked better than they did in a client/server model. For instance, large groupware applications are best maintained from a single point as in the client/server model. However, a distributed application, such as a database, may run better from a series of Windows NT boxes that share their drives with the rest of the network, but are not truly file servers. Or the Engineering workgroup may need to occasionally share files that are too large to e-mail back and forth and do not work well in a common space on the server.

Regardless of the reasoning, many companies, both large and small, began to integrate their homogenous client/server networks with smaller workgroup solutions where they made sense. Both Novell and Microsoft began to take notice of this growing market and introduced products to compete in this area. For the network administrator, it demands a whole group of new issues. This chapter is designed to help you integrate the coming workgroups into your main network.

NetWare Lite

NetWare Lite was originally designed as a way to capture the small (five nodes or less) network market. It was thought these users were not generally going to the added expense of putting in a dedicated file server or that they did not actually need one to share printers and files. Although NetWare Lite was never really a winner in the marketplace, it was used by a lot of NetWare shops as an adjunct to existing NetWare LANs. Integration into the existing network was tedious and required some advance planning. Workstations could be configured as a server, as a client, or as a server/client.

Requirements

The one major complaint with NetWare Lite was its speed. As a result the system has both basic and practical system requirements. The basic requirements were that you had an x286-based computer. Because

NetWare Lite used existing ODI drivers or even the older genned IPX.COM, you could use almost any existing adapter hardware. However, practical limitations were that only a x286 computer or above be used as a server or a client/server. NetWare Lite runs very nicely on 386 or better machines and should be viewed with that in mind. Also, because it takes up a rather large amount of memory, having ample space to load the operating software (CLIENT.EXE and SERVER.EXE) was almost essential. Because this product was seen as a DOS-only product (it would work with Windows, but no utilities for Windows were included), there were no other limitations on the hardware.

Installation and Configuration

Prior to starting the installation of NetWare Lite, you should carefully plan your network. Remember that this type of network is a peer-to-peer network and will not have the same performance characteristics as standard NetWare. You should probably choose workstations that are at least 386/33s with sufficient hard drive space (four megabytes or more free) to install NetWare Lite and hold any additional files and applications you plan to share.

NetWare Lite will operate with any network adapters that have ODI workstation or linkable IPX drivers. Therefore, you should choose your network access method based upon your individual needs. For purposes of this book, we are assuming that you already have a network in place and simply wish to Add NetWare Lite to your existing network structure. For a more serious discussion on network access methods, review the first book in this series—*Networking the Desktop: Cabling, Configuration, and Communications.*

NetWare Lite uses an automated installation utility. An individual copy of NetWare Lite must be installed on each workstation. You can install NetWare Lite as a client, a server, or both. If installed as a server, the workstation can share files with others on the network. If the workstation is installed as a client, it can access the NetWare Lite network but not share its files with the network. If installed as both a server and a client, the workstation can share its files and access the files of other NetWare Lite servers.

First, install your network adapters according to the manufacturer's instructions. Then insert the first disk of your NetWare Lite diskettes and type INSTALL. The installation utility uses a standard NetWare interface. The Main Menu has four available options:

- Make this machine a client.
- Make this machine a client and a server.
- Make this machine a server.
- Verify network connections.

When you planned the NetWare Lite portion of your network you should have decided whether your workstations would be clients, servers, or both. If you choose to make a workstation a server and client, or simply a server, you will need to enter the server name. There is a 15-character limit on server names. The installation utility also changes the FILES= statement in your CONFIG.SYS file to 30.

Note:

If you are going to be running Windows, you will need to increase the number of files allocated by 50 in the CONFIG.SYS file.

NetWare Lite also attempts to change the number of available DOS buffers to 30. This is an acceptable number unless you are using a disk caching program. If you will be using a DOS disk caching program, such as SMARTDRV, you will need to ensure that the number of buffers is sufficient for the disk caching utility.

After these changes have been made the installation utility will allow you to select your network adapter. You must select the settings for your adapter's configuration. Be sure that the settings do not conflict with other devices in your workstation. Finally the installation utility will modify your CONFIG.SYS file to modify your LASTDRIVE statement and your AUTOEXEC.BAT file to add your NetWare path to the path statement and to add SHARE.EXE. SHARE.EXE is required to allow DOS to allow multiple file access. The batch file to load the network operating system software is STARTNET.BAT and is located in the NetWare client subdirectory (typically C:\NWCLIENT). If you complete the installation properly, your configuration files should appear as shown in Figures 6-1, 6-2, and 6-3.

Adding your workstation to existing Novell network requires you to manually edit your STARTNET.BAT file. You will need to Add NETX.EXE to this file as shown in Figure 6-4.

In addition to manual editing of the STARTNET.BAT file to include the network redirector, the LASTDRIVE statement can become important when used in conjunction with NetWare. It sets the number of drives that are available for both DOS and NetWare. There are only 26 drives available under DOS (A–Z). If you are using a NETX redirector, you

```
C:\dos\setver.exe
C:\dos\himem.sys
Files=30
Buffers = 30
Lastdrive=Z
```

Figure 6-1. *CONFIG.SYS.*

```
Prompt $P$G
Path=c:\;c:\dos;c:\nwclient
Set Compsec=c:\command.com (needs to be added manually)
c:\nwclient\startnet.bat
```

Figure 6-2. *AUTOEXEC.BAT.*

```
LSL
IPXODI
share (Required)
server (Starts server services)
client (Starts client services)
```

Figure 6-3. *STARTNET.BAT.*

```
STARTNET.BAT
LSL
IPXODI
share (Required)
NETX
I:LOGIN
server (Starts server services)
client (Starts client services)
```

Figure 6-4. *STARTNET.BAT with NetWare hooks.*

must differentiate the DOS drives from the NetWare drives. NetWare Lite drives are considered DOS drives; you must make allowances for the number of NetWare Lite drives you will need and still maintain the number of NetWare drives you need. If you are using Virtual Loadable Modules (VLMs) this problem is solved not in the CONFIG.SYS file, but in the NET.CFG file. The VLM redirector's first drive is set in the NET.CFG statement. The LASTDRIVE is set to Z and the first NetWare drive is set in the NET.CFG file. (See Figures 6-5 and 6-6.)

```
C:\dos\setver.exe
C:\dos\himem.sys
Files=30
Buffers = 30
Lastdrive=E
```

Figure 6-5. *A sample CONFIG.SYS file.*

```
NetWare DOS Redirector
First Network Drive = G
```

Figure 6-6. *A sample NET.CFG file.*

Configuration Tips

Setting the first NetWare drive when you are using NETX or VLMs with NetWare Lite can be a problem. The default login drive for NetWare is F, set by the system login script as the home directory. The home directory the drive mappings must be set to reflect the settings in the CONFIG.SYS or NET.CFG files. Thus, if you need six NetWare Lite drives, you must set your LASTDRIVE statement to I. This makes your first standard NetWare drive J.

When you set up a NetWare v3.x or 4.x connection, you should establish your standard NetWare connection and log in to the NetWare server prior to starting the NetWare Lite network. Establishing this connection sets the drive mappings to the file server first and allows you to then share drives. This method also appears to be more stable. Because NetWare Lite connections are not dynamic, you cannot load and unload applications from memory.

Quick List

Following is a quick recap of the installation of NetWare Lite.

1. Install network adapters.
2. Start NetWare Lite Installation utility.
3. Assign server name.

4. Add NetWare client directory to path.
5. Add STARTNET.BAT to AUTOEXEC.BAT file.
6. Set BUFFERS statement in the CONFIG.SYS file.
7. Set FILES statement in the CONFIG.SYS file.
8. Set LASTDRIVE statement in the CONFIG.SYS file.
9. Select and configure network adapter.
10. Exit Install.
11. Manually edit the STARTNET.BAT files to Add NETX or VLM and login statements.

Troubleshooting

Troubleshooting is not a necessary part of NetWare Lite installation. As with any installation, be sure to change one thing at a time and start with the most obvious items. Most problems occur with the configuration of the adapter or cabling.

Verify that your cabling is intact and properly connected. Then, verify your adapter settings. Most adapter manufacturers provide configuration and test utilities with their adapters. Use these applications to be sure that you have configured the adapter properly. Then verify that you have not created a conflict in the system. The vendor's utilities should allow you to verify that the adapter is transmitting and receiving properly. If the adapter uses a memory address, as most ARCnet and token-ring adapters do, verify that you have excluded the area of memory the adapter is using.

If you have verified the adapter settings on all the computers, restart the NetWare Lite installation utility. The main menu provides an option to verify the network connection. You will need to enter a name for each machine in the test. The test utility then attempts to transmit IPX packets. If you can see the name of the other machine on your screen and can successfully transmit packets, your network connection is valid. If you cannot see the other machine, repeat your earlier steps or replace the network adapters individually until you can create a successful connection.

Performance

One of the problems inherent in NetWare Lite and other DOS-based peer-to-peer networks is related to file access. DOS only allows single access to drives in turn. Thus, if two users attempt to open the same file simultaneously, NetWare Lite queues the second request until the first is finished. Additionally, because the DOS file access method (FAT or file allocation table) is designed for a single-user system, when a file request is made, the hard drive moves to the outer portion of the drive, picks the location of the file and then moves to the part of the disk that contains the files. This procedure must be repeated for each file access, thus slowing performance. Load-balancing applications and files among the NetWare Lite workstations can help solve this problem.

Printing may also slow performance. When a file is sent to the printer, the entire file must be spooled to the server's disk prior to being sent to the printer. During this period the drive cannot be used for file access by users. Therefore, users should print to a local printer or NetWare print queue instead of the NetWare Lite shared printers when possible.

Performance in NetWare Lite is proportionate to the number of users. The more users on a NetWare Lite network, the slower the network. We recommend a maximum of 25 users.

Personal NetWare

Personal NetWare was designed as a upgrade to NetWare Lite, which would combine the NetWare Client into a Universal Client to allow easy access to Personal NetWare desktop servers, NetWare v2.x, v3.x, and 4.x. The product has two components: the Universal Client and the Desktop Server. For purposes of this book, we will take you through the steps of installing the Personal NetWare client on a NetWare v3.x or 4.x server.

Requirements

Personal NetWare has the same requirements as NetWare Lite. You will need at least an 8086 machine with 640KB of RAM and a hard drive with approximately 5MB of available disk space. For practical purposes, you should have at least a 386 with 2MB of RAM. If the workstation is going to share your drives with other workstations on the network, it will need the added processing power.

Installation and Configuration

From the Personal NetWare installation screen, choose the Networking option. This takes you to the first Networking installation screen. On this screen, you choose and configure the network adapter and basic network options.

Select the type of network adapter in the machine from the list provided. All drivers certified by Novell are included in the list; additional or updated drivers may be added by selecting "OEM-supplied driver." When you choose this option, setup modifies the NET.CFG and STARTNET.BAT files to automatically load the appropriate driver. If this workstation will share its resources with others on the network, check the box next to Share This Computer's Resources.

You also must give the computer a name by which it will be known on the network. This name should be one by which you can easily recognize the computer or its function. Choose the field labeled "User of this computer." As you start to enter the user's name, an entry box pops up. Press Enter when you're finished. When you've completed the initial setup, choose "Select Server types to connect to." This option displays a menu.

On this screen, click the box next to the server type the workstation connects to. Your choice adds statements to the PREFERRED NETWORK statement in the NET.CFG file.

Three client types may be used at the same time, allowing the Universal Client to attach and use all NetWare services concurrently. Let's look at your choices one at a time.

Selecting NetWare v2.x and v3.x Servers places the BIND command in the NetWare PROTOCOL statement in the NetWare DOS Requester section of the NET.CFG file. The Preferred Server field allows you to insert the name of the server you want to use as your primary server. Normally, the Personal NetWare shell connects to the first server to respond to its request to Get Nearest Server. The Preferred Server tells the shell to wait for the named Preferred Server to respond. The shell waits only so long. If it doesn't find the Preferred Server within the time limit, it attaches the workstation to the first server to respond to its Get Nearest Server request. Selecting NetWare 4.x Servers causes the NDS STATEMENT to be used. This statement enables NetWare Directory Services.

Selecting Personal NetWare Desktop Servers places the PNW statement in the NetWare PROTOCOL statement in the NET.CFG file. If the workstation is part of a Personal NetWare workgroup, you can insert the name of the workgroup in the Preferred Personal NetWare

Workgroup field. When the requester is loaded, it attempts to attach the workstation to the workgroup.

On this screen you also choose the location of the first available network drive. The available options are drives A through Z. Base your selection on the number of drives you must allocate for local drives. Typically, drives A through E are designated as local drives. This selection changes the FIRST NETWORK DRIVE option in the NET.CFG file. When you complete this step, choose Accept the Above and continue. You will return to the first Networking installation screen.

From this screen, choose Network Management. Here you install network-management services.

Check the box next to Load SNMP Agent. Setup adds the command that adds the Host Resources Management Information Base to the STARTNET.BAT file, and adds the necessary VLM commands to the NETWARE DOS REQUESTER section of the NET.CFG file. Select the box to load the SNMP AGENT, only if you want to add network management services to your computer. It will take up memory on your system and may reduce performance.

You also are asked whether you want to load the NetWare Manager (NMR) Agent management module. If you want to make your system an agent for Novell's Network Management System, set this option to YES.

When you finish choosing the appropriate network management options, choose Accept the Above and continue. You will return to the first Network installation screen.

The selections available in this section of the Setup utility depend on the information provided by the manufacturer in the driver information file for the adapter. The driver information file provides the configuration for the adapter's Open Data-Link Interface (ODI) driver and modifies the driver section of the NET.CFG file. To make a choice, highlight the individual statement and press the Enter key. You will see the available options. Select one of the options and press the Enter key. Your adapter manufacturer provides help in this section of the installation if you're unclear as to which statements are required.

Select the frame type to bind to the driver. Individual network protocols use their own packet structure. Frame types allow the driver to accept a frame from a number of network types and keep the incoming information straight.

When you've completed the installation steps, choose Accept the Above and continue. The choices you made during installation now are used to create the NET.CFG and STARTNET.BAT files.

Configuration Tips

Remember that you are designing this workstation for an existing NetWare network and that you should set up the workstation accordingly. Personal NetWare will set the BUFFERS and FILES statements to the appropriate setting. If you are using programs that require a different setting, choose the higher setting.

Because Personal NetWare was designed around the Universal Client and VLMs, client installation will set your LASTDRIVE statement to Z. If you intend to use the NETX redirector you must change the statement to reflect the number of DOS and Personal NetWare drives you need. The remaining drives should be allocated to standard NetWare.

If you are using a local printer and want to use Share This Printer on the Network, you will need to allocate more FILES and BUFFERS. Add approximately 20 additional for each statement. If you are using the printer with RPRINTER, you will need to set SPX CONNECTIONS to 60 in the NET.CFG file (see Figures 6-7 and 6-8).

Quick List

Following is a quick recap of the installation of Personal NetWare.

1. Run the Network Installation utility from the first installation disk.
2. Select the Network Adapter.
3. Install the Universal NetWare Client and choose the appropriate redirector.
4. Select the network adapter settings.
5. Select the configuration settings such as First Network Drives.
6. Install Network Management.
7. Select the frame type.

Troubleshooting

The configuration of the adapter or cabling causes most problems with Personal NetWare.

```
Link Support
  BUFFERS 8

Link driver TOKEN
  PORT A20
  SLOT 1
  DATA RATE 16
  MAX FRAME SIZE 4208
   PCMCIA
  FRAME TOKEN-RING MSB
  FRAME TOKEN-RING_SNAP MSB

NetWare DOS Requester
  FIRST NETWORK DRIVE = F
  USE DEFAULTS = ON
  NETWARE PROTOCOL = NDS,BIND,PNW,
  PREFERRED SERVER = ALR_VEISA
  PREFERRED WORKGROUP = WORKGROUP
  WORKGROUP NAME = PNW
  WORKGROUPID HIGH = 0
  WORKGROUPID LOW = 0
  WORKGROUP NET = 00002001:FFFFFFFFFFFF
  VLM = NMR.VLM
  VLM = WSSNMP.VLM
  VLM = WSTRAP.VLM
  VLM = WSREG.VLM
  VLM = WSASN1.VLM
  VLM = MIB2IF.VLM
  VLM = MIB2PROT.VLM
  VLM = PNWTRAP.VLM
  VLM = PNWMIB.VLM
```

Figure 6-7. *The NET.CFG file.*

```
@ECHO OFF
SET NWLANGUAGE=ENGLISH
C:
CD C:\NWCLIENT
LH LSL
LH TCTOKSH
LH IPXODI
LH SERVER
LH VLM
LH STPIPX.COM
LH HRMIB.EXE
CD \
C:\NWCLIENT\NET LOGIN
```

Figure 6-8. *The STARTNET.BAT file.*

After verifying that the cabling is intact, verify your adapter settings. Most adapter manufacturers provide configuration and testing utilities with their adapters. Use these applications to be sure that you have configured the adapter properly. Then verify that you have not created a conflict in your system. The vendors' utilities should allow you to verify that the adapter is transmitting and receiving properly. If your adapter uses a memory address, as do most ARCnet and token-ring adapters, verify that you have excluded the area of memory the adapter is using.

If you have verified the adapter settings on all computers, then restart the Personal NetWare installation utility. The main menu provides an option to verify the network connection. You will need to enter a name for each machine in test. The test utility then attempts to transmit IPX packets. If you can see the name of the other machine and can successfully transmit packets, then the network connection is valid. If you cannot repeat your earlier steps, replace the network adapters individually until your can create a successful connection.

Performance

One of the problems inherent in Personal NetWare and all other DOS-based peer-to-peer networks is file access. DOS only allows single access to drives in turn. Thus, if two users attempt file access simultaneously, Personal NetWare queues the second request until the first is finished. Additionally, the DOS file access method (FAT or File Allocation Table) is designed for a single-user system. When a file request is made, the hard drive must go to the outer portion of the drive, pick up the location of the file, and move to the portion(s) of the disk that contain the file. This procedure must be repeated for each file access. Load-balancing applications and files throughout the Personal NetWare workstations can help solve this problem. Personal NetWare performs a lot of memory management to help alleviate file access problems.

Personal NetWare has a built-in performance monitoring utility called PNWDIAGS, which was developed to help you measure and compare network traffic patterns. It also measures the hard disk access and space available and remote vs. local access. PNWDIAGS not only helps you load-balance individual workstations, but also makes possible comparisons and load-balancing of the entire peer-to-peer network.

Windows for Workgroups (WFW)

Windows for Workgroups or v3.11 is designed as an enhanced-mode operating environment. Windows Enhanced mode is designed for use on 386 or above machines that can take advantage of 32-bit architecture and protected mode memory. Windows for Workgroups has built-in features including 32-bit networking, NDIS 3.0 drivers, and 32-bit disk and file access. As a result, the minimum system configuration recommended by Microsoft is a 386SX with 4MB of RAM. In practice, you should probably have at least 8MB of RAM available. Windows for Workgroups operates from a local hard drive or can be loaded from the network. If you choose to load Windows for Workgroups from a NetWare file server, you should also place your swap file on the network drive.

Installation and Configuration

Windows for Workgroups is installed from eight diskettes. The installation utility, SETUP.EXE, takes you through the complete setup routine. Windows for Workgroups was designed to provide peer services using the Microsoft network. It will also provide client network services for one additional network operating system.

Network services can be installed during the initial installation or afterwards using the Network Setup utility found in the Network group. The installation procedure and screens are nearly the same. The only difference between the standalone setup and a later network setup is that during the initial installation, the setup utility will attempt to discover a network adapter.

Note:

The network adapter discovery process does not work well. It is better to select the adapter manually than to allow the discovery process to take place.

To begin installation, select the Network icon from the Network group. This will bring you to an opening screen. The Network Setup dialog box is on the next page. From this dialog box, you will set up the network(s) you want. You may select to install Microsoft Windows networking alone, Windows support for other network operating systems, or Microsoft networking and a single other network operating system.

Remember that you may only choose Microsoft Windows Network and one other.

Note:

The Microsoft Windows Network encompasses more than Windows for Workgroups peer services. You may also log on to a Windows NT or LAN Manager domain using Microsoft Windows Networking. The limit of a single additional network operating system is resolved in Windows 95.

In this dialog box, you may also choose to share your drives and printers with others and select the network adapter.

Your choices for NetWare support are:

Novell NetWare (Workstation Shell 3.x)

Novell NetWare (Workstation Shell 4.0 and above)

When you select one of these options, you will need to have available your NetWare Client installation diskettes.

Note:

You will need your NetWare Client installation diskettes only because Novell would not allow the client files needed for Windows support to be shipped with Windows for Workgroups. These files had previously been available with Windows v3.1.

Windows for Workgroups will install a series of drivers and make changes to your SYSTEM.INI, WIN.INI, NET.CFG and PROTOCOL.INI files.

When you have completed selecting your network operating system support, select the OK radio button and you will be returned to the main menu. If you selected the Microsoft Windows Network in addition to support for NetWare, you should then select the Sharing radio button. You will be presented with options to select whether you want to share your files and printers with other users on the Microsoft network. Make the appropriate selection for your users and select OK.

You will be taken back to the main menu to select the network adapter driver(s) you need. Windows for Workgroups allows you to select up to two network adapters and a total of three network protocols. After selecting them, clicking on the radio button will take you to the Drivers installation screen. From here, select Add Adapter. (See Figure 6-9.)

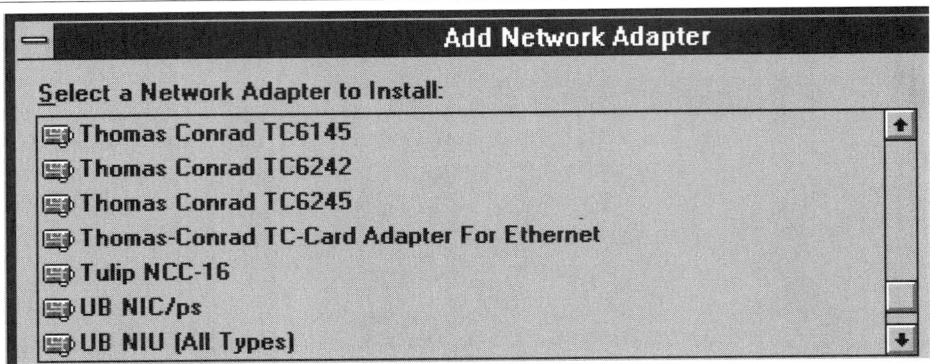

Figure 6-9. *Drivers installation screen.*

The Add Adapter button provides you with a list of driver options. You only need to be concerned with the ones labeled ODI support for ARCnet, Ethernet, or token ring. Select the driver support that makes the access method. Windows for Workgroups uses a shim to hook the ODI drivers into its NDIS interface for use by the Microsoft Network. This allows the ODI driver to be used in peer networking, as well as NetWare networks.

Windows For Workgroups installs the driver support for a standard interface using the access method chosen. It then creates a PROTOCOL.INI file and modifies the existing NET.CFG file or creates a new one if necessary. The installation also modifies your WIN.INI and SYSTEM.INI files. When the installation is complete your installation files should appear as shown in Figures 6-10 through 6-13.

Note:

If the Windows for Workgroups installation finds an existing driver, the modifications will include the name of the driver in appropriate sections of the NET.CFG and the PROTOCOL.INI files if the driver does not use XXXX as a placeholder. If this happens during your installation, you must manually edit the files using a text editor. In addition, the Windows for Workgroups installation procedure sometimes places the ODIHLP.EXE file in the wrong place. It must appear after the ODI driver loads.

If you are installing the NetWare Client software, you can install additional functionality and updated drivers by obtaining the latest

```
DEVICE= C:\DOS\HIMEM.SYS
DOS=HIGH
DEVICE=C:\DOS\SETVER.EXE
DEVICE=C:\WIN31\EMM386.EXE NOEMS X=B000-BFFF X=C800-D1FF
DEVICEhigh=C:\DOS\POWER.EXE
FILES=30
BUFFERS=30
DOS=HIGH,umb
DEVICEhigh=C:\thinkpad\IBMDSS01.SYS /S0=2
DEVICEhigh=C:\thinkpad\IBMDOSCS.SYS
DEVICEhigh=C:\thinkpad\DICRMU01.SYS /MA=C800-CFFF
DEVICEhigh=C:\thinkpad\$ICPMDOS.SYS
DEVICEhigh=C:\AUDIODD\TPAUDDD.SYS
lastdrive=z
STACKS=9,256
rem DEVICE=C:\IBMAUDIO\DIAG\AUDTEST.SYS
 /F=C:\IBMAUDIO\DIAG\AUDTEST.OUT /V=10DE
DEVICE=C:\WINDOWS\IFSHLP.SYS
```

Figure 6-10. *Windows for Workgroups CONFIG.SYS file.*

```
DEVICE= C:\DOS\HIMEM.SYS
DOS=HIGH
DEVICE=C:\DOS\SETVER.EXE
DEVICE=C:\WIN31\EMM386.EXE NOEMS X=B000-BFFF X=C800-D1FF
DEVICEhigh=C:\DOS\POWER.EXE
FILES=30
BUFFERS=30
DOS=HIGH,umb
DEVICEhigh=C:\thinkpad\IBMDSS01.SYS /S0=2
DEVICEhigh=C:\thinkpad\IBMDOSCS.SYS
DEVICEhigh=C:\thinkpad\DICRMU01.SYS /MA=C800-CFFF
DEVICEhigh=C:\thinkpad\$ICPMDOS.SYS
DEVICEhigh=C:\AUDIODD\TPAUDDD.SYS
lastdrive=z
STACKS=9,256
rem DEVICE=C:\IBMAUDIO\DIAG\AUDTEST.SYS
 /F=C:\IBMAUDIO\DIAG\AUDTEST.OUT /V=10DE
DEVICE=C:\WINDOWS\IFSHLP.SYS
```

Figure 6-11. *Windows for Workgroups AUTOEXEC.BAT file.*

client diskettes from a newer version of NetWare, NetWire on CompuServe, Novell's FTP site (FTP.NOVELL.COM), or its WWW site (//WWW.NOVELL.COM). The NetWare Client diskettes install files to your WINDOWS subdirectory and make the necessary changes to your .INI files and creates a NWUSER.EXE file.

```
Link Driver PCMDMCS
   Frame Ethernet_802.3
   Frame Ethernet_II
   Frame Ethernet_802.2
   Frame Ethernet_SNAP
   PCMCIA

link driver token
        data rate 16
        pcmcia
```

Figure 6-12. *Windows for Workgroups NET.CFG file.*

```
[boot]
shell=progman.exe
network.drv=wfwnet.drv
mouse.drv=mouse.drv
language.dll=
sound.drv=mmsound.drv
;comm.drv=comm.drv
comm.drv=C:\AUTOINST\WIN\SSCOMM.DRV
atm.system.drv=system.drv
386grabber=vga.3gr
oemfonts.fon=vgaoem.fon
fixedfon.fon=vgafix.fon
fonts.fon=vgasys.fon
display.drv=vga.drv
keyboard.drv=keyboard.drv
system.drv=atmsys.drv
286grabber=vgacolor.2gr
MAVDMApps=
os2mouse.drv=mouse.drv
useos2shield=1
os2shield=winsheld.exe
os2fonts.fon=vgasys.fon
fdisplay.drv=vga.drv
sdisplay.drv=vga.drv
secondnet.drv=netware.drv
drivers=mmsystem.dll
SCRNSAVE.EXE=C:\WINDOWS\SSFLYWIN.SCR

[keyboard]
keyboard.dll=kbdus.dll
oemansi.bin=
subtype=
type=4
```

Figure 6-13. *Windows for Workgroups SYSTEM.INI file.*

```
[boot.description]
mouse.drv=Microsoft, or IBM PS/2
language.dll=English (American)
system.drv=MS-DOS System
codepage=437
woafont.fon=English (437)
aspect=100,96,96
display.drv=VGA
keyboard.typ=Enhanced 101 or 102 key US and Non US key-
boards
network.drv=Microsoft Windows Network (version 3.11)
fdisplay.drv=VGA
secondnet.drv=Novell NetWare (Workstation Shell 4.0 and
above)

[386Enh]
EMMExclude=D000-DFFF
;
REM============================== PCMCIA Drivers
==============================
device=C:\AUTOINST\WIN\SSVRDD.386
device=C:\AUTOINST\WIN\SSVCD.386
COM1Base=3F8
COM1Irq=4
COM2Base=02F8
COM2Irq=3
COM3Base=3E8
COM3Irq=4
COM4Base=2E8
COM4Irq=4
TimerCriticalSection=10000

device=*vpd
mouse=*vmd
woafont=dosapp.fon
display=*vddvga
EGA80WOA.FON=EGA80WOA.FON
EGA40WOA.FON=EGA40WOA.FON
CGA80WOA.FON=CGA80WOA.FON
CGA40WOA.FON=CGA40WOA.FON
device=vpmtd.386
device=lpt.386
device=serial.386
device=vcomm.386
device=vtdapi.386
device=vshare.386
device=vcache.386
device=ifsmgr.386
device=C:\BH\DRIVERS\BHSUPP.386
device=C:\BH\DRIVERS\VBH.386
```

Figure 6-13. *Windows for Workgroups SYSTEM.INI file, continued.*

```
device=C:\WINDOWS\SYSTEM\WIN32S\W32S.386
DEVICE=CS48BA11.386
32BitDiskAccess=OFF
device=*int13
device=*wdctrl
network=*vnetbios,*vwc,vnetsup.386,vredir.386,vserver.386
ebios=*ebios
keyboard=*vkd
device=*vpicd
device=*vtd
device=*reboot
device=*vdmad
device=*vsd
device=*v86mmgr
device=*pageswap
device=*dosmgr
device=*vmpoll
device=*wshell
device=*BLOCKDEV
device=*PAGEFILE
device=*vfd
device=*parity
device=*biosxlat
;device=*vcd
device=*vmcpd
device=*combuff
device=*cdpscsi
local=CON
FileSysChange=off
netheapsize=20
InDOSPolling=FALSE
secondnet=vnetware.386
OverlappedIO=off
netmisc=ndis.386,msodisup.386
transport=nwlink.386,nwnblink.386,netbeui.386
PagingFile=C:\WINDOWS\WIN386.SWP
MaxPagingFileSize=5233
ReflectDOSInt2A=TRUE
UniqueDOSPSP=TRUE
PSPIncrement=5

[standard]

[NonWindowsApp]
localtsrs=dosedit,ced

[mci]
CDAudio=mcicda.drv
Sequencer=mciseq.drv
WaveAudio=mciwave.drv
```

Figure 6-13. *Windows for Workgroups SYSTEM.INI file, continued.*

```
[drivers]
midimapper=midimap.drv
WAVE=CS48BA21.DRV
timer=timer.drv

[vcache]
minfilecache=512

[Network]
FileSharing=No
PrintSharing=No
LogonDisconnected=yes
EnableSharing=No
winnet=wfwnet/00025100
multinet=netware4
UserName=user3
Workgroup=ENTERPRISE
ComputerName=THINKPAD_750
Comment=Mark Anderson
logonvalidated=no
PreferredRedir=FULL

[DDEShares]
CHAT$=winchat,chat,,31,,0,,0,0,0
SCHAT$=winchat,chat,,31,,0,,0,0,0
CLPBK$=clipsrv,system,,31,,0,,0,0,0
HEARTS$=mshearts,hearts,,15,,0,,0,0,0

[NetWare]
NWShareHandles=TRUE
RestoreDrives=TRUE

[network drivers]
devdir=C:\WINDOWS
LoadRMDrivers=No
netcard=
transport=

[Password Lists]
*Shares=C:\WINDOWS\Share000.PWL
MARKANDE=C:\WINDOWS\MARKANDE.PWL
USER3=C:\WINDOWS\USER3.PWL



;============================================================
=====================
[NWNBLINK]
LANABASE=0
```

Figure 6-13. *Windows for Workgroups SYSTEM.INI file.*

The following files are contained on the NetWare Client diskettes:

NETWARE.DRV	NWUSER.EXE
NETWARE.HLP	PNW.DLL
NWCALLS.DLL	TASKID.COM
NWGDI.DLL	TBM12.COM
DWIPXSPX.DLL	TLI_SPX.DLL
NWLOCALE.DLL	TLI_TCP.DLL
NWNET.DLL	TLI_WIN.DLL
NWPOPUP.EXE	VIPX.386
NWPSRV.DLL	VNETWARE.386

These files are the drivers, dynamic link libraries, and applications that link NetWare with standard Windows applications. Two of the applications are present as programs: NWPOPUP.EXE provides support for NetWare messages, and NWUSER.EXE allows you to map drives and printers as well as use some of the more common Novell utilities such as USERLIST.

The driver files VIPX and VNETWARE allow virtual sessions in 386 Enhanced mode. This allows you to use the interface in 386 Enhanced mode for Virtual Network Services.

The files provided in the NetWare DOS Client Kit include additional functionality for File Manager, Print Manager, and the new NWUSER.EXE.

Configuration Tips

There are two ways to configure your computer to log in to the NetWare server. You may choose to include the login statements in your AUTOEXEC.BAT or STARTNET.BAT files, or you may allow the NetWare graphical interface to present you with a login screen while Windows is loading. This screen is similar to the Windows for Workgroups Microsoft Windows Login screen. Either login method is acceptable. If you do not spend much time in Windows, you may want to log in to the network prior to running Windows. This will maintain your login and drive mappings when you leave Windows. If however, you do spend most of your time in Windows, we suggest that you log in from the graphical interface provided by NetWare for Windows.

During the installation procedure, Windows for Workgroups is sometimes careless about where it puts the ODIHLP.EXE statement in your AUTOEXEC.BAT or STARTNET.BAT file. It must be placed after NET START and after the driver. The proper order is:

NET START
LSL
adapter driver
ODIHLP

You may want to load IPXODI prior to ODIHLP, but it is not necessary. In any event, be sure to check your batch file prior to restarting your computer.

When selecting a protocol, keep in mind what you will be doing on the network. The available protocols are:

IPX/SPX COMPATIBLE TRANSPORT
IPX/SPX COMPATIBLE TRANSPORT WITH NetBIOS
MICROSOFT NetBEUI
ODI ARCnet Support Transport with NetBIOS

If you do not need NetBIOS support or NetBEUI, do not select them. NetBIOS is required for some applications and for other older Microsoft network products such as LAN Manager. Microsoft NetBEUI is not a routable protocol. However, IPX/SPX Compatible Transport with NetBIOS allows NetBIOS to be routed through a router that supports IPX/SPX or through a NetWare server. This lets Windows for Workgroups clients be on disparate networks and still share files and printers.

Quick List

Following is a quick recap of the installation of Windows for Workgroup clients.

1. Select Network Setup from the Network Group.
2. Select Network Setup and select the appropriate Network Support.
3. Select Share Files and Printers if you chose Microsoft networking.
4. Select the appropriate adapter driver and settings to match the workstation.
5. Verify and select new protocols if needed.
6. Restart the workstation.

Troubleshooting

Troubleshooting a Windows for Workgroups installation is more difficult than Personal NetWare or NetWare Lite because there is no installation verification utility. You must rely on standard troubleshooting techniques.

First, verify adapter settings. Most adapter manufacturers provide configuration and testing utilities with their adapters. Use these applications to be sure that you have configured the adapter properly. Then verify that you haven't created a conflict in your system. The vendors' utilities should let you verify that the adapter is transmitting and receiving properly. If your adapter uses a memory address, such as most ARCnet and token-ring adapters, verify that you have excluded the area of memory the adapter is using.

As Windows starts, it maintains a file named BOOTLOG.TXT. This is running under the Windows boot process. If any part of the boot process fails, you will receive an error code in this text file. Microsoft of the LAN adapter vendor will often need to interpret the error code. If you are running the Microsoft Network or NDIS drivers, a second file called NDISLOG.TXT is also maintained. This file provides you with information specific to the NDIS portion of the boot process. A listing of error codes provided by the BOOTLOG.TXT and NDISLOG.TXT is available using the Windows for Workgroups Resource Kit from Microsoft. However, the log is also useful in pointing you in the direction of the error condition. Once you know what is failing, it is a simple matter to discover the cause. Be sure to keep clean copies of all .INI files so that you may refer to them as well. Also, if you feel that your network driver or settings on the adapter are incorrect, you may decide to load Windows with the WIN /N switch. This will load Windows without loading the network features. If your machine is hanging when it is attempts to load other drivers, you can use this to stop network operations.

Performance

One of the best improvements of Windows for Workgroups over standard Windows is the performance enhancement. The 32-bit disk and file access increase internal application speed and provide greater speed for disk access. Unfortunately, the 32-bit disk access will do nothing to speed network drives. The limiting factor, unless you are using a 100Mbps network solution, is the speed of the network and not the drive access.

The caching utility (VCACHE.386) provided with 32-bit file access provides a great enhancement over any other method. If you are running Windows, you will notice a tremendous performance improvement.

These performance features will attempt to run by default during installation. To verify whether these features are operating, select the Control Panel from the Main group and then select the 386 Enhanced Mode icon. Then, select the Virtual Memory radio button. When the Virtual Memory dialog box is displayed, you will see the Disk Access and Swap File settings. To change these settings, select the Change radio button. The 32-bit Disk Access and File Access check boxes are located at the bottom of the dialog box. (See Figure 6-14.) Click the check boxes to activate the features. If the features are grayed out, your hardware will not support 32-bit access.

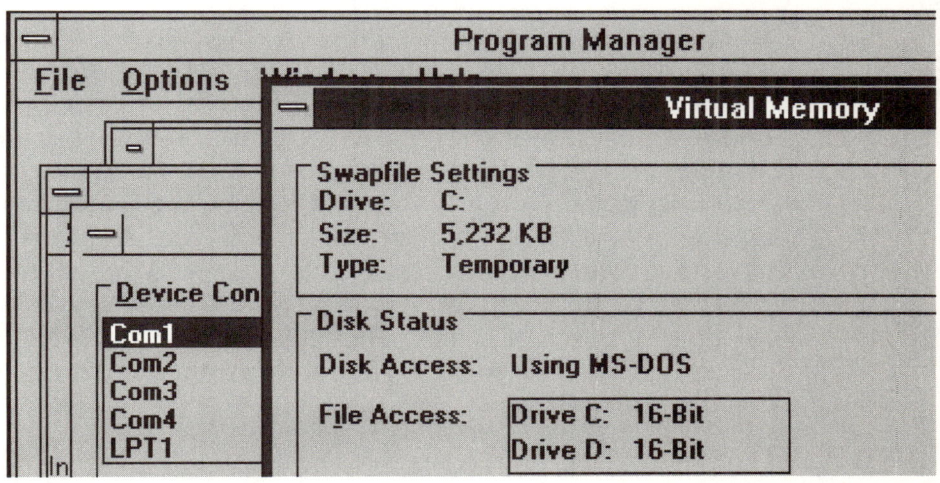

Figure 6-14. *Virtual Memory Change dialog box.*

Windows NT

Windows NT, the successor to LAN Manager, was designed as a high-end, yet scaleable, operating system that provides the power for future needs. It provides the perfect operating system for an integrated LAN and operating system functions.

Requirements

In keeping with its function as a high-end operating system, the minimum system configuration is a 386/33 with 12MB of RAM and enough hard disk space to accommodate the operating system and a 27MB swap file. For use as a server, we recommend at least a 486/50 with 24MB of RAM; for a workstation we recommend a 486/33 with 16MB of RAM. These recommendations are obviously higher than the traditional NetWare workstation, but the Windows NT workstation is far more capable than the traditional DOS workstation. If you are planning on using Windows NT, you should be prepared for the higher workstation cost.

Installation and Configuration

Support for NetWare under Windows NT can be divided into three areas: Microsoft Client Services for NetWare, Microsoft Gateway Services for NetWare, and the Novell Client for NT. Microsoft Windows NT products for NetWare use NDIS 3.0 drivers and the Microsoft IPX/SPX protocol. Microsoft Client Services provide standard integration with NetWare so a user on the Windows NT machine can log in to a NetWare server and use its file- and print-sharing services. The Microsoft Gateway Services for NetWare allow a Windows NT client to provide NetWare services to non-NetWare clients on an existing Microsoft network. The Novell Client for NT is designed to provide client access to a NetWare server from a Windows NT workstation using ODI drivers.

Microsoft Client Services for NetWare

Microsoft Client Services for NetWare are provided as part of the base operating system. The package is installed through the Network icon in the Control Panel. From the Network Installation dialog box, select Add Software. The drop-down dialog box provides a list of available options. Select Client Services for NetWare. At this point you will need to have the Windows NT CD-ROM available. You will also need to select the IPX/SPX Compatible Protocol or IP as one of the protocols you will use for connecting to the network. If you use IPX/SPX, you will need to select a valid frame type or allow the frame type to be autodetected.

Note:

If you are using the Autodetect for frame type selection, you will need to be careful, especially on a switched network. In autodetect mode, the Windows NT protocol stack sends out broadcast packets on each frame type. This has the potential, especially on an Ethernet network with all frame types loaded, to cause broadcast storms on routed networks.

The available frame types are:

Frame	Use
ETHERNET_802.2	NetWare Default
ETHERNET_802.3	Old NetWare Default
ETHERNET_II	Generally used for IP
ETHERNET_SNAP	Macintosh or IP frametype
TOKEN_RING	NetWare default
TOKEN_RING_SNAP	NetWare IP and Macintosh
Novell_RX-NET	

You should also select a preferred server. The preferred server acts in a similar fashion to the Preferred Server in a NetWare NET.CFG file. In this case, when the preferred server is not available, Windows NT will not attach to any server and will ask you through a Login dialog box if you want to attach to another server. Your Windows NT username should be the same as your NetWare username. With the Windows NT Universal Client, when you enter your username and password on Windows NT you will be simultaneously logged into the preferred NetWare server.

The Microsoft Client will not run NetWare login scripts and will not operate with NetWare Directory Services (NDS). It uses a bindery emulation. Therefore, the Novell administrative clients for NDS will not operate under Windows NT. NetWare drives must be mapped using the File Manager utility, and NetWare print queues must be attached using Print Manager.

Gateway Services Installation

Gateway Services for NetWare are installed in the same manner as Microsoft Client Services. Select the Network icon from the Control Panel and, in the Network dialog box, select Add Program. Select the Gateway Services for NetWare option from the list. Be sure you have your Windows NT CD handy. You will then see the Gateway Services for NetWare appear in the list of programs. When the installation is complete, you must reboot the Windows NT machine.

Gateway Services for NetWare will now appear as an icon in the Control Panel. Click on the icon to bring up the Setup dialog box. You will need to enter your preferred server and user. This connection to the server must have sufficient rights to access the volumes and print service you want to share. You will also need to select the volumes and printing resources you wish to add to the Gateway Share list. Remember that this will be the only connection that the NetWare server sees. The Windows NT machine will act as a true gateway to allow the Microsoft Network Client users to see this machine.

It is a good idea to create a group of Microsoft Network users who will have access rights to NetWare shared resources. This group will act as an easy means to maintain security for the shared NetWare resources. You may also want to create a similar group on the NetWare server, allowing you to have several Windows NT machines acting as gateways and maintain additional security at the NetWare servers.

Note:

Remember, all gateway printing services are managed through the Print Manager.

As of this writing, the Novell Client for NT is still in beta. The client interface is available on NetWire or directly from your Novell dealer. Please be warned, however, that it is still a beta product, and you may encounter some problems, particularly with heavy use across the link.

The Novell Client for NT uses existing ODI LAN drivers and shims them into the NDIS 3.0 Windows NT interface. This provides a 32-bit Novell driver for the Windows NT machine. Also, remember that this is an all-or-nothing proposition. If you use this interface, you will not be able to use the Microsoft Client or Gateway Services. Novell learned quite a bit about writing interfaces for Windows with Windows 3.1 and Windows for Workgroups. Therefore, you will notice much similarity between those interfaces and the Novell Client for NT.

Novell Client for NT Installation

As with Microsoft clients, the Novell Client for NT is installed through the Network icon from the Control Panel. The Novell Client comes on two diskettes. Select the Add Programs radio button and select Other. When prompted, place the first disk in the appropriate drive. When the installation is completed, it will appear in the list of available programs. Also, two icons are placed in the Control Panel: a NetWare Client icon and a DOS icon.

The NetWare icon is used to select the preferred server and username. You do not need to have the same username for your NetWare and Windows NT login. The Novell client does not take advantage of the Windows NT login procedure and uses its own login dialog box. You must enter your password each time you log in to the Novell network.

NetWare volumes and directories are accessed through the Windows NT File Manager. When you select the Connect Network Drive icon, the subsequent dialog box has a Network icon from which NetWare drives are selected. This feature is not as integrated as the Microsoft Client, but is similar to existing clients for Windows and WFW.

NetWare printers are attached through the Printer icon in the Control Panel. As with the file access method, printer attachment is exactly as it was in previous versions of NetWare clients. Use the Connect button to select the printer; be sure to have the Windows NT CD handy. Then use the Network radio button to select the Novell print queue. Printing tasks may be managed through the Windows NT Print Manager, although it is not necessary. By using the Print Manager, you queue the print job at the Windows NT machine and send it to the network printer. This frees the machine to perform other tasks while the job is sent to the NetWare queue.

The additional DOS prompt box provides compatibility for NetWare DOS utilities. Novell noticed a problem with some of its utilities such as SYSCON or RCONSOLE. This DOS prompt provides the ability to use these utilities.

Configuration Tips

If you are using Microsoft Client Services, several configuration options can be made. First, be sure to select only the IPX/SPX frame types you need, especially if you are on a routed network. Second, do not install Gateway Services for NetWare unless you need it. The Gateway Services for NetWare are an excellent method for allowing non-NetWare clients to access NetWare services, but take a toll on the Windows NT machine's performance.

As with any Windows NT machine, the faster the machine and the more memory, the better your performance will be. If you are installing standard client services, we recommend a minimum of 16MB of RAM; if you are installing Gateway Services for NetWare, we recommend 24MB.

Quick List

Following is a quick recap of installing Windows NT clients on NetWare LANs.

1. Select the Main group.
2. Select the Control Panel icon.
3. Select the Network icon.
4. Install your network adapter—Microsoft Client products only.
5. Select the appropriate protocols—Microsoft Client products only.
6. Select Add Software.
7. Select the appropriate Client or Gateway Services. If you are using Novell, Select "Other" and install the service from diskette.
8. If you are using the Novell client, select the network adapter.
9. Configure the client service for Preferred Server and Username where appropriate.
10. Select the appropriate frame type and IP address.
11. Reboot the computer.

Troubleshooting

The main troubleshooting tool for Windows NT is the Event Viewer. The Event Viewer starts on boot and logs error and event messages generated by Windows NT or one of its add-on components. If there is a hardware problem with the adapter, the driver will generate an error condition that is logged by the Event Viewer. These messages are often specific to the error condition. The adapter vendor should have a list of the error conditions its driver generates. A list of error codes generated by Windows NT is available in the Windows NT Resource Kit. However, most of the error messages are self-explanatory and provide an excellent source for troubleshooting problems.

If the adapter driver loads, but you still cannot find the NetWare server, verify that you have bound the appropriate frame types. To check the frame type, go to the Network icon in the Control Panel and select the IPX/SPX Compatible Protocol. Then, click on the Configure radio button. This will bring you to the Configuration Options for the protocol. Verify that the frame type you have selected is bound to IPX at the server. If you are in doubt, select Autodetect and reboot the Windows NT workstation. If you are using IP, select the IP protocol and press the Configure radio button. This will take you to the IP configuration utility from which you must verify the IP address and netmask.

Be sure that you also verify all cable connections. Remember that the majority of network problems are associated with cable issues. In most cases, this is the first place to look for problems.

Performance

When working with a NetWare environment under Windows NT, acceptable performance has more to do with the horsepower of your client workstation than with the network adapter. The more powerful the workstation, the better the overall performance. Windows NT includes an excellent performance monitor. This utility can be found in the Network Administration group. Select the Performance Monitor and then use the Add function to add specific items for it to monitor. While there are a host of selections to choose from, you will want to look specifically at the number of bytes transmitted and received by the workstation and the number of interrupts generated by the adapter, as well as the amount of processor time spent servicing interrupts. Measured over time, you can determine how much of your workstation's resources are spent servicing the network adapter and the amount of data your adapter is transmitting.

When you have an overall idea of how much of your workstation's time is spent servicing the network connection, you can determine where the bottleneck for your workstation lies. It may turn out that there is a lack of memory or that you simply need a faster machine. Windows NT generates a lot of overhead on the operating system. The more memory available and the faster the machine, the better your performance will be.

When the workstation is properly tuned, then turn to the network adapter. If you are using an access method such as token-ring or FDDI, try changing the packet size and measuring its effect on total bytes transmitted and received and workstation performance. It may turn out that you simply need to turn to a faster access method, or that you can tune some of the settings on your adapter to get more out of your system. Be careful, however; it is easy to get wrapped up in tuning your system and forget that the goal is to actually get some work done.

Windows 95

Microsoft's latest Windows adventure is Windows 95. It offers the user a vastly improved user interface and a full 32-bit operating system. Unlike Windows NT, which was designed as an operating system for high-end workstations that will work with any major chip platform, Windows 95 is an Intel chip-only replacement for DOS and Windows 3.x.

Note:

Microsoft now offers the Windows 95 interface as a replacement for the existing Windows NT interface.

A true 32-bit operating system, it offers fast and reliable multitasking and a easier setup. The user will also find that, like Windows for Workgroups, it offers built-in networking and also a built-in client interface for the majority of third-party network operating systems, including NetWare.

Requirements

Like Windows NT, Windows 95 abandons any pretense of operating with earlier Intel chip designs. The recommended base platform is a 386/DX 33MHz. You must also have a VGA adapter and monitor, as well as 4MB of RAM. Having listed the requirements as recited by Microsoft, let's get realistic. We would not recommend using anything less than a 386/DX 40MHz with 8MB of RAM. While the best performance is obtained with the fastest possible machine with the most memory you can put in it, a good working system is a 486/DX 50MHz with 16MB of RAM and a Super VGA adapter and monitor.

Installation and Configuration

Depending on the driver you use, installing NetWare on Windows 95 is extremely quick and easy. There are three possible drivers from which to choose: NDIS 3.0, NDIS 2.0, and ODI. NDIS 3.0 drivers are 32-bit drivers designed especially for Windows NT and Windows 95. The network portion of the operating system is built around this specification. It provides the fastest interface for network operations. NDIS 2.0 drivers are 16-bit older NDIS drivers that operate with an NDIS 2.0 to NDIS 3.0 wrapper. When Windows 95 makes calls to the NDIS 2.0 driver, it must drop out of protected mode. This slows the network interface considerably. ODI drivers are written to the Novell Open Data-link Specification and 16-bit drivers as well. They are included for compatibility with adapters that do not have NDIS spec drivers. As with the NDIS 2.0 driver, the ODI driver will slow the network functionality. There are two possible NetWare clients to choose from: Microsoft or Novell. Windows 95 will allow multiple clients and adapters, so you could also include another client if necessary.

Driver Installation

The basic installation procedure is the same for all drivers. Each adapter has its own installation file. These files are named with an .INF extension and contain the various settings required for the driver installation and configuration. Those that are included with Windows 95 are copied to the WINPATH\INF subdirectory during installation. This is a hidden subdirectory; however, you can find it by going to your Windows path and typing CD\INF. The NDIS 3.0 drivers are contained in the WINPATH\SYSTEM subdirectory and may contain a .VXD, .386, or .SYS extension. NDIS 2.0 drivers are copied to the \WINPATH subdirectory and have a .DOS extension. ODI drivers are copied by the Windows 95 installation utility to the subdirectory in which the other Novell utility files are located or to the \WINPATH subdirectory if no other subdirectory is reported.

Note:

There should be no need to actually look into the .INF subdirectory. However, if you have trouble using the installation utility or the .INF file does not properly copy drivers, you can copy the .INF file to the \INF subdirectory and the drivers to the appropriate subdirectories, and then proceed with the installation. Windows 95 will rebuild the adapter table and allow you to install the driver.

Drivers are chosen by adding adapters during the initial installation or later. During installation, the utility will bring up a Network dialog box that is identical to the installation utility contained in the Control Panel. Therefore, this discussion will be limited to post-installation driver addition.

To begin driver installation, gather the adapter with its installation diskette and the Windows 95 CD. If the network adapter is a Plug and Play, PCI, Micro Channel, or EISA adapter, you should install the adapter and configure the adapter under DOS. When Windows 95 comes up the next time, it will discover the adapter and allow you to install the driver without trouble. If it is an ISA adapter, it is still preferable to install it prior to attempting to set up the adapter.

If you have an adapter that installs the driver through the discovery process, much of your setup work is done for you. To finish installing the drivers, select the Control Panel from the Your Computer icon or the Settings item from the Start menu. From the Control Panel folder, select the Network icon. The Network Setting dialog box will list all of the installed items. (See Figure 6-15.) The Network Settings dialog box is concerned with four classes of items:

Clients
Adapters
Protocols
Services

Client Installation

Clients are the elements necessary to connect the Windows 95 operating system to the network operating system. This includes the redirec-

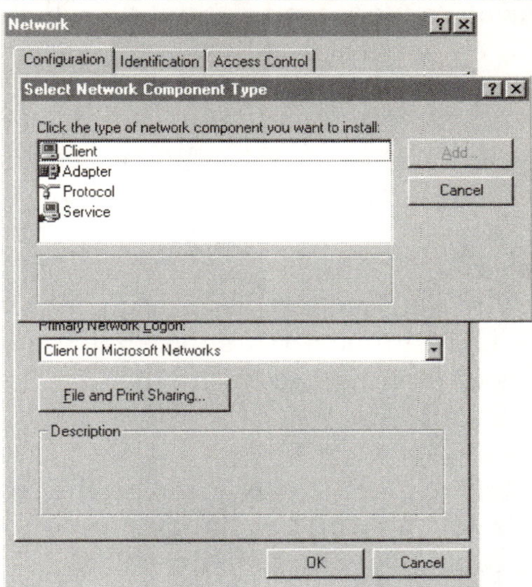

Figure 6-15. *Network Settings dialog box.*

tor for the particular operating system, as well as the file- and print-sharing utilities to connect to network devices. The default clients are the Microsoft Network and Novell Network options. The Novell Network option is the Microsoft version of the Novell Network client. The Microsoft NetWare client is a 32-bit redirector and network service utility that relies on an NDIS 2.0 or 3.0 driver. The combination of the Microsoft NetWare interface and the NDIS 3.0 driver makes the fastest possible network connection on NetWare networks. The one drawback to using the Microsoft client is that it is not yet compatible with NetWare 4.0 specification NetWare Directory Services (NDS). To change the way this client operates, highlight the client listed in the dialog box and select the Properties radio button.

The second type of network client for NetWare is the Novell NetWare client. This client must use ODI drivers. You must also remove the existing Microsoft Network client. To remove a client, highlight it in the Network Settings dialog box and select the Remove radio button. To add the Novell client, select the Add button on the Network Settings dialog box. You will be presented with a list of possible components. Select Clients and double-click. You will be taken to the Network Client dialog box. Select the Novell option, and choose between the NetWare v3.x and 4.x Client. You will need to have your NetWare Client Kit handy, as well as your Windows 95 CD.

If you choose the NetWare v3.x client, you will be asked to provide the NETWARE.DRV file from the Novell Client Kit. If you select the NetWare 4.x client, you will be asked to actually install the complete Novell Client Kit.

Note:

For NetWare 4.x clients using VLMs, the client installation will not continue if Windows 95 does not find the client installed. It will force you to install the client and then continue the client installation.

If you have previously installed the NetWare client, the Windows 95 installation will make changes to your STARTNET.BAT file. It will remove the following statements:

STARTNET.BAT
LSL.COM—Novell Link Support Layer
TCTOKSH.COM—Driver MLID
REM—Removed by Windows 95—IPXODI.COM
REM—Removed by Windows 95—VLM.COM

The ODI-compliant MLID is shimmed into the Microsoft redirector and will then use the Microsoft Universal Client for logging on to the Novell network. When you use the Novell client, you should also use the Novell IPX/SPX protocol. This is different from the Microsoft IPX/SPX-Compatible Protocol that is used by default with the Microsoft client, in that it is designed to work with ODI-compliant drivers. To select this protocol, start from the Network Settings dialog box and select Add. Then choose Protocol and choose the Novell option. The only protocol listed is the Novell IPX/SPX protocol. (See Figure 6-16.) Highlight this option and select OK.

When you have completed installing the various clients, you should configure the clients. Select the Network icon from the Control Panel and highlight the client you wish to configure. Then select the Properties radio button. You will be presented with a list of properties to change. For the Novell settings you will need to select the first network drive and determine if you want to process your login script. If you choose not to process your login script, you will need to map all your local drives NetWare drives, printers, and other network devices

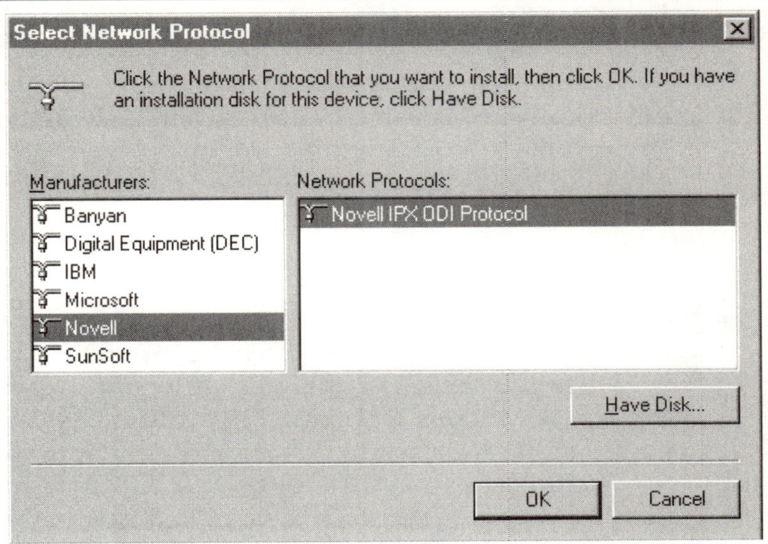

Figure 6-16. *Available protocols.*

separately through the Explorer, the My Computer icon, or the Network Neighborhood icon. Either way, you can tell Windows 95 to restore the connections on all subsequent logins.

Adapter Installation

Adapters are installed in the same fashion as clients. If you have a Plug and Play, Micro Channel, EISA, or PCI adapter, you should only have to turn off your computer, install the adapter, and turn it back on. If you have a Micro Channel or EISA adapter, you will need to run your computer's configuration program. When Windows 95 is started again, it will automatically discover the new device and attempt to install the driver. If it cannot find an .INF file for the adapter, you will need to have the vendor's driver disk ready with an appropriate .INF file and driver disk. If the adapter does not have an NDIS 3.0 driver, you can install an existing ODI driver and use this as the driver for your adapter.

If you are installing an ISA adapter, you will need to install the driver through the standard process. Select the Network icon from the Control Panel. Then choose the Add button and select Adapters. Locate the name of the vendor and open its folder. Choose the adapter you are using and highlight it. Select OK. You will need to have ready either the Windows 95 CD or your manufacturer's driver disk. Windows 95 will install the driver. The driver will now appear in the Network Settings dialog box. To configure the driver, highlight the driver and select the Properties radio button. Verify your adapter's settings and select OK. As with any change to the operating system, you will need to restart your computer.

Note:

If your vendor does not have an NDIS 3.0 driver, you can select an NDIS 2.0 driver. If all you have available is an ODI driver and an .INF file is not available, you can still install the adapter. Go back to the top of the Adapter menu choices and select Existing ODI Driver. You will then need to install the Novell client software as described later in this chapter.

Protocol Installation

Protocols are the rules that govern communication between network workstations. Each network operating system has it own set of protocols. In Microsoft networking products, the default protocols are NetBEUI and Microsoft's IPX/SPX-compatible protocol. Novell's NetWare uses IPX/SPX. Both vendor's products operate with TCP/IP. Windows 95 comes with the following protocol support:

IPX/SPX-compatible	Microsoft default for NT, Windows for Workgroups, and Windows 95
IPX/SPX-compatible with NetBIOS	Microsoft default with NetBIOS
Novell IPX/SPX	Novell default protocol
NetBEUI	Microsoft default with LAN Manager and other NDIS-based network operating systems
TCP/IP	Used for the Internet

Prior to the introduction of Windows NT and Windows for Workgroups, the default communication protocol used by Microsoft was NetBIOS. The problem with this protocol was that you could not internally route it. Today the default protocol is IPX/SPX. This allows it to be routed by a NetWare router.

If you choose the default Microsoft NetWare and Microsoft network clients, the default protocols are IPX/SPX and NetBEUI. If you choose the Novell client, the default protocol remains the same. To add protocols, choose the Network icon from the Control Panel. Select Add and Highlight Protocol in the dialog box. Either double-click on Protocol or choose OK. Select the vendor—Microsoft or Novell. Microsoft has a number of choices including IPX/SPX-compatible, NetBEUI, and TCP/IP. Novell has only the IPX/SPX protocol. The Novell protocol can only be used with ODI drivers.

Once you have configured all the various items you may now restart your computer. When you first log in, Windows 95 attempts to discover the Novell servers on the network. You will then be presented with a Network Login screen. Select the Preferred Server, User Name, and Password. Windows 95 will remember these settings and you will only be presented with the main Windows 95 login screen after this.

Note:

If your password requires periodic changes, you will be presented with a screen that says your password has expired. You will still be given a grace login. When you are logged in, go to a DOS prompt and use the SETPASS command line utility to change your password. The next time you start Windows 95, NetWare will not accept your old password. Change your password in the dialog box and Windows 95 will remember your new password.

Configuration Tips

Given the large number of possible clients, drivers, and protocols, your best choice is to choose only what you absolutely need. The Microsoft 32-bit NetWare client is by far the fastest of the clients. If you use the Microsoft client you will need to use the IPX/SPX Compatible Protocol. If you are not connecting to an existing LAN Manager or other older NetBEUI network, you will not need this protocol. If you are using the Novell client, you should choose the Novell IPX/SPX protocol. The adapter driver choice depends on the client you are using; however, if you are planning on using the Microsoft client, you should choose an NDIS 3.0 driver.

Quick List

Following is a quick recap of installing a Windows 95 workstation on a NetWare LAN.

1. Select the Control Panel through the My Computer icon or Start menu.
2. Select the Network icon.
3. Select the Add button.
4. Select the Client folder and choose a client.
5. Select the Adapter folder and choose an adapter or existing ODI driver.
6. Select the Protocol folder and choose the protocols you need.
7. Return to the Network Settings dialog box and choose the Configure radio button to configure your selections.
8. Restart your computer.

Troubleshooting

Troubleshooting with a graphical interface is both easier and more difficult. If the driver does not start properly, you will be presented with an information box that tells you that the XXX did not load. Typically, XXX is the adapter driver. Unfortunately, if the adapter driver does not load, everything cascades from there and no network drivers will load. The graphical interface provides you with the message, but no idea of what actually went wrong. Therefore, you will need to rely on some other indications.

If you select F8 when you see the statement Starting Windows 95 on your screen, you will be presented with a menu list. Select the Normal Start with Logging. Windows 95 will log each step of the boot process in a text file called BOOTLOG.TXT. When the boot is complete, you can view this log file to find which driver failed to load. Additionally, if a problem occurs with any of the network drivers, a second log file called NDISLOG.TXT is created. This contains error codes generated by the drivers. To adequately use this log file, you will probably need to contact the technical support department for the vendor.

If the driver does not load, be sure to use your standard troubleshooting techniques. Be sure that the cable is attached and then verify that the settings of the driver are correct in Windows 95. Also, if the vendor supplied a diagnostic utility, either use the F8 key during boot or use a boot diskette to boot the machine to DOS and run this utility. Verify that there are no conflicts with other devices in the machine.

Performance

Performance is key for Windows 95. Those of us who grew accustomed to slow performance under Windows will be impressed. The 32-bit network utilities provide excellent performance. Even the performance using 16-bit drivers is acceptable when compared with previous versions of Windows.

However, as with Windows NT, the performance of the network connection is only one aspect of overall system performance. Also, remember that the Windows 95 client will most likely also be part of a peer network, as well as a NetWare network. To measure performance, Microsoft provides three monitors: NetWatcher, System Monitor, and Resource Meter. NetWatcher is used to monitor who is accessing your system and what files they have open. System Monitor is used to measure the individual system resources being used. Resource Meter provides a quick visual display of the memory utilization of the computer. With System Monitor you can select from various systems resources such as the file system, kernel, memory manager, and Microsoft or NetWare Network client. With this utility you can gain an understanding of the computer's usage and then determine the best configuration for each. Remember, however, that the System Monitor uses system resources to operate and may already contribute to any performance problem you may have.

chapter 7

Diskless Workstations

A diskless workstation is simply what the name implies—a computer that has no floppy or hard drive to boot the machine from. When you boot a machine, you load the base operating system from a disk drive. In the case of a diskless workstation, you will boot the machine initially from a device called a boot ROM or remote reset ROM, and then from a file contained on the server. The ROM contains code to boot the machine, initialize the network adapter, and then download the operating system files from the server. The ROM will send out a request frame that is answered by a server. The ROM then sends a request to send the boot image file. This file is downloaded into the computer's system memory and executed. It contains the boot files, configuration files, and any other files, such as HIMEM.SYS and EMM386.EXE, necessary to run the machine.

A diskless workstation is used for one of two reasons. Either the network administrator does not trust the users to properly boot from a floppy or a hard disk, or, more importantly, it is the highest-security workstation available. With no floppy drive from which to boot the machine, you cannot gain any unauthorized entry. There are no confidential files that can be accidentally left on the local drive, and you cannot accidentally take home unauthorized software. Likewise, you cannot bring in a copy of Doom and put it on the local or network drive.

In addition to security reasons, there are administrative ones as well. You have one file or a set of files that can be used to boot all the workstations on the network. When you need to change the boot files you simply regenerate the workstation boot file on the server and you have changed the boot files for all the users.

Requirements

The requirements for a diskless workstation are fairly simple and are designed to be used on almost any machine. In fact, you will probably find that it is the less powerful machines you want to boot from boot ROMs. It is much easier to have a print server boot from a ROM than to worry about a floppy getting lost or damaged, especially when you may only check it once a month when someone complains that the printer isn't printing. In addition, you will need a network adapter that supports a boot ROM. The ROM will cost approximately $50 per workstation. If you are planning on remote booting OS/2, you will need to have a workstation capable of running OS/2 and a copy of OS/2 installed on the server.

At the server you will need to have the remote initial program load (RPL) files in the \LOGIN directory and RPL.NLM loaded and bound to the adapter to the network you are booting from. You will also need to generate a boot image file. This is the file that the ROMs download into the system memory of the remote workstation.

If you are remote booting OS/2, you will need to have a ROM that supports the RPL specification, as well as an OS/2 workstation with the Novell OS/2 Utilities installed.

Installation

The first requirement of installing a machine to be remote booted is to set up the server. You will need to know the difference between older Novell remote reset and RPL. Starting with NetWare v3.x, Novell supported the RPL specification for remote workstations. This is the same method used for remote workstations under IBM LAN Server, Microsoft LAN Manager, and Banyan VINES. This specification allows a remote reset ROM written to the standard RPL specification to remote boot into any server. This method, however, only works for Ethernet, token-ring, FDDI, and access methods that support RPL. ARCnet does not support RPL. In addition, Novell wanted to support all its legacy ROMs. Therefore, they also support the older Novell remote boot specification.

Note:

At present it is possible to remote boot both DOS and OS/2. We will discuss DOS and OS/2 remote setups in this chapter.

To install the remote reset ROM, look for a ROM socket on the adapter. If there is more than one, consult the adapter's manual to find out which one you should use. Locate the notch on the socket and on the ROM. Line up the notches and slide the pins into the holes in the socket. You may want to use a chip installation tool. If you bend the pins you will likely damage the ROM.

Note:

Do not install the ROM backwards. If you reverse the notch with the one on the socket, you will very likely short the ground and hot leads of the ROM. This will immediately burn out the ROM. You only have to lose a few of these to run into some serious money problems.

Each ROM uses a memory address to communicate with system memory and transfer data to and from the adapter to the machine. You must set a memory address on the adapter when installing the ROM.

If you are using RPL ROMs, you must have the appropriate .RPL file located in the LOGIN subdirectory. In addition, you must have the RPL.NLM loaded and bound to the adapter from which the workstations will boot. The process can be automated by putting the commands in the AUTOEXEC.NCF file:

```
LOAD TCTOKH FRAME=TOKEN-RING NAME=RPL1
BIND IPX RPL1 NET=123
LOAD RPL
BIND RPL RPL1
```

Note:

A network number is associated with the binding of RPL. This does not create a new network, but simply binds a protocol to an existing one.

You must also create a boot image file for the workstation's ROM to download. The default name for the file is NET$DOS.SYS. It is contained in the LOGIN subdirectory. You can have more than one boot image file, but we will discuss that later.

To create a boot image file, you must have access to a machine with a boot floppy that is logged on to the network. You must also have SUPERVISOR rights. Create a system diskette with the version of DOS that you want to use. This diskette must also contain all the files necessary to boot the system, including:

COMMAND.COM (and system files)
AUTOEXEC.BAT
CONFIG.SYS
NET.CFG
LSL.COM
MLID (adapter driver)
IPXODI
VLM.EXE (or NETX.EXE)
.VLM FILES

The typical AUTOEXEC.BAT file would appear as follows:

```
LSL.COM
TCTOKSH (MLID)
IPXODI
VLM
F:LOGIN
```

If you are using VLMs, you must have a CONFIG.SYS file with the LASTDRIVE set to Z. You must also have a NET.CFG file, which lists the first network drive and VLMs you are going to load. You might also need a memory manager.

After you have created the boot floppy, log in to the server as SUPERVISOR. Map the \LOGIN and \SYSTEM subdirectories as follows:

```
MAP F:=SYS:SYSTEM
MAP G:=SYS:LOGIN
```

Change the drive to the \LOGIN subdirectory by typing G: and then execute the DOSGEN utility from the G: prompt:

```
G:F:DOSGEN
```

This will create the boot image file. Copy the AUTOEXEC.BAT file from the boot diskette to the \LOGIN subdirectory. It might also be necessary to do the same for the home directory of each user that will use the boot image file. You must also flag the NET$DOS.SYS file as

Shareable Read Only. After the file is created, execute the following command:

`FLAG NET$DOS.SYS S R O`	On NetWare v3.x systems
`NDIR NET$DOS.SYS S R O`	On 4.x systems

Custom Boot Image Files

It may be necessary, especially on a large network or one with users that require different configurations, to create multiple boot images on the server. This can be done by creating a series of boot image files. You must also create a text file to cross-reference a node's address to the boot image file that it needs to boot from. This file is called a BOOTCONF.SYS file.

First create a boot diskette with all the files necessary for each different type of workstation. Think of a unique name for each file. Create a batch file on each diskette that refers to this name. This batch file should include all the statements normally contained in the AUTOEXEC.BAT file. Then create an AUTOEXEC.BAT file that refers to the batch file. The AUTOEXEC.BAT file should appear as follows:

```
AUTOEXEC.BAT
TCC1.BAT
```

in which TCC1 is the batch file that contains the statements for the drivers and login. Then, log in to the network as SUPERVISOR and map the drives as before. This time, at the G: prompt, type:

```
G:.F:DOSGEN A: filename.SYS
```

in which the *filename* is the unique name you called this boot image file. Then, flag the new boot image file as before.

Once you have created a boot image file for each unique boot, create the BOOTCONF.SYS cross-reference file. When the RPL ROM first looks for a boot image file, it will look to see if there is a BOOTCONF.SYS file. If it finds one, it will look for its unique network and node ID. If it finds it, then it opens the corresponding boot image file. If it does not find it, it will attempt to open and use the NET$DOS.SYS file. The BOOTCONF.SYS file should appear as follows:

```
0x1,00801C456789=TCC1.SYS
```

The 0x is required at the beginning. The 1 represents the network number, and the remaining numbers after the comma represent the node ID of the remote boot workstation.

Remote Booting OS/2

If you have OS/2 workstations you will need to start from an OS/2 workstation logged into the server with SUPERVISOR rights. Run the NetWare installation utility. Select the menu option Installation on Server. This will install a copy of OS/2 on the NetWare server and set up the installation for remote booting. Then, select the menu item to set up remote workstations. You will need to know the node ID of the adapter in the remote workstation. The utility will set up a basic installation of OS/2 for this workstation. It will also create a \MACHINES subdirectory under the main OS/2 subdirectory. This subdirectory will contain a subdirectory for each workstation to be remote booted. The name of the subdirectory is the node ID of the workstation. The individual configuration files such as CONFIG.SYS are copied to this subdirectory.

Note:

You will need to have approximately 40MB of disk space to install OS/2 on the server. You will also need a good deal of patience.

Note:

A separate subdirectory is set up on the server for each workstation to be remote booted. The subdirectory is designated using the node ID. This subdirectory contains the individual configuration files for each machine. The installation utility should set all this up for you, but it may be necessary to set up each workstation by hand. If so, you will need to locate the \MACHINES subdirectory. It is located off the root of the OS/2 subdirectory created to hold the copy of OS/2 on the server. There, you will need to copy the configuration files to a subdirectory designated by the workstation's node ID and modify the configuration files for each individual machine.

For the most part, the OS/2 remote boot works fine. However, the process is not foolproof, and unless there is an extreme need to remote boot OS/2, we suggest that you not try to do it.

Configuration Tips

Planning is essential. It is a good idea to group the workstations according to the files that are necessary to run each station. If you need some with memory managers, try to be consistent. Have as few different configurations as possible. This will minimize the amount of administration you will have to do. After you have an idea of the number of different boot image files you will need, create the boot image files and record the node IDs and boot image file names. Name the custom boot images in a manner that gives you a mnemonic to remember the image and its use.

It will also be necessary to have the batch file for the custom boot image files in the \LOGIN subdirectory. You may also need to put the batch file in the home directory of each user.

Quick List

Following is a quick recap of installing remote boot capabilities on an OS/2 workstation:

1. Plan the network with remote booting in mind. Be as consistent as possible in the use of configuration files.
2. Record the node ID of each workstation to be remote booted.
3. For RPL booting, copy the .RPL files to the \LOGIN subdirectory.
4. For RPL booting, LOAD and BIND the RPL.NLM.
5. Install the ROMs on each workstation to be remote booted.

Under DOS:

1. Create boot diskettes for each different type of workstation configuration.
2. Generate the NET$DOS.SYS file or custom boot image files.
3. Create the BOOTCONF.SYS file if necessary.

Under OS/2:

1. Install the OS/2 utilities on the server.
2. Generate workstation configuration files for each workstation to be remote booted.

Troubleshooting

As with any LAN connection, look to the obvious first. Be sure that you have the cable and connections properly made. Remember, RPL and remote boot ROMs take up space in memory. Verify that there is no memory conflict.

The other common mistake is to mistype the node ID in the BOOTCONF.SYS file. If the ROM is working properly it will first try to open the BOOTCONF.SYS file. Then, if it cannot find its node ID, it will attempt to open and use the NET$DOS.SYS file. If you thought you set this adapter in the BOOTCONF.SYS but it is using the NET$DOS instead, you have probably mistyped the node ID in the file.

RPL ROMs typically have a short message string that runs when the ROM is booting. It will generally show the adapter node ID, the settings of the adapter, and the number of server request frames it is sending out. When it finds a server and requests the boot image file, you should then see a second number appear that increments rapidly. If you do not see this, or if the ROM times out and generates an error, you should immediately verify that it can indeed find a server at all. You might want to carry a disk drive and boot floppy with you to verify that you can indeed find a server.

chapter 8

IBM LAN Support

Many times network users need more than NetWare connectivity. In the development of NetWare, people needed to connect to IBM mainframes and minicomputers. During this period, IBM had developed the IBM LAN Support Program to provide IEEE 802.2 connectivity in a DOS environment for its token-ring products. By adding the proper NetBIOS support, you can connect to an IBM PC LAN, a 3270 controller, an IBM AS/400 using PC Support, and to IBM's OS/2 LAN Server.

Note:

IBM's OS/2 LAN Server v4.0 is the first of these products to use the Network Driver Interface Specification (NDIS), a mechanism that lets a single driver on a LAN adapter communicate with multiple protocol stacks. As a result, you do not need LAN Support.

The current version of IBM LAN Support is 1.35. Starting with version 1.3, IBM supported NDIS drivers using a Protocol Manager that allowed it to connect to a wider range of products and allow additional protocol support other than IEEE 802.2 and NetBIOS. Previous to this release, IBM began to support Ethernet, as well as token-ring.

IBM developed its version of token-ring as a way to allow the PCs it was selling to act as terminals to IBM mainframe computers. Prior to this, PCs used 3270 adapters to allow them to emulate 3270 terminal environments. Emulation, however, was a waste of processing power. Users wanted to be able to use their PCs to connect in a LAN and still use them as terminals for other IBM minicomputer and mainframe applications. The LAN operating system of choice during this time period was the IBM PC LAN. Novell, in a desire to gain some of this market, jointly developed a driver with IBM that would interoperate with both NetWare and IBM LAN products. Called the LANSUP driver, it is still the preferred method of communication between NetWare clients and IBM products.

Requirements

LANSUP.COM provides NetWare connectivity for the following adapter types:

Token-ring
Ethernet
PC Adapter
PC Adapter /A

Depending upon the version of LANSUP and IBM LAN Support you are using, you should be able to run on any 286 or higher processor workstation. The latest version, 2.01, requires LSL.COM v2.11 and a 386 or higher processor.

You will also need to run IBM LAN Support v1.25 or higher. Some vendors, including Madge Networks, Olicom, and Compaq Computer, provide their own versions of the Interrupt Arbiter and Logical Link Control (LLC) drivers that take the place of IBM LAN Support and interoperate with LANSUP.COM.

Installation and Configuration

An installation utility called DXMAID installs IBM LAN Support. This utility installs the drives in the \LSP directory and makes changes to your CONFIG.SYS file. To begin the installation, insert the installation disk and type DXMAID. You will see a series of screens explaining the requirements for using IBM LAN Support. (See Figures 8-1 through 8-3.)

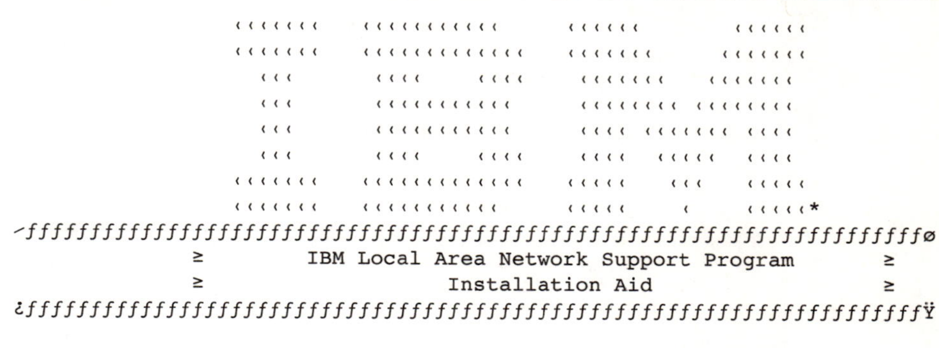


```
          (C) Copyright IBM Corporation 1987, 1993
       Program property of IBM - all rights reserved.
          US Government Users Restricted Rights -
         Use, duplication or disclosure restricted
        by GSA ADP Schedule Contract with IBM Corp.
       * Trademark of International Business Machines

      Press Enter (□ƒƒŸ) to continue or Esc to cancel.
```

Figure 8-1. *First IBM LAN Support installation screen.*

```
                    LAN Support Program Installation Aid
Information

The Installation Aid lets you configure and install the IBM LAN Support
Program (LSP). LSP consists of device drivers and supporting files that
enable application programs to communicate with an adapter. The
Installation Aid copies the required files to a working disk, edits
CONFIG.SYS and other control files, and saves the original versions of
these files.

LSP supports Network Driver Interface Specification (NDIS) adapters,
which work with the DXME0MOD.SYS and DXMJ0MOD.SYS protocol drivers.
Selecting DXMJ0MOD.SYS is recommended if you do not need 802.2
support.

See the README.LSP file and the LSP User's Guide for more information.


  F3=Exit   Enter=Continue
```

Figure 8-2. *Second LAN PC Support installation screen.*

```
                        LAN Support Program Installation Aid
ƒInformationƒƒƒƒƒƒƒƒƒƒƒƒƒƒƒƒƒƒƒƒƒƒƒƒƒƒƒƒƒƒƒƒƒƒƒƒƒƒƒƒƒƒƒƒƒƒƒƒƒƒƒƒƒƒƒƒƒƒƒø

  ≥  To configure and install LSP, you will need:
  ≥  - A backup copy of the original LSP diskettes (Note: Any copy of
       LSP must contain all the files and preserve the original
       subdirectories)
  ≥  - A formatted system diskette, if LSP will be installed on diskette
  ≥  - A driver diskette, if your adapter needs NDIS support. The driver
      diskette contains the NDIS MAC driver, the Network Information
      File (NIF), and associated files.

¿ƒƒƒƒƒƒƒƒƒƒƒƒƒƒƒƒƒƒƒƒƒƒƒƒƒƒƒƒƒƒƒƒƒƒƒƒƒƒƒƒƒƒƒƒƒƒƒƒƒƒƒƒƒƒƒƒƒƒƒƒƒƒƒƒƒƒƒƒƒƒƒƒƒƒŸ

  F3=Exit   F7=Previous panel   Enter=Continue
```

Figure 8-3. *Third LAN PC Support installation screen.*

You will then reach the main installation screen. At this point you have to select whether you are updating an existing installation or performing a new installation. If you are creating a new installation, you will be asked for an installation disk. An installation disk contains an OEMSTUP.INF file and a Network Driver Interface Specification (NDIS) 2.0-compliant LAN driver. This diskette allows you to install a driver for an Ethernet, token-ring, or other adapter that does not have an LLC driver. (See Figure 8-4.)

When you select the driver you want, you will see the installation screen. At this screen you need to select an LLC driver; if you are using an NDIS driver, the LLC driver should accompany your NDIS driver. (See Figure 8-5.)

When you have completed the installation requirements, the DXMAID installation utility copies the necessary drivers to the \LSP directory or to a subdirectory you created, and edits the CONFIG.SYS and AUTOEXEC.BAT files. If you have completed the installation correctly, your CONFIG.SYS file should appear as follows:

```
DEVICE= C:\DOS\HIMEM.SYS
DOS=HIGH
DEVICE=C:\DOS\SETVER.EXE
DEVICE=C:\WINDOWS\EMM386.EXE NOEMS X=B000-BFFF X=C800-D1FF
FILES=30
BUFFERS=30
DOS=HIGH,umb
lastdrive=z
```

```
                         LAN Support Program Installation Aid

Use the arrow keys to move between fields. Make changes as needed to the
information below; then, press Enter.
⁄ƒSetupƒƒƒƒƒƒƒƒƒƒƒƒƒƒƒƒƒƒƒƒƒƒƒƒƒƒƒƒƒƒƒƒƒƒƒƒƒƒƒƒƒƒƒƒƒƒƒƒƒƒƒƒƒƒƒƒƒƒƒƒƒƒƒƒƒƒƒƒƒƒø

  ≥ Use the Space bar to toggle between 'Yes' and 'No':

  ≥ Are you updating an existing configuration?                          Yes
  ≥ Do you have driver diskettes?                                        Yes

  ≥ Type changes as needed to the information below:

  ≥ Target for LSP:                                                   C:\LSP
  ≥ CONFIG.SYS to update:                                      C:\CONFIG.SYS
  ≥ AUTOEXEC.BAT to update:                                  C:\AUTOEXEC.BAT

¿ƒƒƒƒƒƒƒƒƒƒƒƒƒƒƒƒƒƒƒƒƒƒƒƒƒƒƒƒƒƒƒƒƒƒƒƒƒƒƒƒƒƒƒƒƒƒƒƒƒƒƒƒƒƒƒƒƒƒƒƒƒƒƒƒƒƒƒƒƒƒƒƒƒƒƒŸ
  F1=Help   F3=Exit   F7=Previous panel   Enter=Continue
```

Figure 8-4. *Driver selection screen.*

```
                         LAN Support Program Installation Aid

Press F4 to install the drivers shown below. To change the drivers, use
the arrow keys to move to the desired field; then, press F6.

⁄ƒPrimary Adapter: ADAPTER DRIVERƒƒƒƒƒƒƒƒƒƒƒƒƒƒƒƒƒƒƒƒƒƒƒƒƒƒƒƒƒƒƒƒƒƒƒƒƒƒƒø

  IBM Token-Ring Adapters (DXMC0MOD.SYS)

/ƒPrimary Adapter: PROTOCOL DRIVERSƒƒƒƒƒƒƒƒƒƒƒƒƒƒƒƒƒƒƒƒƒƒƒƒƒƒƒƒƒƒƒƒƒƒƒƒƒ≥

  IBM DOS NETBIOS (DXMT0MOD.SYS)

¿ƒƒƒƒƒƒƒƒƒƒƒƒƒƒƒƒƒƒƒƒƒƒƒƒƒƒƒƒƒƒƒƒƒƒƒƒƒƒƒƒƒƒƒƒƒƒƒƒƒƒƒƒƒƒƒƒƒƒƒƒƒƒƒƒƒƒƒƒƒƒƒƒƒƒƒŸ

⁄ƒAlternate Adapter: ADAPTER DRIVERƒƒƒƒƒƒƒƒƒƒƒƒƒƒƒƒƒƒƒƒƒƒƒƒƒƒƒƒƒƒƒƒƒƒƒƒø

/ƒAlternate Adapter: PROTOCOL DRIVERSƒƒƒƒƒƒƒƒƒƒƒƒƒƒƒƒƒƒƒƒƒƒƒƒƒƒƒƒƒƒƒƒƒƒ≥

  F1=Help   F3=Exit   F4=Install   F5=Change parameters
  F6=Driver choices   F9=Restart setup
```

Figure 8-5. *Driver installation screen.*

```
STACKS=9,256
rem DEVICE=C:\IBMAUDIO\DIAG\AUDTEST.SYS /F=C:\IBMAUDIO\DIAG\AUDTEST.OUT
   /V=10DE
DEVICE=C:\WINDOWS\IFSHLP.SYS
DEVICE=C:\LSP\DXMA0MOD.SYS 001
DEVICE=C:\LSP\DXMC0MOD.SYS N ,d800,0,0,0
DEVICE=C:\LSP\DXMT0MOD.SYS O=YES
```

If you are using an NDIS 2.0 driver, your CONFIG.SYS file will appear as follows:

```
DEVICE= C:\DOS\HIMEM.SYS
DOS=HIGH
DEVICE=C:\DOS\SETVER.EXE
DEVICE=C:\WINDOWS\EMM386.EXE NOEMS X=B000-BFFF X=C800-D1FF
FILES=30
BUFFERS=30
DOS=HIGH,umb
lastdrive=z
STACKS=9,256
rem DEVICE=C:\IBMAUDIO\DIAG\AUDTEST.SYS /F=C:\IBMAUDIO\DIAG\AUDTEST.OUT
   /V=10DE
DEVICE=C:\WINDOWS\IFSHLP.SYS
DEVICE=C:\LSP\PROTMAN.DOS /I:PROTMAN.DOS
DEVICE=C:\LSP\DXMA0MOD.SYS 001
DEVICE=C:\LSP\TCCTOK.DOS
DEVICE=C:\LSP\DXME0MOD.SYS
DEVICE=C:\LSP\DXMT0MOD.SYS O=YES
```

Note:

You can also use this configuration to create a DOS boot diskette under OS/2 to use the IBM LAN Support drivers in OS/2 for specific connectivity applications.

In either instance, the device drivers load the Arbiter, the device drivers and LLC driver, and, if necessary, the NetBIOS driver. The drivers represent the following:

PROTMAN.DOS—Protocol manager for NDIS environments
DXMA0MOD.SYS—Interrupt Arbiter for IBM LAN Support
*.DOS—IS 2.0 driver
DXMC0MOD.SYS—N Support driver for IBM token-ring adapters
DXMT0MOD.SYS—NetBIOS driver for IBM LAN Support

The connection to a NetWare network with the IBM LAN Support program requires the use of LANSUP.COM as the Multiple Link Interface Driver (MLID) in place of the adapter driver. The IBM LAN Support MLID can be placed in the AUTOEXEC.BAT or STARTNET.BAT files in the following manner:

```
STARTNET.BAT
LSL
LANSUP
IPXODI
VLM
```

Command Summary

The IBM LAN Support program provides several configuration options for the Arbiter (DXMA0MOD.SYS) and the Adapter driver, DXMC0MOD.SYS.

DXMA0MOD.SYS

DXMA0MOD.SYS has only one setting, the number of adapters that the arbiter must configure:

> OOX—The number of the adapter, 1 or 2, in which X represents the number of the adapter.

DXMC0MOD.SYS

DXMC0MOD.SYS has the following commands available:

addr0	Replace with the locally administered address for the primary adapter
mem	Replace with the RAM location for the primary or only adapter
etr0	In which 0 is specified for Early Token Release and 1 disables Early Token Release (parameter is ignored if adapter data rate is 4 megabits per second [Mbps])

addr1	Replace with the locally administered address for the alternate adapter
mem1	Replace with the RAM location for the alternate adapter

These parameters are placed at the end of the statement in the CONFIG.SYS file. The commands can be chained to set all the various commands you need to set.

LANSUP.COM

There are only three configuration options for LANSUP.COM, which are placed in the NET.CFG file. These settings are as follows:

SAPS number
This parameter represents the number of Service Access Points. The available parameters are 1–255. The default is 1. Only change this option if the application you are using recommends it.

LINK STATIONS number
This parameter represents the number of Link Stations. The available parameters are 1–255. The default is 1. Only change this option if the application you are using recommends it.

MAX PACKET number
This parameter represents the packet size. The default is four kilobytes for token-ring. The maximum is 17,960 bytes. Only change this option if the application you are using recommends it.

Configuration Tips

The basis for using IBM LAN Support is to provide dual connectivity with NetWare and another IBM network function. This could include IBM 3270 or 5250 terminal emulation or connectivity to an IBM OS/2 LAN Server network. As a result of configuring for two networks and the IBM LAN support drivers and the NetWare drivers loading, you can easily take up RAM. To alleviate this, all the drivers including the LAN Support and NetWare drivers will load high. We recommend that you load as many of the drivers as possible into high memory.

Quick List

1. Obtain the IBM LAN Support program.
2. Determine which LAN driver (LLC or NDIS) you will use.
3. Use the DXMAID utility to install the IBM LAN Support program.
4. Set up any other connectivity products, such as IBM PC Support, that you need.
5. Install the NetWare Client Software using LANSUP.COM.

Troubleshooting

There should be no other problems related to the use of LAN Support drivers. If the IBM LAN Support drivers load, you should have no problem loading the NetWare drivers. You may need to adjust the number of SAPS and Link Stations depending on the application you are using. If you are using DXMT0MOD.SYS to provide NetBIOS support and you also set the number of Link Stations and SAPS, you will need to adjust the number in your NET.CFG file. Also, if you adjust the packet size in the DXMT0MOD.SYS line, you will need to adjust the packet size in your NET.CFG file using the MAX PACKET statement.

Performance

If you are using IBM LAN Support your goal is connectivity, not screaming performance. You can count on a ten percent reduction in normal performance. You can sometimes increase performance by adjusting the packet size. The default is 4KB; by increasing that to 16KB, you can gain back a bit of performance.

chapter 9

TCP/IP

TCP/IP is the most widely used network transport protocol and part of a larger suite of protocols called TCP/IP. It is the protocol used by the Internet and UNIX installations. To the NetWare user, IP will be the second most important protocol next to IPX, and over the years it will become more and more important as the average NetWare network joins the rest of the world.

Novell has several packages that allow connections with IP-based networks. Among them are LAN WorkGroup and LAN WorkPlace.

LAN WorkGroup

Novell's LAN WorkGroup provides NetWare workstations with TCP/IP connectivity, applications, and utilities from the NetWare server. It has all the utilities of the single-user version LAN WorkPlace, including file transfer (FTP), remote login (Host Presenter), and remote printing (LPR). LAN WorkGroup differs from LAN WorkPlace in that it dynamically assigns IP addresses to the workstation requesting IP services.

LAN WorkPlace

LAN WorkPlace was designed as a nonshared, single-user version of IP software that is installed on the individual workstation or the server. It is administered from the local workstation and provides complete TCP/IP connectivity with DOS and Windows utilities for file transfer (Rapid Filer, FTP, RCP, and TFTP), Telnet and remote login (Host Presenter), and remote printing facilities. It also provides a NetBIOS Application Programming Interface (API) that lets users run network applications that require a NetBIOS interface.

REQUIREMENTS

The maximum requirements of LAN WorkGroup and LAN WorkPlace are a minimum 8088 or above PC. The Windows 3.1x utilities require a 80286 or above. The minimum memory requirements are 512 kilobytes (KB). The Windows utilities require 2MB with 4MB of RAM recommended. Additionally, 4.5MB of hard disk space at the server or workstation is required.

THE EVOLUTION OF TCP/IP

TCP/IP closely followed the evolution of the Internet. It started as a low-level experimental packet-switching protocol and evolved to a connection-oriented protocol with an added connectionless end-to-end layer. TCP was a media-specific frame and addressing scheme. IP was specifically designed to be easy to introduce into a group of switching nodes as a media-independent communication protocol.

The TCP/IP router was developed specifically to handle the packet switching needs of a wide-ranging media-independent internetwork. The idea was to encase the address of the gateways in the message. An upper layer protocol, such as FTP or Telnet, passes information to IP for transmission. The host's IP stack examines the network address of the frame, also known as the IP address, and determines if the destination node is on the local network or a remote network. If the destination is on a remote network, the frame, or datagram as it is called, is relayed to a locally attached IP router. The router looks up the address in its routing table and relays the frame to another IP router or to the local network host. Each frame is routed individually based on the table lookup in each router. The intelligence was built into the routers to open the frame, address it to the next router, and send the message on its way. In this manner, the frame could travel through many different routers to its final destination.

Tip:

On an IP network, the host is any computer running TCP/IP software. Each computer maintains a list of known hosts.

With the development of the packet-switched network, the Internet took its basic shape. However, the equipment to maintain an Internet connection was still extremely expensive, and TCP/IP was not a widely used protocol, except on the Internet. Simultaneous with the development of TCP/IP was the development of the UNIX operating system. When the initial AT&T UNIX was developed into Berkeley UNIX, it included TCP/IP as the network transport protocol for LANs. TCP/IP underwent more changes to accommodate the needs of LANs and became the widespread network transport protocol of choice for the UNIX environment. As LANs grew and moved into non–UNIX-based operating environments, TCP/IP has moved into these areas as well.

In addition to basic packet-switching, additional functionality was developed for remote login (RLOGIN), file transfer (FTP), and electronic mail. These functions are described by a series of additional protocols that were added to the basic TCP/IP package:

ARP	Address Resolution Protocol. Provides IP address to physical adapter address resolution. RFC 826
RARP	Reverse Address Resolution Protocol. Provides physical adapter to IP address resolution. RFC 903.
ICMP	Internet Control Message Protocol. Provides diagnostic features. RFC 792.
SNMP	Simple Network Management Protocol. Provides management features. RFC 1065.
SMTP	Simple Mail Transfer Protocol. The Internet mail protocol. RFC 821.
TELNET	The standard TCP/IP remote login protocol. RFC 854.

TCP/IP has evolved through the work of hundreds of persons. The protocol standardization process has also evolved as an open system. A researcher wishing to make a change publishes a Request for Comment (RFC). The RFC is debated and criticized prior to implementation. Standards are thus developed over a long period of test and evolution. Regardless of the quality of the Internet, the final standards are promulgated from meetings of engineers who are members of the Internet Engineering Task Force (IETF), who meet on a regular basis to finalize the standards and publish the results.

The Transmission Control Protocol (TCP)

TCP provides a virtual circuit connection-oriented end-to-end transmission between end-user applications. Additionally, TCP can provide support for end-to-end connections for host processes. It has all the reliability features not found in IP, such as flow control, sequencing, checksum, acknowledgment, and retransmission.

To establish a TCP connection, the upper layer protocol, such as FTP, must be identified to a TCP socket. A socket is the end-to point of a communications link between two applications. In the case of a network application, such as TCP, it is the connection between two or more applications running on separate computers attached to the network. Sockets provide a full-duplex communication link between the two systems. In the case of TCP, a stream socket is used. A socket consists of two separate addresses. The first is the address of the specific application or process running on the computers; the second is the IP address of the workstation on the network. Some common sockets are:

- FTP 21
- TELNET 23
- SMTP 25

Thus, the upper layer connection is identified by the port address and the IP address. The process continues with the error control and detection of out-of-sequence packets. Flow control is used to ensure that the sender of data does not overwhelm the receiver. This is accomplished by the two systems cooperating to establish a sliding window of data. The stream is increased until retransmissions are required; then the speed of transmission is reduced. The connection control features are also responsible for the establishment, termination, and interruption control of the connection.

In the case of TCP, the transmission of data from the upper layer protocol, such as FTP, is treated as a continuous stream of data. TCP divides this stream into segments of up to 65KB octets. Each octet is assigned a sequence number for reassembly. The segment is then passed to the IP layer, which creates and passes the datagram to the lower layers for additional header information and transmission.

The TCP header contains a minimum of 20 octets. The fields are:

Source Port	16 bits. Contains the port address of the application process using the TCP service.
Destination Port	16 bits. Contains the port address of the called port.
Sequence Number	32 bits. Used to ensure reliable reassembly. This number represents the byte sequence number of the first octet in the TCP block and is increased by one for each block transmitted in the TCP segment.
Acknowledgment Number	32 bits. Provides indication of receipt so retransmission can be completed if necessary.
Data Offset	4 bits. Indicates the size of the header in 32-bit words.
Reserved	6 bits. Set to all zeros.
Flags	6 bits. Provides control functions such as setup and termination of the session. Flags include URG—Urgent pointer; ACK—Acknowledgment; PHS—Push function; RST—Reset connection; SYN—Synchronize sequence numbers; FIN—Data transmission completed.
Window	16 bits. The receive windows size indicates the number of octets the receiver can accept.
Checksum	16 bits. A checksum based upon the IP fields, plus the TCP header information.

Urgent Pointer	16 bits. Points to the first octets that follow the urgent data so the receiver can determine how much urgent data is coming.
Options	Variable size. Set aside for future options. Currently only one option has been defined—the maximum TCP segment size.

While TCP does provide a reliable end-to-end connection, it does so at the expense of much higher overhead. In addition to the standard TCP connection, an additional connection protocol known as Serial Line IP (SLIP) has been defined to support serial line connections.

The User Datagram Protocol (UDP)

When TCP was split into TCP and IP, a new protocol was developed to provide the transport protocol for applications that did not need extensive error checking—the protocol developed was the User Datagram Protocol (UDP). The Simple Network Management Protocol (SNMP) is an example of an upper-layer application that uses UDP. SNMP is used to communicate status and parameter values between a remote device and a network management station. In this case, complete reliability is not a requirement, thus UDP is the better choice for transmitting data.

The UDP header contains only four fields:

Source Port	16 bits. The address of the calling port.
Destination Port	16 bits. The address of the port being called.
Length	16 bits. Length of the UDP datagram.
Checksum	16 bits. Checksum for the UDP header.

As you can see from the header information, UDP is not a guaranteed delivery system. There are no fields that would provide the reliability, such as sequence and acknowledgment numbers. This kind of delivery is also known as a best-effort delivery. Any error checking and calls for retransmission must be performed by upper-layer protocols.

IP ADDRESSING

TCP/IP was intentionally designed as an internetwork that would not depend on any particular hardware. Any hardware had to be able to join the network and function properly within the protocol. As a result, the addressing scheme had to allow for a large number of hosts (individual nodes) and was independent of any other addressing method. The Internet address consists of a 32-bit (4-byte) address that identifies both the network and the local host. In an address that is going to join the Internet, the network portion of the address is provided by the Defense Data Network (DDN) Information Center. The host portion of the address is provided by the local administrator.

The address is written as a series of four decimal numbers separated by dots, such as 192.124.119.33. Each of the four fields represents eight bits of the 32-bit address and can have a value from 0 to 255. The possible range of IP addresses is split into five classes. The classes are labeled from A to E. The classes divide the groups as follows:

Class A	Bit 0 = 0. Range from 1 to 127. Network field of eight bits with 24 bits for host IDs.
Class B	First octet begins with 10. Range from 128 to 191. Network field of 16 bits and a host field of 16 bits.
Class C	First octet begins with 110. Range from 192 to 254. Network field of 24 bits and host field of eight bits.
Class D	First octet begins with 1110. Used for IP multicast addressing.
Class E	First octet begins with 1111. Used for experimental purposes.

For all classes, the addresses 0 and 255 are reserved.

As you can see, the number of host addresses available to the network depends upon the class of the IP address. Class A addresses will support 16 million hosts, but only 127 networks. Class B addresses will support 65,000 hosts and 16,000 networks. Class C addresses will support two million networks, but only 254 hosts.

However, many computers can have the same host number as long as the network number is different. The actual number of computers that can attach to the Internet is therefore immense. Yet even with the number of addresses available, the end of the line is within sight. In order to solve the problem of address shortages, a new protocol called the Simple Internet Protocol or SIP has been proposed. SIP uses a 64-bit address rather than IP's 32-bit addressing. SIP will be fully compatible with IP.

Subnetworking the Net

Once an address is obtained, it is necessary to fit the available hosts on the system. If the network is divided into smaller subnets, it is necessary to also subnet the IP address. To do this you take a portion of the IP address reserved for hosts and give it over to the network address. You will generally take between 1 and 3 bits of the host address and assign it to the network. The rest of the host address is then divided among the subnets depending upon the number of bits used to make the subnet. The bits used to create the subnet are called the subnet mask. While the bits used to define a subnet are generally taken from the most significant bits and are contiguous, they don't need to be. However, if you decide to use noncontiguous bits, you run the risk of a strange layout of the host address. Also, the addresses that coincide with the bits 00 and 11 are unavailable, and this effectively cuts down the available number of hosts available to you.

Let's assume you have a network with a Class C address of 192.124.119. You have to divide the network into six subnets. A subnet represents an actual piece of wire that forms a network. You take the three most significant bits as the subnet. This gives you a subnet mask of 224. Since a subnet cannot use the binary equivalent of 11 or 00, you have effectively divided the network into six subnets with subnet 1 using hosts between 32 and 63; subnet two using hosts between 65 and 95; subnet 3 using hosts between 97 and 127; subnet 4 using hosts between 129 and 160; subnet 5 using hosts between 161 and 191; and subnet 6 using hosts between 192 and 223. Hosts 0–31 and 225–255 are illegal.

Tip:

You will now actually get a chance to use some of the higher math you learned in school. The subnet mask is the decimal representation of the binary number you create with the bits you plan to use as the mask. Take the decimal number and "AND" it to the proposed host. You will get the number of the subnet it is on. You can use this formula to arrive at the subnet for any host address you want to use. It doesn't get much more complicated than this. We promise.

FTP

The File Transfer Protocol (FTP) is an application layer protocol designed to facilitate the moving of files between workstations. FTP is actually the name of a utility designed to allow you to access files and directories on remote hosts, transfer files, and perform other file and directory functions. FTP requires the use of passwords for security. Rapid Filer is a Windows-based utility based upon the File Transfer Protocol that performs the FTP functions from a Windows application. In addition, another utility, Remote Copy Protocol (RCP), allows you to move one or more files between remote hosts that have RSH and RCP. LAN WorkPlace also provides utilities for Trivial File Transfer Protocol (TFTP) that allow file transfers without the use of passwords.

You can also use the workstation as a file server using the Serving FTP, a Windows-based utility that allows you to set up the workstation to allow others to access it using FTP or TFTP file transfer protocols. A utility, FTPD, allows DOS users to set up their workstations for remote file transfers.

Note:

If you are going to set up a computer to allow others to access files on it, be conscious of security. You can restrict access to the computer by requiring a password or restricting users to only a few directories.

Telnet

Both LAN WorkPlace and WorkGroup allow you to log in to and operate another workstation, such as a DEC VT220, VT100, VT52, or ANSI terminal. The Windows utility is called Host Presenter. Host Presenter also allows you to run multiple host sessions to one or more remote hosts. With Host Presenter, you can also write scripts using any standard ASCII text editor to let you log in using the script language. For instance, you might write a script to log in and send the password to the remote host.

X-Windows

Both LAN WorkPlace and LAN WorkGroup provide support for X-Windows, which is a UNIX-based Windows-like graphical user interface (GUI). The user will be able to use the Remote Login (RLOGIN) function to run a Telnet session from the remote session and then start X-Windows to provide a graphical interface for the use of X-Windows-based programs and other functions.

SLIP and PPP

TCP/IP supports asynchronous serial line communications via two protocols: the Serial Line Internet Protocol (SLIP) and the Point-to-Point Protocol (PPP). Configured properly, LAN WorkPlace and LAN WorkGroup can use these protocols and a modem to communicate through an Internet Service Provider (ISP) with a remote site.

Installation and Configuration

Installation of LAN WorkPlace or LAN WorkGroup requires some knowledge of IP and IP addressing. Therefore, if you skipped the sections on the evolution of TCP/IP and IP addressing, we suggest you go back and read them.

The installation of LAN WorkPlace and LAN WorkGroup are somewhat similar. They each modify or create the following files:

NET.CFG	Contains the configuration parameters for the protocols.
LANWP.BAT	The batch file to load the drivers and protocols for LAN WorkPlace.
LANWG.BAT	The batch file to load the drivers and protocols for LAN WorkGroup.
CONFIG.SYS	The system configuration file.
AUTOEXEC.BAT	The system batch file used to call the other batch files.
PROGMAN.INI	Controls the program groups and icons in Windows.

WIN.INI	Contains the program extension names for Windows.
SYSTEM.INI	Contains the Windows system configuration.

Note:

The .INI files for Windows are only modified if they are present when you install the LAN IP software. If you install Windows after the installation, you must make the modifications.

In addition, prior to any installation you will need to have the following information available:

- Target drive
- Local username for remote login utilities
- IP address for target workstation
- Subnet mask for target workstation
- Network router
- Domain name if using Domain Name Services
- Domain Name Server IP address

LAN Workplace Workstation Installation

LAN WorkPlace uses a DOS-based installation routine. The basic procedure is simple. Place the disk in the drive and type INSTALL. However, before you begin, you must know certain requirements of the system. First, verify where you want the files. Typically the location is the C: drive, but you can perform an installation to a network drive. Second, know where the network files are located. If you installed the workstation using the NetWare Client Kit, this subdirectory will be C:\NWCLIENT. Third, be certain you have the information on the system configuration describe above. If you have all the above information, simply follow the step-by-step procedure and provide the information required.

As you can tell, the majority of the installation goes on behind the scenes and creates or modifies files without a great deal of user intervention. This is where you can get into serious trouble. Prior to leaving the installation, it is best to understand and verify what the program has added and modified in the system. The first place to start is to verify the NET.CFG file. This file is the main configuration file for the network settings. In LAN WorkPlace, the file resides where the ODI driver loads—typically the C:\NWCLIENT subdirectory. In LAN WorkGroup, the file is located in a shared directory on the server.

A typical NET.CFG is shown in Figure 9-1. The NET.CFG file is divided into sections by the driver it is designed to modify. The first section it modifies is the Link Support section to add the BUFFERS and MEMPOOL statements. If the ODI driver does not have a frame type that supports TCP/IP, it will add one, as well as an appropriate PROTOCOL statement to load the correct driver for IPX. It will then add the PROTOCOL TCPIP statement as shown in Figure 9-1.

The TCPIP statement has various sections internal to it. The first four statements are the location of the script and profile files, as well as the location of the LWP_CFG and TCP_CFG configuration files. This location is by default C:\NET, however, it can be anything you wish. The next section is the BIND statement to tell TCP/IP which LINK DRIVER statement to bind with. The final section contains the configuration for the TCP/IP driver. IP address are shown in decimal dot notation. The settings are as follows:

IP_ADDRESS	The IP address of the workstation.
IP_ROUTER	The default router, where all packets destined for remote networks are sent.
IP_NETMASK	The subnetwork mask if subnets are used.
TCP_SOCKETS	The maximum number of concurrent TCP connections. The default is 8. The range is 0–64.
UDP_SOCKETS	The maximum number of UDP connections. The default is 8. The range is 0–32.
RAW_SOCKETS	The maximum number of raw IP connections. The default is 1. The range is 0–1.
NO_BOOTP	Specifies whether to bypass BOOTP and use the Reverse Address Resolution Protocol (RARP) to identify a LAN WorkGroup server.

Remember, for the sockets, that the total number of sockets set are shared among multiple adapters. The NO_BOOTP setting is only seen in LAN WorkGroup configurations. The network name shown in the NET.CFG file in Figure 9-1 is only used if multiple nets are bound.

A change will also be made to the CONFIG.SYS file to add the following line:

```
DEVICE=c:\path\ANSI.SYS
```

```
Link Support
   Buffers 8 1500
   MemPool 4096

Link Driver NE2000
   Int #1 2
   Port #1 340 10
   Frame Ethernet_II
   Frame Ethernet_802.3
   Protocol IPX 0 Ethernet_802.3

Link Driver SLIP_PPP
   Int 4
   Port 3F8
   Baud 9600
   MRU 800
   TCPIPcomp VJ
   Frame PPP
   Direct No
   Dial 836-1935

Protocol TCPIP
   tcp_sockets 8
   udp_sockets 8
   raw_sockets 1
   ip_address  192.124.119.69    DIAL-NET
   ip_router   192.124.119.61    DIAL-NET
   ip_netmask  255.255.255.224   DIAL-NET
   ip_address  195.124.119.18    SOFTWAREENG-NET
   ip_router   195.124.119.1     SOFTWAREENG-NET
   ip_netmask  255.255.255.0     SOFTWAREENG-NET
   bind slip_ppp #1 PPP DIAL-NET
   bind ne2000 #1 ETHERNET_II SOFTWAREENG-NET
```

Figure 9-1. *The NET.CGF file.*

ANSI.SYS is required for TNVT220 to operate in ANSI mode. TNVT220 will send an escape sequence to the screen to determine if an ANSI driver is loaded.

Finally the AUTOEXEC.BAT file is modified to call the LANWP.BAT file located in the \NET directory. A sample LANWP.BAT file appears in Figure 9-2. It first gives you the option to load the network software. If you answer No, it goes to the end of the batch file and releases control back to AUTOEXEC.BAT file without loading any of the IP networking software. It then appends the NET\BIN path to the existing path and loads the IP networking drivers. If LSL.COM and the ODI drivers have previously been loaded, they will not appear in the batch file.

```
C:\yesno "Do you want to load the networking software?"
if errorlevel 1 goto noload
path c:\NET\BIN;%path%
C:\LSL.COM
C:\NE2000.COM
C:\SLIP_PPP.COM
TCPIP.EXE
SET NAME=BJOHNSTON
BREAK ON
:noload
```

Figure 9-2. *The LANWP.BAT file.*

Command Summary

Internetworking with TCP/IP requires a rudimentary knowledge of UNIX and TCP/IP commands. Following is a list of the commands you may use when your workstation uses IP to communicate with UNIX workstation, X Windows machines, or the Internet.

FTP Commands

The TCP/IP suite uses a number of commands for file transfers between machines:

FTP	Enter FTP utility.
APPEND	Append a local file to a remote file.
ASCII	Set the file transfer type to ASCII.
BELL	Sound bell after each file transfer is complete.
BINARY	Set the file transfer type to support BINARY image transfer.
BYE	Terminate all sessions.
CD	Change current directory.
CLOSE	Terminate the FTP session.
COPY	Copy files to a specified destination.
DEBUG	Enter debugging mode.
DEFAULTS	Restore DEBUG, SENDPORT, and VERBOSE commands to default settings.
DELETE	Delete a single file from the remote host.

DIR	Give a detailed listing of the current working directory on the remote host.
EXEC	Execute a specified command on a remote host.
FILE	Set the file transfer structure to FILE (as an unstructured byte stream).
FORCE	Select whether the file transfer parameters associated with the current connection or the file types are determined automatically.
FORMAT	Display the file transfer format.
GET	Copy a file from remote host to workstation.
HASH	Print a # mark to indicate progress made during file transfer.
HELP	List all FTP commands.
LCD	Change current working directory on workstation to the specified directory.
LDIR	Give detailed listing of current working directory on the workstation.
LEXEC	Escape to DOS on workstation and allow execution of DOS commands.
LLS	List contents of working directory of workstation, in brief.
LPWD	List the name of current drive and working directory on workstation.
LS	List the brief contents of the current working directory on workstation.
MDELETE	Delete one or more files from the remote host.
MDIR	List contents of current working directory on remote host.
MGET	Copy one or more files from remote host to current working directory on remote host.
MKDIR	Create a directory on the remote host.
MLS	List the contents of working directory on remote host, in brief.
MODE	Display the current mode.
OPEN	Open a connection with the FTP server.
PROMPT	Set interactive prompting.

PWD	Display the name of the current working directory on the remote host.
QUIT	Terminate the FTP session with all remote servers.
QUOTE	Send an FTP protocol element to the server, bypassing normal command parsing.
RECORD	Set the file transfer structure to RECORD.
RECV	Copy a remote file from remote host to file on workstation.
REMOTEDIR	Enable or disable the usage of remote directories with GET or PUT commands.
REMOTEHELP	Display help documentation from the remote server.
REMOTESTATUS	Display the status of remote server.
RENAME	Rename a file on remote host.
RGET	Copy a remote file from the host to a file on workstation.
RMDIR	Delete a directory on remote host.
RPUT	Copy a local file to a file on the remote host.
SEND	Copy a file from workstation to the remote host.
SENDPORT	Specify the PORT protocol element.
STATISTICS	Select the display of transfer statistics.
STATUS	Display the current state of all FTP options.
STRUCTURE	Display the current file transfer structure.
TYPE	Display the current file transfer type.
USER	Log in to the remote FTP server.
VERBOSE	Toggle verbose mode on or off.
?	List all FTP commands.
!	Suspend the FTP session.

FTPD Command

FTPD	Start the SERVER on the workstation to enable other systems to use FTP to transfer files.

KEY220 Command

One command, in particular is used to map the PC keyboard to that of a VT220 terminal:

KEY 220	Define a file for mapping workstation keys to VT220 function keys for Host Presenter and TNVT220.

L—Printer Utilities

For printing on TCP/IP networks, three commands are used to direct print jobs to printers:

LPQ	Report the status of a print job.
LPR	Send a print job to a remote printer.
LPRM	Delete a print job on remote printer.

Miscellaneous Commands

Several other commands are used for a variety of purposes:

RCP	Copy files or directories between a workstation and remote host.
REXEC	Execute a single command on a remote host.
RSH	Execute a single command on a remote host.
TELAPI	Load the Telnet Application Programming Interface (API).
TFTD	Transfer one or more files to or from a remote host.
TFTPD	Run the Trivial File Transfer Protocol server program on a DOS workstation to let other workstations running the TFTP command to transfer files.

Remote Printer Utilities

In addition, three printer utilities are also used for directing output to remote printers in TCP/IP networks:

RPD	Delete print job placed in remote printer queue.
RPR	Send a print job to a remote printer.
RPS	Report status of job on a remote printer.

TNVT220 Commands

In terminal emulation, you will use the following commands to perform tasks on a PC acting as a TNVT220 terminal:

TNVT220	Start the terminal emulation command.
ASCII	Request ASCII mode sessions to the remote server.
BINARY	Request a binary mode session on the remote server.
CHARLOCAL	Send characters to the server while locally echoing them.
CHARREMOTE	Send characters to the server, with remote echo.
CLOSE	Close a session to a remote host.
HELP	List and provide help for TNVT220 commands.
LINEMODE	Buffer characters until a line terminator is sent.
OPEN	Establish a session with a host.
QUIT	Close all sessions and exit to DOS.
RECVEOL	Specify how end-of-line sequences are received.
RESUME	Resume the current or indicated session.
SELECT	Select a session.
SETIP	Set the interrupt process character.
SENDEOL	Specify how end of line sequences are translated.
SESSIONS	Display a summary of all sessions.
SGA	Request that remote host not suppress go-aheads.
STATUS	Display the status of a session.
?	Briefly list TNVT220 commands.
!	Suspend the TNVT220 session.

Configuration Tips

The largest consideration in configuring the TCP/IP workstation is one of memory management, particularly if you are going to be loading IP with IPX. It may well be necessary to load as many programs as possible into upper memory. If you are using DOS 6.x with EMM386.EXE, you can use MEMMAKER to increase the amount of lower memory available. If you are using another memory manager, try running its memory configuration utility. Otherwise, experiment with loading various drivers high until you get an acceptable memory configuration. The following are some memory requirements.

Memory-resident Software

The following memory requirements are necessary for TCP/IP workstations:

NetBIOS	45KB
LSL	26KB
TCPIP	23KB
TELAPI	22KB for two sessions (default); 2KB for additional sessions.

Windows Programs

For Windows-based workstations, the following programs take varying amounts of RAM:

Finger	31KB
Finger Daemon	27KB
IP Resolver	25KB
Serving FTP	49KB plus 2KB per session

DOS Programs

The following programs require these amounts of RAM on the workstation:

FTP	155KB to 200KB
TNVT220	169KB plus 2KB per session
TSU	85KB
XPC	14KB with EMM installed; 59KB if loaded in conventional memory.

Troubleshooting

The problems related to TCP/IP will generally occur within two areas. First, the TCPIP stack will either not load or not bind to the driver. This is related to a mistake in the NET.CFG file. The driver is bound to the wrong ODI driver or the driver is attempting to bind to the wrong frame type. IP will bind only to the following protocols:

Ethernet
ETHERNET_II
ETHERNET_SNAP

Token-Ring
TOKEN-RING_SNAP

ARCnet
RX-NET

Verify all the settings for the NET.CFG file. If you are using Ethernet, be sure that the frame type is consistent with the frame type of other workstations, including the NetWare server.

The other problem you may encounter is that all drivers will appear to load and bind properly, but will not locate any other IP workstations on the network. This is generally related to a problem with either the IP_ADDRESS, IP_NETMASK, or IP_ROUTER settings in the NET.CFG file.

If you are using BOOTP to obtain an address from the NetWare server, be sure you are attached to the BOOTP server with the proper username. If you have set the individual address in the NET.CFG file, be sure that you have entered all the information properly. Verify the netmask and address. You might also want to review the earlier sections of this chapter related to IP addressing and netmasks.

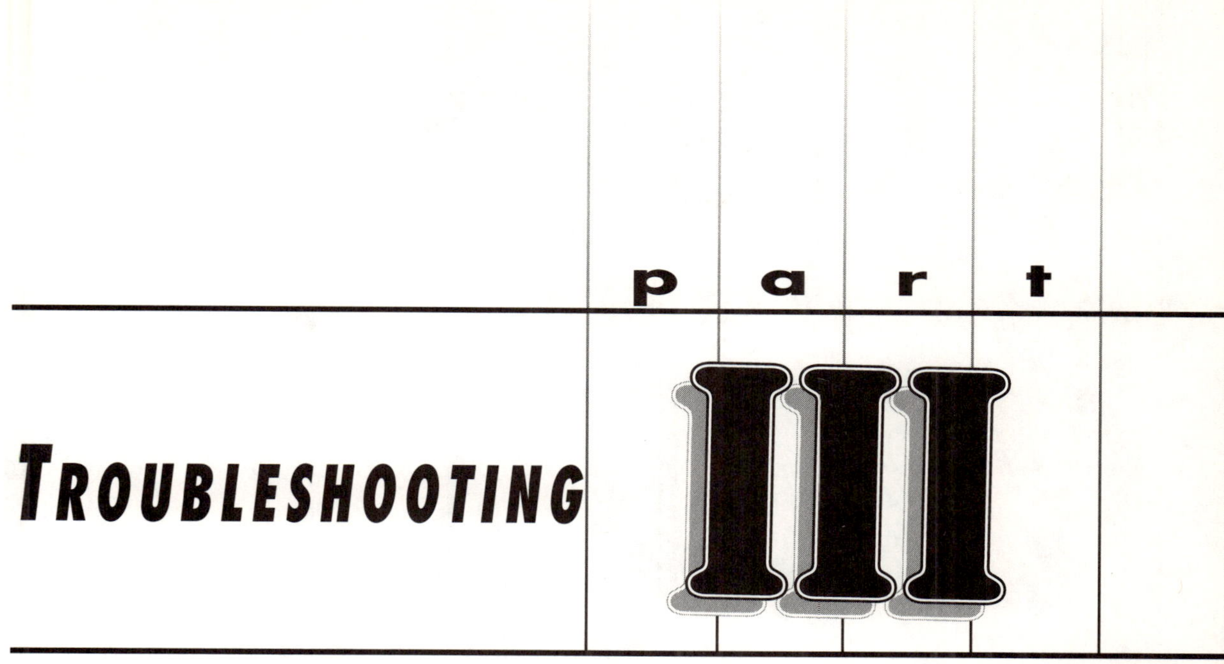

Part III: Troubleshooting

Inevitably, if things can go wrong, they will. Your phone will ring and you can almost be sure it's a user on the other end with a problem. This is the scenario: "I tried to log in, and I can't." You're faced with these questions:

> "Did something change from the night before?"
>
> "Did someone move the machine?"
>
> "Can other users in the same area log in?"

Fixing this problem involves a logical sorting out of the possible causes. This section helps you isolate those causes, reason through the solution, and fix the problem.

Troubleshooting Workstations

Many people think troubleshooting a computer network is a black art performed by those with a great amount of specialized information, training, and access to the gods. In reality, troubleshooting takes a bit of knowledge, some experience, and the ability to think logically. Troubleshooting a workstation problem is more work than almost any other network problem, because it involves a large number of variables. You need to consider cable and connectors, network adapters, multiple operating systems, third-party drivers, applications, and a variety of computer hardware to arrive at the cause of the problem. Regardless of the problem, the steps are the same—identify the problem, isolate the cause, arrive at a solution, and fix the problem. If you approach every problem in this order, you will find you can fix problems more quickly and easily.

Identify the Symptoms

The first step is to identify the problem. Typically, but not always, this is a simple task. It involves an overt symptom, such as inability to attach to the network or an application that will not load. The process of identification begins with gathering information. If an error message is generated, be sure to read it carefully. Let's use the example of a workstation that cannot find the server. The error message "A file server cannot be found" appears at a workstation. You receive a call from the user.

Isolate the Cause

The next step is to isolate the problem. Begin the problem isolation phase of your investigation by dividing the potential causes of the problem into different areas. A newly installed workstation that cannot find the server has a large number of potential causes. By dividing them into smaller units, you can more easily eliminate causes and isolate the location of the problem. In this phase, you should start with the easiest possible cause and work toward the more difficult. In our example, the following potential causes exist:

- A problem at the server
- A poorly terminated cable or connectors or a cable break
- A hardware failure
- A hardware conflict
- An improperly configured workstation
- A software or driver problem

Once you have divided the problem into smaller and more manageable units, you can begin to collect more information and perform simple experiments to isolate the problem. Start with the first problem on your list and verify it. In this case, a quick look at the server tells you that it is up and running and other users can log in. Therefore, the problem is more than likely not at the server.

You can easily eliminate a cable problem by plugging the cable from the problem workstation into a known working machine and seeing if it can log in to the server. You have now eliminated two broad categories of problems rather quickly and saved a lot of time.

The next steps, looking for a hardware failure or conflict, can be a little more trouble. Most network adapters come with test software that lets you verify basic adapter and machine operation. Armed with this diagnostic software, you may discover that the hardware is fine, but that you have an interrupt conflict with COM2.

Note:

In your attempts to isolate the problem, remember to change only one variable at a time. Changing the cable and putting in a new adapter may well solve the problem, but you still will have no idea why the first configuration failed. You will have to do more work later to find that the cable is good and the adapter works in another machine. You have then learned nothing by the experience.

Resolve and Fix the Problem

The final step is to resolve the problem. In our example, we change the interrupt to a known free interrupt and the workstation begins operating normally. In many cases, knowing the cause of the problem may not yield an immediate resolution. Many times the resolution will not be so easy and may involve as much experimentation as the isolation phase.

Perhaps the hardest problem is a series of problems. You fix one problem only to discover that something else is wrong. In that case, you begin the process again until all problems are resolved.

Basic Hardware

Before you begin to troubleshoot workstations, you should gather a set of tools. At a minimum you should have the following:

A toolkit

This should include screwdrivers (straight, Phillips, and star), nut drivers, needle-nose pliers, diagonal cutters, and a simple chip removal tool. From here, you can get expansive with power tools and a soldering iron. Your kit should also include a series of screws, bolts, computer slot covers, and drive bay components. This is where it is nice to be a pack rat for materials not used with other machines. They will come in handy.

A cable kit

This kit should be designed around the cabling type you use. For UTP cable, you will need a large number of RJ-45 connectors, cable, and a crimping tool. For RG-58 and RG-62 cabling, you will need appropriate cable ends, a cable cutting tool, crimpers, T-connectors, and terminators. For fiber-optic cable, you will need a much more extensive kit that can be purchased from your cable dealer. You should also keep on hand plates for the wall and wiring closet.

A cable scanner

A scanner is recommended to monitor and check cable you normally use. We would suggest you evaluate the equipment from several manufacturers before making a decision. Microtest and Fluke are among the best. If you are on a budget, this is the one expensive concession you should make.

A volt ohm meter (VOM)

A Fluke VOM is essential for verifying proper voltages on the wire or voltages coming from a power supply to the appropriate pins on an adapter in the workstation. The amount of resistance on a cable can be used to verify its length or quality.

Spare equipment

You should have at least one or two network adapters, a spare disk controller, video adapters, and any other adapter you routinely use on the network, workstation, or server. The more mission-critical the device is on the network, the more need you have for a spare.

Diagnostic software

A good diagnostic program like CHECKIT or Norton's diagnostic software is essential. Also, a bootable DOS diskette with FDISK, FORMAT, and CHKDSK is necessary. Many vendors now supply diagnostic software with their equipment; keep it handy.

Novell software

A complete set of Novell client disks for your version of the operating system is necessary.

Protocol analysis software and/or hardware

A product such as LANalyzer for Windows or other protocol analysis tool is useful. If you choose the more expensive hardware analyzer, you should consider a device like Network General's Sniffer.

Vendor software

The latest drivers and setup software for all of the equipment on your LAN are an absolute requirement. For EISA and Micro Channel machines, be sure to have the latest setup software.

Manuals

You need to have the documentation for every piece of equipment on the network. A complete set of Novell manuals, specifically the system and error message manuals, is necessary. At a minimum, you should have a copy of the Novell Support Encyclopedia (NSEPro) on CD-ROM.

A CompuServe account

Be sure to join NetWire, the Novell forum. Also, equipment vendors maintain their own forums on CompuServe. You can often find these by typing GO NVENA, NVENB, or PCVENA through PCVENK. *NetWare Solutions* magazine also has a forum on CompuServe (GO NWSFORUM).

Network documentation

A list of equipment, user information, network map, and workstation documentation is an absolute necessity.

Trade publications

Of course, don't forget that several magazines give excellent technical information on NetWare LANs. Among them are *NetWare Solutions* (see subscription card in the back of this book) and the Network Professional's Association's *Networking Journal*.

Tip:

Maintaining spare network adapters is essential. This is also true for hubs, concentrators, and hard drives. Most vendors will cross-ship products, but that means that you will be down a minimum of 24 hours. If your network is critical to your business operation, the cost of a spare is small compared to the cost of 24 hours without the network.

Where to Get Help

The sample problem was a fairly simple example of the steps and solutions you'll need to solve problems. Problems can, and will, get much harder. In that case you should be ready to ask for help. There are a plethora of places to get help from and all should be used from time to time:

Vendor technical support

If your problem is with a specific product, hardware or software, you should contact the vendor for support. Its technical support representatives should know the product better than you and be able to give sound advice. The vendor will also have access to technical expertise that you don't. Many vendors have forums on CompuServe, WWW sites on the Internet, or BBSes from which to get the latest drivers and software patches.

Novell Technical Support

If the problem has been isolated to a potential bug in NetWare or a component, contact Novell. Remember that Novell Technical Support is fee-based.

Technical Support Alliance

Many vendors of Novell-certified products are also members of the Technical Support Alliance. The members of the TSA are extremely useful in multivendor problems that otherwise would be difficult to solve through one vendor. They will share information and equipment between the members to help isolate and solve your problem.

NetWire

Novell's fee-based forum on CompuServe is an excellent opportunity to speak with others that may have encountered similar problems. It is also a great place to get upgraded software and patches. NetWire is extremely useful for generic problems or those intermittent problems that are hard to pinpoint. There are many NetWire sysops who will answer your questions in less than 24 hours.

Generic Network Problems

Although many of the problems you will find on a network are specific to a particular vendor's product, you will find that there are also many problems that are generic to networking that you should look at first.

Cabling

Malfunctioning cabling represents the majority of problems on a network. A good cable scanner is essential to isolating the problems you will encounter. However, there are a few simple rules to go by:

Verify the cable ends

The termination point of the cable is where the majority of stress on the cable will occur. Good terminations are essential.

Cable terminators

The terminators for bus segments can degrade over time and should be checked with a volt ohm meter to verify the termination value. Also, remember that one of the ends of a 10BASE-2 or 10BASE-5 segment should be grounded.

Cable specifications

Be sure that you are using the proper type of cable for your network. UTP cable that worked well for 4Mbps token-ring networks may be out of specification for 16Mbps token-ring networks and cause immediate or intermittent problems.

Protocol specifications

Verify that you have not exceeded the cabling specifications for your topology. The 10BASE-T specification of 100 meters and the 5,4,3 rule should not be ignored. Exceeding these specifications can cause immense problems.

Power Problems

Although rare, power problems will crop up from time to time on a network. When you encounter them, they will be of two varieties: power supply, and AC power and grounding.

Power Supply and Related Problems

A problem with a device's power supply can cause a variety of problems on your network. An errant power supply can cause problems such as sending unfiltered or over-voltage power down the network line; a noisy power supply can cause data corruption. The first problem can cause havoc on your network that is immediate and devastating. The second can cause intermittent problems that are almost impossible to detect and cure.

Tip:

One of the hardest problems we have encountered with power was related to the voltage line on a bus that had gone bad. The adapter would not get the proper power on initial startup, but if warm booted would initialize and work normally. This was later traced to a bad 5-volt line on the bus.

A problem power supply will often cause other problems on the computer unrelated to network problems. Replacing the power supply on a computer is a simple operation. Do not attempt to replace the supply on a concentrator, multistation access unit (MAU), or hub. Send it back to the manufacturer.

AC Power and Grounding Problems

Problems related to AC power and wiring are also rare. However, you can run into them from time to time and should be prepared to deal with them. If you suspect a problem with the AC power, you can rent monitoring equipment, or in many cases, the local power company will come in and verify the line for you. An AC power line monitor is an expensive piece of equipment that you should consider renting if you feel you need one. AC power problems are often related to consistent low voltages or voltage fluctuations. Some of these problems can be eliminated by power conditioning equipment or battery backup systems. If brownouts or blackouts are a problem in your area, consider purchasing one of these systems.

Another potential problem related to AC power is proper grounding. In a properly grounded system, there should be little or no voltage on the ground line. Computer networks use the AC ground as part of the reference signal. If voltage is too high on the ground line or fluctuates between devices on the network, the result is a signal that is disrupted or corrupt. This will cause data corruption, and over time, damage your equipment. Have the local power company or a qualified electrician verify the grounding on the outside of the building and verify that the AC outlets are properly grounded.

The problem with AC grounds increases dramatically if you attempt to use copper cable between buildings or between areas of the same building that are on a different AC ground. There is no guarantee that the different buildings or the areas have the same ground potential (the amount of voltage to ground). If you must run a cable between buildings or to different areas of a building on a different AC ground use fiber optic cable if at all possible. This will eliminate any potential problem. Fiber optic cable transmits the signal as a pulse of light and does not require a ground plane for reference.

Tip:

An improperly grounded system invites another problem—lightning-related power problems. Most systems, including surge suppressors, that arrest or prevent lightning problems are tied to the building's AC ground. If the AC ground is faulty or nonexistent, they will not operate properly. No power system will be unaffected by a direct lightning strike to a building.

Workstation Problems

On the workstation, problems are often related to the software configuration or hardware conflicts. LAN adapters, in particular, may cause problems related to one or more of the following features:

- Base I/O port
- Interrupt
- Shared RAM address
- DMA channel

A conflict can occur with any of these. However, the most likely causes of conflicts are the interrupt, shared RAM address, or DMA channel. Interrupt conflicts are the most likely to occur with modems and video cards. A program designed to poll the machine for devices and ports in use will be helpful in isolating the problem.

One of the most common conflicts involves interrupt channels. Most adapters in a computer will generate an interrupt. ISA machines cannot share interrupts, so each interrupt must be unique. Many Micro Channel, EISA, and PCI devices are designed to share interrupts with like devices. This makes a lot of the problems easier to work with. The following is a list of the most common interrupt conflicts with ISA machines:

Interrupt 2/9	Video cards, other LAN adapters, mouse
Interrupt 3	COM 2
Interrupt 4	COM 1
Interrupt 5	LPT 2, mouse
Interrupt 6	Floppy controller
Interrupt 7	LPT 1
Interrupt 10	Hard drive controller, PS/2 mouse
Interrupt 11	Hard drive controller
Interrupt 12	Hard drive controller

Shared RAM address can also conflict with the machine or other devices in the machine. Many machines shadow the BIOS and video into RAM, which can cause conflicts with the RAM address space of network adapters. Also, VGA controllers use the space from C000-C7FF for adapter RAM space.

Tip:

Another problem can occur between VGA controllers and 16-bit shared RAM adapters. This involves the way in which the adapters send information along the bus. Data is sent in blocks. Sixteen-bit adapters that occupy the same 128KB memory segment (i.e., from D000 to DFFF) must decode the information in the same way. The available sizes are 16KB and 128KB. If the sizes are different, only one of the adapters will work. The majority of video cards and shared RAM adapters allow you to adjust this size to allow them to match.

Another source of problems with shared RAM adapters is memory managers. You must exclude the area of memory that the adapter will be using. Thus, if the card is using the address range C800 to CBFF, you must exclude this area of memory. The exclusion statements for memory managers are different, but must include a statement of exactly how much memory to exclude.

Tip:

For Windows and Window 95 users, you may also have to exclude the area of memory for shared RAM adapters in the SYSTEM.INI file. To do this, place the following statement in the [386enh] section of the SYSTEM.INI file:

```
EMMEXCLUDE=XXXX-YYYY
```

in which XXXX is the beginning point of the shared RAM address and YYYY is the end.

Tip:

For ARCnet users, most vendors require that a 16KB address space be set aside for shared RAM. However, only the first 8KB is critical. The last 8KB is reserved for a boot ROM. If you are not going to remote boot, then you need only exclude the first 8KB.

DMA conflicts occur with other ISA devices using direct memory access, such as SCSI device controllers. An additional problem can occur with bus-mastering devices. Bus-mastering devices will hold the bus until they have completed the DMA data transfer or until the next video refresh cycle. When multiple bus-mastering cards are in place, they must give up the bus more often. The criteria for releasing the bus are based on the priority of the DMA channel and an algorithm called fairness. Most of the drivers for bus-mastering devices invoke fairness. For those that do not invoke fairness, sometimes you can manipulate the time on and off of the bus. Another alternative is to place the device that is not operating properly at a higher-priority DMA channel. To do this, place the device at a channel with a lower number than the device that will not invoke fairness.

Another problem related to DMA bus-mastering in ISA machines is that some machines will not support ISA bus-mastering. In that case, you must disable bus-mastering on the machine. The majority of these problems do not appear with EISA machines or with EISA bus-mastering. With Micro Channel machines, you must set an arbitration level. The arbitration level automatically sets bus priority between multiple bus-mastering adapters.

PCI adapters have their own problems. The standards for PCI are still evolving and can cause unlimited problems. Many machines alter the way PCI slots are configured or do not allow you to configure them. Some limit the number of bus-mastering slots. If a PCI adapter does not work the first time you plug it in, be sure to verify the configuration, and if necessary, change slots. Also, verify that your adapter can share interrupts. It may be necessary to manually configure each PCI slot for a different interrupt. Finally, be sure that you have the latest PCI BIOS from the computer manufacturer. PCI BIOS versions change on an almost weekly basis, and you should be sure that you have the latest version, particularly if you have a problem.

NET.CFG Problems

The NET.CFG file contains parameters for the NetWare components of the workstation. The values placed in this file are designed to override the default configuration. Most times, the default configuration will work well. However, if you change the network adapter's default settings, you must make the changes in the NET.CFG file. If the settings in the NET.CFG file do not patch the driver, it will not load. The driver settings are placed in the LINK DRIVER section of the NET.CFG file. The options include:

DMA number
This option is used to configure the DMA channel for the adapter.

INT number
This option is used to configure the Interrupt.

MEM number
This option specifies the beginning memory address for shared RAM adapters.

PORT address
This option is used to configure the starting port address for adapters using a port address.

FRAME type
This option is used to override the default frametype. The driver will load if this option is incorrec. However, unless it matches the option set at the file server, the workstation will not be able to find the file server.

There are more settings for network adapters, but they should not stop the adapter from being initialized by the driver. The various settings in the NET.CFG are discussed in detail in Appendix A.

Protocol Analysis and Troubleshooting

Protocol analysis is provided through a protocol analyzer. A protocol analyzer uses the access method's promiscuous mode chipset to capture all the packets traveling along the media. This analysis is available at two levels. The captured frames can be used to calculate various network functions including bandwidth utilization and frames on the network or it can be used to make general decisions about the network. You should use this feature of the protocol analyzer to get a baseline of your network's performance and then set the analyzer to look for items that exceed the baseline you determined.

Tip:
One of the things you should look for in a protocol analyzer is the ability to generate network traffic. By generating network traffic in a controlled experiment, you can determine the result of making a change in your network before you actually make the change. For instance, if you have 30 nodes on your network and performance is acceptable, you can use the analyzer to increase your traffic by 50 percent and see what happens when you add the additional 15 workstations that you want.

The other essential feature is the ability to capture all packets and let you do packet level analysis. This level of analysis is not available with other analysis tools and is best used to solve specific problems such as a protocol that is not routing properly or why a particular node cannot find the network. You cannot use this analysis for an extended period of time, as it takes a great deal of memory to store the packets. Most analyzers allow you to set aside an amount of memory that is filled on a first in, first out basis. The most popular protocol analyzers include Triticom's LAN Decoder /E and /TR and Novell's LANalyzer for Windows.

SNMP Management and Troubleshooting

The Simple Network Management Protocol is a common communications protocol for collecting information from devices and allowing the status of the devices to be changed. The information is collected by *agents.* An agent is used to control a managed device. The agent can either be software built into the managed device, such as a bridge or a router, or a program run on the device, such as a computer that has an adapter in it. The agent collects the information and responds to queries from a management console to provide the information. SNMP is the transport protocol that allows the console to access the agents to obtain information and change the status of the device for which the agent is collecting information. As originally written, the SNMP protocol had to use TCP/IP as the network protocol. However, in 1992 SNMP was expanded to include support for IPX, OSI, and AppleTalk. This greatly expanded the number of networks that could take advantage of SNMP for network management.

The information is collected by the console and stored in a management information base or MIB. The MIB is written to the SNMP specification by the manufacturer of the device being managed. While they must be written to work within SNMP, they can contain information specific to the devices, allowing the user to control almost every aspect of the device.

Typical Information Functions

Network mapping
Event trapping with alarms
Traffic monitoring
Diagnostic functions

Report generation
Historical management of information

Typical Management Functions

Automatic disconnection of nodes
Network segmentation
Connect or disconnect workstations based on factors such as time of day, etc.
Device management
Protocol analysis
Offsite management

Tip:
Remember that in order to be generic enough to be managed by almost any management console the device opens itself to be abused. For instance, you can query the MIB for a great deal of information, much of which can be used only by someone with extensive training. In addition, you might accidentally shut down the entire device without knowing what you did or why.

Tip:
A feature of this ability, however, is that you can gather information on almost any type of device on the network. One school has attached all of the soda machines on campus to the net via Ethernet. An SNMP module running on the machines is constantly queried as to the number of drinks of each variety in the machine. When a particular variety is out the agent sends an alert to the management console. This is the same console that runs the school's network.

Management consoles are generally written to be as generic as possible, allowing them to work with almost any MIB. The console uses SNMP to query the agent based upon the MIB loaded on the console. It will then display the information to you in an understandable manner. The devices are displayed as icons to represent devices on the network. The network can also be displayed according to a graphical interface. In many you can even display the icons on a map of the area to illustrate the relationship between devices. Using the console you can monitor each agent and set traps to warn you of events on the network, such as increased utilization or excessive collisions. In addition, you can set the trap to issue a warning or to shut down an offending node entirely.

The information supplied by the agents can be garnered over an extensive period of time, allowing you to do trend analysis on your network. You can customize reports to provide the information most needed on your network. SNMP is best used in conjunction with a managed hub in a structured wiring system. With all of your stations connected through a managed hub that uses SNMP, you can gather information on the entire network and then use the information to control the network. In addition, you can set traps to warn you of problems on the network and, in extreme cases, to control individual ports on the network to stop problems.

Almost every device today is supplied with an agent to allow SNMP management. The leading vendors of SNMP consoles are Hewlett-Packard's Open View, SunConnect's Sun Net Manager, and IBM's NetView 6000. However, as configurable and extensible as SNMP is, there are improvements on the horizon, the most important of which is CMIP. CMIP is the OSI Common Information Management Protocol. This protocol is more extensive and configurable than SNMP, but the interface is more proprietary. As a result, SNMP has retained and expanded its popularity.

Final Words

Once you have mastered the basics of network troubleshooting, time and experience will provide you with the additional skills you need to become an expert at network problem resolution. The more you see of problems on a network workstation, the more easily you can solve them. Also, the more information you get about your network and the workstations on it, the more quickly you can isolate and solve problems before they occur.

Document your network carefully. Configuration management software and metering software will help you keep track of the configuration of each of your workstations. Use this information to keep your workstations' software and drivers up to date.

Take a holistic approach to your network. Use your analysis tools to maintain a complete picture of your network. Once you have that picture, begin to use it to identify network bottlenecks and potential problems. Remember that prevention is the best troubleshooting tool you have.

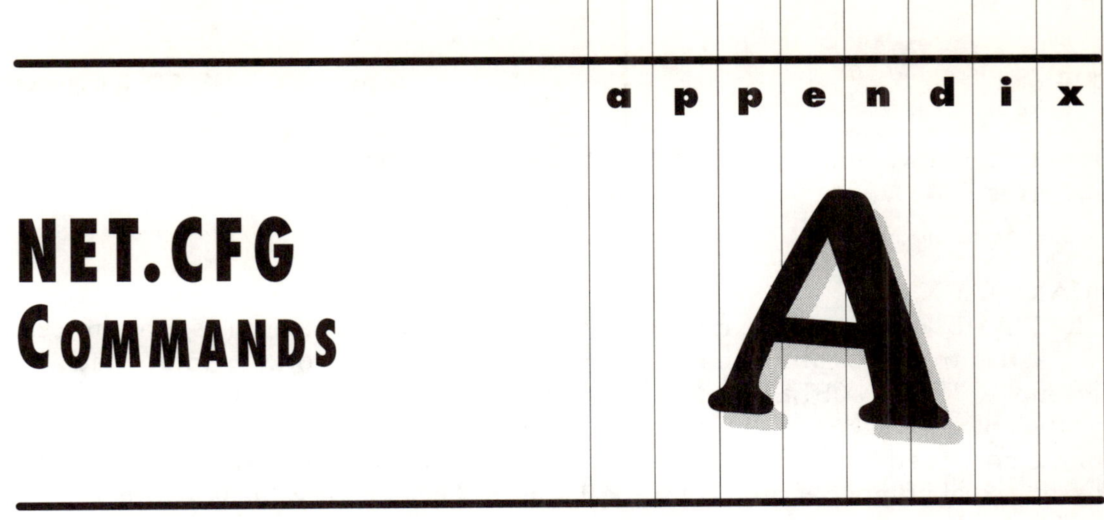

NET.CFG Commands

Following is a list of the commands used in the NET.CFG file arranged by their position in the file.

The Link Support Layer (LSL) (LSL.COM)

BUFFERS

The BUFFERS statement sets the number of receive buffers the LSL will maintain. The number of communications buffers must be large enough to hold all the media headers and the maximum data size of a frame. The default value for BUFFERS is 0. This parameter is not used for IPX. For IP, we suggest a value of 1,514 for Ethernet and 4,096 for token-ring. The buffer size may also be set with the BUFFERS command. The minimum size is 628 bytes. The total buffer space must fit into approximately 59 kilobytes (KB). The total buffer space is determined by multiplying the number of buffers by the size of the buffer. The syntax is

```
BUFFERS number, size
```

MAX BOARDS

The MAX BOARDS statement configures the maximum number of logical boards (adapters) the LSL can handle. Each LAN driver logical board uses one board resource. A logical board is used each time a FRAMETYPE is loaded. An Ethernet driver should support all four logical FRAMETYPES for a maximum of four logical boards per adapter. The default value is 4 with a range of 1 to 16. For example, you have two adapters in the machine. Board 1 is bound to ETHERNET_802.2, ETHERNET_802.2, and ETHERNET_SNAP. Board 2 is bound to two token-ring frame types. The maximum number of boards will be five, one for each frame type. The syntax is

```
MAX BOARDS number
```

MAX STACKS
The MAX STACKS statement configures the maximum number of logical protocol stack IDs the LSL can utilize. Each protocol stack uses one or more stack ID resources. The MAX STACKS statement also controls the amount of resident memory the LSL uses, which is directly proportional to the number of stacks. The amount of memory used by the LSL can be controlled by reducing the MAX STACKS value to the actual number of protocol stack IDs used. The default value is 4 with a range of 1 to 16. The syntax is

```
MAX STACKS number
```

MEMPOOL
MEMPOOL configures the size of the memory pool buffers maintained by the LSL. The IPXODI protocol stack does not use the MEMPOOL buffers. IP does. The syntax is

```
MEMPOOL number
```

Driver Parameters

Each driver also has a specific set of parameters that can be specified in the NET.CFG file. The list of parameters includes:

DMA
This setting represents the DMA channel used.

MEM
This parameter is the memory address of the adapter.

NODE ADDRESS
This is the locally administered node ID of the adapter.

PCMCIA
This is the type of PCMCIA device.

PROTOCOL
This is the first protocol used by the adapter.

LINK STATIONS
This setting is used by LANSUP.COM to set the link stations.

MAX FRAME SIZE
This setting represents the largest frame size used by the driver.

INT
This is the interrupt used by the the adapter.

PORT
This is the port the adapter uses.

SLOT
This setting is the slot used for EISA and PCI adapters.

FRAME
This is the frame type the adapter uses.

SAPS
This setting is used by LANSUP.COM to set the number of Service Access Points.

ALTERNATE
This setting is used to designate a second adapter for token-ring adapters.

DOUBLE BUFFER OFF
This setting allows double buffers for transmitting and receiving packets.

IPX Parameters

BIND
IPXODI binds to the first board it finds in the NET.CFG file. If you want to bind the IPX/SPX protocol to a different board, add the BIND statement to the PROTOCOL IPXODI section of the NET.CFG file, which forces IPXODI to bind to a subsequent logical board. To add the BIND statement to the IPXODI section, simply place the statement: *BIND [driver]* under the heading PROTOCOL IPXODI section. The *[driver]* represents the name of the adapter driver you are using. For an NE3200 Ethernet adapter, the syntax of the BIND statement is:

```
PROTOCOL IPXODI
BIND NE3200
```

INT64
The INT64 parameter allows applications to use Interrupt 64h to access IPX services. This parameter is used for older applications that do not use INT64.

INT7A
The INT7A parameter allows applications to use Interrupt 7Ah to access IPX services. Only specific applications must use this interrupt.

IPATCH

The IPATCH parameter allows any address in the IPXODI.COM file to be patched with any specified byte offset value. This statement should be used only when an application requires a specific byte offset value.

IPX PACKET SIZE LIMIT

The IPX PACKET SIZE LIMIT parameter reduces the maximum packet size set by each LAN driver. The default setting is the lesser of 4,160 bytes or the size specified by the LAN driver. The range is 576 to 6,500 bytes.

IPX RETRY COUNT

The IPX RETRY COUNT parameter sets the number of times IPX allows the DOS shell and SPX to resend a packet. The default is 20 retries. You may want to increase this parameter when you have a lot of traffic, or if you are sending traffic over a wide-area network.

IPX SOCKETS

The IPX SOCKETS parameter configures the maximum number of sockets IPX can have open at the workstation. IPX-specific programs may require that this number be increased. The default number of sockets is 20. You rarely need more than 20 sockets unless you are running an application on a workstation that is communicating with several other workstations.

MINIMUM SPX RETRIES

The MINIMUM SPX RETRIES parameter determines the number of unacknowledged transmit requests that will be allowed before it is assumed that the connection is bad. This parameter should be increased if an application that uses SPX loses its connection. The range for this parameter is 0 to 255.

SPX ABORT TIMEOUT

The SPX ABORT TIMEOUT parameter adjusts the amount of time SPX waits without receiving any response from the other side of the connection. The value for this parameter is the number of clock-ticks (approximately 1/18th of a second) that SPX waits. The default value is 540 ticks, approximately 30 seconds. It should be used when SPX programs time-out too quickly.

SPX CONNECTIONS

This parameter configures the maximum number of SPX connections a workstation can have open at one time. If you plan to use RPRINTER.EXE to use a local printer on a NetWare v2.x, v3.x, or 4.x network, you will need to increase this parameter to 60.

SPX LISTEN TIMEOUT

This parameter sets the time SPX waits without receiving a packet from the other side of the connection before it requests a packet from the other side to assure the connection. The timeout values is also specified in number of ticks. The default value is 108 ticks. You should change this setting only if you experience time-outs on your SPX link.

SPX VERIFY TIMEOUT
This parameter configures the frequency at which SPX sends a packet to the other side of the connection to indicate that the connection is still alive. SPX sends the alive packet when no other SPX traffic is sent by the session. The value is measured in ticks. The default value is 54 ticks.

NetWare DOS Requester

AUTO LARGE TABLE
When AUTO LARGE TABLE is enabled, AUTO.VLM allocates a table of 178 bytes per connection for bindery reconnects. The default setting is OFF. When disabled, the setting is 34 bytes per connection. The parameter BIND RECONNECT must also be set to ON.

AUTO RECONNECT
The AUTO RECONNECT parameter sets AUTO.VLM to reconnect a workstation to a NetWare server and rebuild the workstation's environment after a connection loss. If AUTO RECONNECT is set to OFF, reconnection is manual. The default value is ON.

AUTO RETRY
The AUTO RETRY parameter sets the number of seconds AUTO.VLM waits before attempting a retry after receiving a network error. When you set AUTO RETRY to 0, AUTO.VLM will make no retry attempts. The default time is 0 and the range is between 0 and 3,640 seconds.

AVERAGE NAME LENGTH
The AVERAGE NAME LENGTH parameter reserves space for a table of NetWare server names based on the AVERAGE NAME LENGTH and the value of the CONNECTIONS parameter. You may save additional memory by setting the length to a lower value. The default value is 48 characters.

BIND RECONNECT
BIND RECONNECT automatically rebuilds the bindery connection and restores drives and printer connections. This parameter also requires that AUTO RECONNECT be set to ON. BIND RECONNECT's default value is OFF.

CACHE BUFFERS

CACHE BUFFERS determines the number of cache buffers the requester allocates for local caching of nonshared, nontransaction-tracked files. This parameter allows the DOS Requester to cache one file. Increasing the number of cache buffers increases the speed of sequential reads and writes, and thus performance, but also increases memory use. The default is five cache blocks and the range is from 0 to 64.

CACHE BUFFER SIZE

The CACHE BUFFER SIZE sets the size of the cache buffer. Increasing the size parameter increases performance, but also increases memory usage. The parameter should never be set to a size larger than the MAXIMUM PACKET SIZE set for the network adapter driver. The default is 512 bytes and the range is from 64 to 4,096 bytes.

CACHE WRITES

The CACHE WRITES parameter may be set to ON or OFF. If the parameter is set to OFF, performance will decrease, but data integrity will increase. Setting the parameter to ON potentially causes data loss if the server runs out of disk space between writes. The default value is ON.

CHECKSUM

The CHECKSUM parameter forces NCP packet validation. There are various levels of security for this parameter:

0	Disabled
1	Enabled but not preferred
2	Enabled and preferred
3	Required

Setting the parameter to 2 or 3 increases data integrity, but decreases system performance. The default is 1. The ETHERNET_802.3 frame type does not support checksums.

CONNECTIONS

The CONNECTIONS parameter sets the maximum number of connections the requester supports. The range of values is 2 to 50. A value larger than necessary increases memory use without increasing performance. Setting the value to a number larger than 8 can also affect NETX compatibility with older versions of NetWare. The default value is 8.

DOS NAME

DOS NAME sets the name of the operating system the shell uses. This %OS variable in the login script uses this parameter to map search drives to the network's DOS directory. The requester automatically recognizes the name DRDOS and

NWDOS without setting the DOS NAME parameter. Setting this variable disables the autorecognition feature. The maximum number of characters is five.

FIRST NETWORK DRIVE
The FIRST NETWORK DRIVE parameter sets the first network drive letter specified when a connection is made. The default is the first available DOS drive found. The range is from A to Z.

HANDLE NET ERRORS
HANDLE NET ERRORS determines the method for handling network errors. A network error is generated whenever the workstation does not receive a response from the server. If HANDLE NET ERRORS is set to ON, INT24h handles network errors. If HANDLE NET ERRORS is set to OFF, a NET_REC_ERROR return is made on a network error. Some applications may not recognize NET_REC_ERROR returns.

LARGE INTERNET PACKETS
LARGE INTERNET PACKETS determines the size of packets used when crossing bridges and routers. Previously NetWare set the MAXIMUM PACKET SIZE to 576. When set to ON, the maximum packet size is negotiated between the destination NetWare server and the workstation when crossing bridges and routers. The access method used determines the maximum packet size.

LOAD CONN TABLE LOW
The LOAD CONN TABLE LOW parameter is used with the initial release of NetWare 4.0 utilities. When set to ON, the connection table loads in low memory, increasing memory usage. The default setting of OFF loads the table in upper memory.

LOAD LOW CONN
The LOAD LOW CONN parameter set to OFF loads the CONN.VLM into upper memory, saving memory but decreasing performance. The default is ON, which loads the VLM into conventional memory.

LOAD LOW IPXNCP
The LOAD LOW IPXNCP parameter designates where the IPXNCP.VLM is loaded in memory. Set to ON, the VLM loads into conventional memory. Set to OFF, the VLM loads in upper memory, increasing conventional memory space and decreasing performance.

LOCAL PRINTERS
LOCAL PRINTERS overrides the number of local printers determined by the system BIOS. Normally the BIOS allocates one local printer for each parallel port. The default is 3 with the range from 0 to 9.

LONG MACHINE TYPE

The LONG MACHINE TYPE tells the requester the type of machine used when the %MACHINE variable is accessed. This variable sets the machine's search path to the correct version of DOS on the server. The default is IBM_PC.

MAX TASKS

MAX TASKS configures the maximum number of active tasks. The default is 31 tasks; the range is from 20 to 128 tasks.

MESSAGE LEVEL

The MESSAGE LEVEL sets the amount of information displayed with load time messages. Each message level implies the previous level's message. The default is 1. The values are as follows:

0	Always display copyright message and critical errors
1	Display warning messages
2	Display program load information for VLMs
3	Display configuration information
4	Display diagnostic information

MESSAGE TIMEOUT

MESSAGE TIMEOUT sets the timeout in ticks before broadcast messages are cleared from the screen without user intervention. The default 0 requires you to clear the message. The range is from 0 to 10,000 ticks.

NAME CONTEXT

The NAME CONTEXT parameter allows you to set the current position in the NetWare Directory Services tree structure and applies only to NetWare 4.x networks. The default NAME CONTEXT is the root directory. Quotation marks must enclose the directory name. The complete syntax is

```
NAME CONTEXT = "name context"
```

NETWARE PROTOCOL

NETWARE PROTOCOL sets the network protocols that will be bound at the workstation. Available protocols are

NDS	NDS allows use of NetWare Directory services
BIND	BIND allows use of NetWare bindery for NetWare v2.x and v3.x
PNW	PNW is used to define Personal NetWare

NETWORK PRINTERS

The NETWORK PRINTERS parameter sets the number of LPT ports the NetWare DOS Requester can capture. The range is from 0 to 9 with a default of 3. Setting the value to 0 specifies that the PRINT.VLM does not load.

PB BUFFERS

PB BUFFERS sets the number of packet burst protocol buffers. Packet burst is automatically enabled in the requester. Setting the value to 0 disables packet burst. The default is 3 with a range from 0 to 10. Setting the number to a higher value increases memory usage. Setting the value to 0 decreases memory usage and in some cases may decrease performance.

PREFERRED SERVER

PREFERRED SERVER sets the NetWare v2.x or v3.x server to first attach if the server has a connection available. If both the PREFERRED SERVER and PREFERRED TREE parameters are specified, the first protocol to successfully build an attachment is used.

PREFERRED TREE

PREFERRED TREE sets the tree to connect to in a NetWare 4.0 network environment if the tree specified has a server with a free connection. If both the PREFERRED SERVER and PREFERRED TREE parameters are specified, the first protocol to successfully build an attachment is used.

PREFERRED WORKGROUP

PREFERRED WORKGROUP sets the name of the Workgroup for Personal NetWare to search and attach to.

PRINT BUFFER SIZE

The PRINT BUFFER SIZE determines the print buffer size in bytes. The default is 64 bytes and the range is from 0 to 256 bytes. Increasing this value increases printing output and memory usage.

PRINT HEADER

PRINT HEADER sets the size of the buffer that holds the information used to initialize a printer for each print job. This parameter should be used if print jobs with many instructions, such as forms, are used. The default is 64 bytes and the range is from 0 to 1,024 bytes.

PRINT TAIL

PRINT TAIL sets the size of the buffer that holds the information used to reset the printer after print jobs. The default is 16 bytes and the range is from 0 to 1,024 bytes. You should only need to change this if the printer does not reset properly.

READ ONLY COMPATIBILITY

READ ONLY COMPATIBILITY determines if a file marked Read Only (RO) can be opened with a read/write access call. Prior to NetWare v2.1, a program could open a Read Only file with write access without an error. To maintain compatibility with DOS, NetWare v2.1 and above do not allow a Read Only file to be opened for write access. Setting the parameter forces the shell to allow the open request to succeed. The default is OFF. You should only need to reset this if you are using an older version of DOS.

SEARCH MODE

SEARCH MODE changes the way the NetWare requester searches for .EXE and .COM files that are not in the current directory. Valid search modes are 0–7. In previous versions of NetWare, the default drive had to be a network drive. The DOS Requester will search all drives regardless of the current drive.

SET STATION TIME

SET STATION TIME synchronizes the workstation date and time with the NetWare server that the workstation initially attaches to. The default is ON; setting the parameter to OFF disables synchronization.

SHOW DOTS

SHOW DOTS shows the DOS directory entries for . and ..; this setting is used with Windows 3.x to show the DOS dots for directory searches.

SHORT MACHINE TYPE

The SHORT MACHINE TYPE parameter is used with the %MACHINE variable in the login script. The SHORT MACHINE TYPE is used specifically with overlay (.OVL) files. The default SHORT MACHINE TYPE is IBM and is limited to four letters.

SIGNATURE LEVEL

SIGNATURE LEVEL sets the level of enhanced security support. The available values are as follows:

0	Disabled
1	Enabled, but not preferred
2	Preferred
3	Required

Setting the option to 2 or 3 increases the level of security but decreases performance.

TRUE COMMIT

The TRUE COMMIT variable selects whether the commit NetWare Core Protocol (NCP) is sent on DOS commit requests. The option should be set to ON to guarantee integrity when processing critical data. This variable also sacrifices performance for integrity. The default value is OFF.

USE DEFAULTS
USE DEFAULTS overrides the default VLMs that VLM.EXE loads. If USE DEFAULTS is set in the NET.CFG file, then the DOS Requester installs VLMs to control NetWare services. The default VLMs are

CONN.VLM	IPXNCP.VLM
TRAN.VLM	SECURITY.VLM
NDS.VLM	BIND.VLM
NWP.VLM	FIO.VLM
GENERAL.VLM	REDIR.VLM
PRINT.VLM	NETX.VLM

If this parameter is set to ON and the default VLMs are specified in the NET.CFG file, they will attempt to load twice, generating an error during the load. The default value is ON.

VLM
VLM specifies the VLMs that the VLM.EXE should load. This allows VLMs not listed in the default for VLM.EXE to be added. The syntax for the parameter is

```
VLM = [path]\*.VLM
```

The .VLM extension must be used. A maximum of 50 VLMs can be loaded.

Link Driver LANSUP

SAPS
This parameter represents the number of Service Access Points. The available parameters are 1–255. The default is 1. Only change this option if the application you are using recommends it. Used with IBM LAN Support.

LINK STATIONS
This parameter represents the number of link stations. The available parameters are 1–255. The default is 1. Only change this option if the application you are using recommends it. Used with IBM LAN Support.

MAX PACKET
This parameter represents the packet size. The default is four kilobytes for token ring. The maximum is 17,960 bytes. Only change this option if the application you are using recommends it. Used with IBM LAN Support.

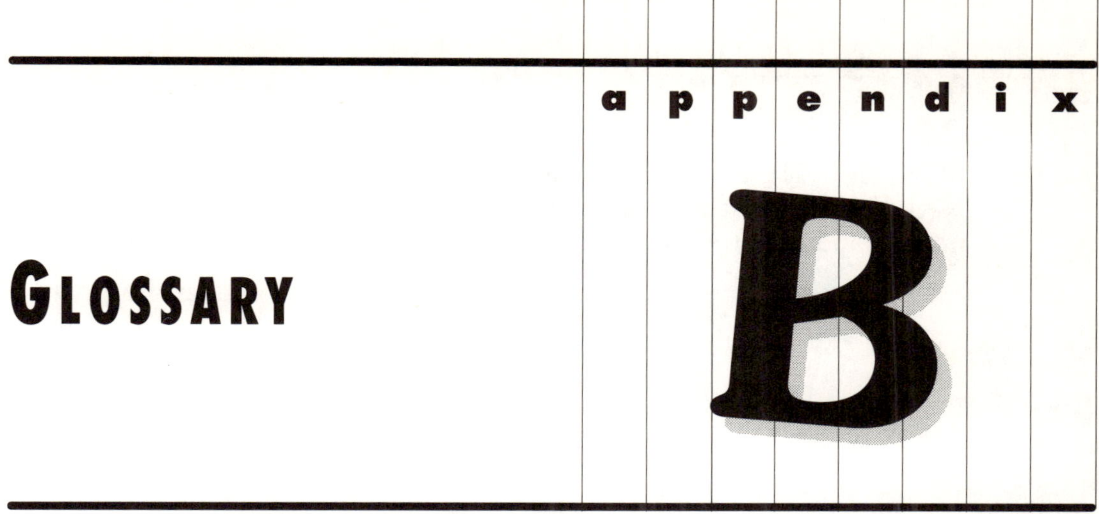

Glossary

A

Address Resolution Protocol (ARP)
The Address Resolution Protocol, part of the TCP/IP suite, provides IP-address-to-physical-adapter address resolution. It is specified in RFC 826.

AppleShare
AppleShare is Apple Computer's network operating system for the Macintosh. It uses the AppleTalk protocol suite.

AppleTalk Zone
In AppleTalk, nodes are grouped in zones, much like NetWare's groups. These zones may be departmental, graphical, or functional.

Application Program Interface (API)
APIs consist of a collection of function calls that provide access to an operating system or application.

ARCnet
ARCnet is a media access method with a transmission speed of 2.5 megabits per second (Mbps). Although at one time ARCnet was very popular, it has been replaced by Ethernet and token-ring networks.

AUTOEXEC.BAT
The AUTOEXEC.BAT file sets how the system looks and runs programs. Within the AUTOEXEC.BAT file, you will set the system path and run programs such as SMARTDRV.EXE, the drive caching program for MS-DOS and PC-DOS.

AUTOEXEC.NCF The AUTOEXEC.NCF file is a batch file that configures the NetWare server. It is used to load modules (NLMs, etc.), execute commands, and load LAN and disk drivers.

B

Bindery
The bindery is a database in NetWare v2.x and v3.x that contains information about the resources on the network. For a user, it contains the user's rights and attributes, his or her password, and information on the resources available.

Bindery emulation
In NetWare 4.x, NetWare Directory Services (NDS) replaces the NetWare bindery. Bindery emulation is the mechanism that allows NetWare v3.x networks to operate in a NetWare 4.x environment.

Boot image file
The boot image file is used in diskless workstations to boot the workstation to the network. It is downloaded into the computer's system memory and executed. The boot image file contains the boot files, configuration files, and any other files, such as HIMEM.SYS and EMM386.EXE, necessary to run the machine.

Boot ROM
A boot ROM is a hardware chip used in diskless workstations that allows them to boot to the network. It fits into a socket on the network adapter.

BOOTCONF.SYS
The BOOTCONF.SYS file is a text file that can be used to cross-reference node address to the boot image file they need to boot from.

BOOTP
The boot protocol is used in TCP/IP networks to allow the workstation to find its IP address.

Buffer
A buffer is a temporary storage area in memory used to store data until the device can process it.

Bus-mastering
In bus-mastering, the network adapter takes control of the system bus, allowing the CPU to perform other processing. Bus-mastering is performed in ISA, Micro Channel, and EISA machines and can increase performance.

C

CHKDSK
CHKDSK is a DOS utility used to analyze the data on a disk and report on the number of bad sectors, lost clusters, free space, and volume information.

Client
In networking, client refers to the operating system a workstation is using or emulating. NetWare supports DOS, OS/2, Macintosh, and UNIX clients.

COMMAND.COM
The COMMAND.COM file translates DOS commands into actions. For example, when you type DIR to look at a directory of the files in a subdirectory, the command interpreter issues the command to the DOS filing system to display a list of the files in the current subdirectory.

CONFIG.SYS
The CONFIG.SYS file governs the configuration of the operating system, such as the number of files and buffers available to the system and the basic memory structure. Device drivers, such as memory managers, run from the CONFIG.SYS file.

Connection-oriented
Connection-oriented protocols such as SPX and TCP require that a connection between peer partners be established before transmission begins and that the connection be disconnected after.

Connectionless
Connectionless protocols such as IP and IPX do not require that a connection exist before data transmission. Connectionless transport protocols prove best-effort, nonguaranteed delivery.

D

Direct Memory Access
Some network adapters use DMA to transfer data to or from system memory without using the CPU.

Domain
A domain is a grouping of objects or elements for administrative purposes. Microsoft's network implementations are domain-based.

Dynamic
Dynamic refers to the ability of the file server to allocate memory as needed, by loading and unloading modules. It also refers to the network's ability to reroute data transfers between nodes in response to traffic patterns.

E

Ethernet
Ethernet is a media access method with a theoretical maximum transmission speed of 10Mbps. It is a contention-based access method that has been codified as IEEE specification 802.3.

ETHERNET_802.2
ETHERNET_802.2 is the default NetWare frame type used in NetWare v3.1x and 4.x networks. It replaces ETHERNET_802.3 as the default frame type.

ETHERNET_802.3
ETHERNET_802.3 was formerly the default NetWare frame type used in NetWare v2.x.

ETHERNET_II
ETHERNET_II is the frame type often used for IP.

ETHERNET_SNAP
ETHERNET_SNAP is the frame type most often used for Macintosh or IP.

EtherTalk
EtherTalk is Apple Computer's Ethernet implementation for the Macintosh environment.

F

Fairness
Generally bus-mastering devices will hold the system bus until they have completed the DMA data transfer or until the next video refresh cycle. However, when multiple bus-mastering adapters are installed in the same machine, they must give up the bus more often. The criteria for doing this are based upon the priority of the DMA channel on the adapter and an algorithm called fairness. Most of the drivers for bus-mastering devices invoke fairness. For those drivers that do not invoke fairness, you can sometimes manipulate the adapters' time on and off the bus.

FDDI
The Fiber Distributed Data Interface (FDDI) is a media access method with a theoretical maximum throughput of 100Mbps. FDDI uses a token-passing protocol and consists of a ring topology of fiber-optic connected nodes.

File Transfer Protocol (FTP)
The File Transfer Protocol (FTP) is an Application Layer protocol designed to facilitate the moving of files between workstations.

Flow control
Flow control is used to ensure that the sender of data does not overwhelm the receiver. This is accomplished by the two systems cooperating to establish a sliding window of data. The stream is increased until retransmissions are required; then the speed of transmission is reduced.

H

High Performance File System (HPFS)
HPFS is the name of the file system employed by OS/2. It allows long file names.

I

IBM LAN Support IBM developed the IBM LAN Support Program to provide IEEE 802.2 connectivity in a DOS environment for its token-ring products.

ICMP
The Internet Control Message Protocol provides diagnostic features in the TCP/IP protocol suite.

INTERLNK
Some versions of MS-DOS and PC-DOS include the program INTERLNK, which lets you connect your laptop to your desktop machine through a null modem cable and use the drives from your laptop as if they were drives on your local machine. The need for this program is obviated by a network.

Internetwork Packet Exchange (IPX)
IPX is the network transport protocol NetWare uses.

L

LANSUP
In a desire to gain some of the IBM connectivity market, Novell jointly developed a driver with IBM that would interoperate with both NetWare and IBM LAN products. Called the LANSUP driver, it is still the preferred method of communication between NetWare clients and IBM products.

LocalTalk
LocalTalk is the media access protocol for Apple networks. It has a transmission speed of 230 characters per second and uses twisted-pair cable. LocalTalk is a contention-based network.

Logical Link Control (LLC)
The OSI Data-Link layer is divided into two sublayers: the Logical Link Control layer and the Media Access Control Layer. The LLC provides access to the OSI Network Layer protocols.

M

Media Access Control (MAC)
The OSI Data-Link layer is divided into two sublayers: the Logical Link Control layer and the Media Access Control layer. The MAC provides access to the OSI Physical Layer.

MEMMAKER.EXE
The MEMMAKER program optimizes a computer's memory. This program evaluates a system and determines the most effective memory scheme. It attempts to load as many programs into upper memory as possible to provide you with as much free memory in the lower 640KB for running programs. MEMMAKER.EXE will also configure expanded and extended memory to your specifications.

Miniport
A Miniport driver is an NDIS driver that relies on a tighter integration with Microsoft code and a wrapper that handles a lot of the operations contained in the full MAC version driver. As a result, you have a smaller faster driver. Many of the drivers written for Windows NT are Miniport drivers.

MSD.EXE
MSD is a utility for users of MS-DOS or Windows that shows you most of the system and configuration files, and also displays a memory map of the system it is run on. MSD can be useful in determining interrupt and address conflicts within your system. It also contains an editor to allow you to edit your configuration files, including the CONFIG.SYS, AUTOEXEC.BAT, and Windows .INI files.

Multiple Link Interface Driver (MLID)
The MLID represents the LAN adapter driver in Open Data-Link Interface implementations.

N

NET.CFG
After installation is completed, you will need to create the configuration file for NetWare, called the NET.CFG file, with an ASCII text editor. This file contains the settings for the Open Data-Link Interface (ODI) Link Support Layer (LSL), IPXODI, the adapter driver, and the Virtual Loadable Modules (VLM) or NETX.

NET$DOS.SYS
In diskless workstations, you must create a boot image file for the workstation's ROM to download. The default name for the file is NET$DOS.SYS. It is contained in the LOGIN subdirectory.

NetBEUI
NetBEUI, developed by Microsoft, is a variant of IBM's NetBIOS. With Windows for Workgroups and Windows 95, Microsoft abandoned NetBEUI as its default net-

work transport protocol. They now use a Microsoft version of IPX/SPX that is fully compatible with NetWare and is routable.

NetBIOS
NetBIOS is the protocol and API IBM developed for the IBM PC Network.

NetWare Core Protocol (NCP)
NCP is Novell NetWare's request/response protocol.

Network Driver Interface Specification (NDIS)
NDIS is a driver specification that allows a single driver to communicate with multiple protocol stacks. It is used in both Microsoft and Novell network implementations.

O

Open Data-Link Interface (ODI)
ODI is Novell and Apple's driver specification that allows a single driver to communicate with multiple protocol stacks. It is used in both Microsoft and Novell network implementations.

P

Point to Point Protocol (PPP)
PP provides support for asynchronous serial line communication in IP networks.

R

RARP
The Reverse Address Resolutions Protocol (RARP) provides physical-adapter-to-IP address resolution.

Redirector
In networking, redirection is the process that diverts data from its original destination to another. For example, in NetWare, the redirector accepts requests and determines if they are for a network drive or for a local DOS driver.

S

SCANDISK
SCANDISK is a graphical utility that verifies the entire hard drive as well as performs surface scans.

Serial Line IP (SLIP)
Serial Line IP (SLIP) has been defined to support serial line connections in IP networks.

Sequenced Packet Exchange (SPX)
SPX is Novell's connection-oriented guaranteed delivery protocol, used primarily for diagnostics and printing.

Simple Internet Protocol (SIP)
To solve the problem of address shortages in IP networks, a new protocol called the Simple Internet Protocol or SIP has been proposed. SIP uses a 64-bit address rather than IP's 32-bit addressing. SIP will be fully compatible with IP.

Simple Mail Transfer Protocol (SMTP)
SMTP is the Internet mail protocol.

STARTNET.BAT
STARTNET.BAT is located in the \NWCLIENT subdirectory or the directory you specify and loads the NetWare drivers.

T

TELNET
TELNET is the standard TCP/IP remote login protocol.

Token-ring
Token-ring is a media access method with a theoretical maximum throughput of 4 or 16Mbps. It employs a token-passing protocol and is configured in a star-wired ring topology. It has two implementations: IEEE 802.5 or IBM Token-Ring.

TOKEN_RING
TOKEN_RING is the NetWare default frame type.

TOKEN_RING_SNAP
TOKEN_RING_SNAP is the frame type used for NetWare IP and Macintosh connections.

TokenTalk
TokenTalk is the token-ring implementation for Apple networks.

U

User Datagram Protocol (UDP)
When TCP was split into TCP and IP, a new protocol was developed to provide the transport protocol for applications that did not need extensive error checking—the protocol developed was the User Datagram Protocol (UDP).

V

Virtual Loadable Modules (VLMs)
In NetWare, the VLM has replaced NETX as the module that allows a workstation to communicate with a NetWare server.

Acronym List

A

API	Application Programming Interface
ARP	Address Resolution Protocol

D

DLL	Dynamic Link Libraries
DMA	Direct Memory Addressing
DPMI	DOS Protected Mode Interface
DPMS	DOS Protected Mode Services

E

EISA	Extended Industry Standard Architecture

F

FAT	File Allocation Table

FDDI	Fiber Distributed Data Interface
FTP	File Transfer Protocol

H

HPFS	High Performance File System

I

ICMP	Internet Control Message Protocol
IETF	Internet Engineering Task Force
IPX/SPX	Internetwork Packet Exchange/Sequenced Packet Exchange
ISA	Industry Standard Architecture

L

LLC	Logical Link Control
LSL	Link Support Layer

M

MAC	Media Access Control
MLID	Multiple Link Interface Driver

N

NCP	NetWare Core Protocol
NDIS	Network Driver Interface Specification

NDS	NetWare Directory Services
NFS	NetWare File System
NFS	Network File System
NTFS	Windows NT File System

O

ODI	Open Data-Link Interface

P

PPP	Point to Point Protocol

R

RARP	Reverse Address Resolution Protocol
RFC	Request for Comment

S

SAPS	Service Access Points
SIP	Simple Internet Protocol
SLIP	Serial Line IP
SMTP	Simple Mail Transfer Protocol
SNMP	Simple Network Management Protocol
SPX	Sequenced Packet Exchange

U

UDP	User Datagram Protocol (UDP)
UMB	Upper Memory Block

V

VLM	Virtual Loadable Modules

Vendor List

3Com Corp.
5400 Bayfront Plaza
Santa Clara, CA 95052-8145
(800) NET-3COM; (408) 764-5000
Fax: (408) 764-5032

A

Accton Technology Corp.
1962 Zanker Road
San Jose, CA 95112
(800) 926-9288; (408) 452-8900
Fax: (408) 452-8988

Accu-Tech Corp.
200 Hembree Park Drive
Roswell, GA 30076-3890
(404) 751-9473
Fax: (404) 475-4659

Acculogic
13715 Alton Parkway
Irvine, CA 92716
(714) 454-2441; (800) 234-7811
Fax: (714) 454-8527

ADC Kentrox
14375 NW Science Park Drive
Portland, OR 97229
(800) 733-5511; (503) 643-1681
Fax: (503) 641-3341

Addtron Technology Co. Ltd.
47968 Fremont Blvd.
Fremont, CA 94538
(800) 998-4638; (510) 770-0120

Allied Telesis
575 E. Middlefield Road
Mountain View, CA 94043
(800) 424-4284
Fax: (415) 964-8250

Alta Research Corp.
600 S. Federal Highway
Deerfield Beach, FL 33441
(800) 423-8535; (305) 428-8535
Fax: (305) 428-8678

Andrew Corp.
10500 W. 153rd St.
Orland Park, IL 60462
(800) 328-2696
Fax: (800) 861-1700

Artisoft
2202 N. Forbes Blvd.
Tucson, AZ 85745
(800) 233-5564
Fax: (602) 670-7359

Asante Technologies
821 Fox Lane
San Jose, CA 95131
(800) 662-9686; (408) 435-8388
Fax: (408) 432-7511

Attachmate Corp.
3617 131st Ave. SE
Bellevue, WA 98006
(800) 426-6283; (206) 644-4010
Fax: (206) 747-9924

B

Bay Networks
4401 Great America Parkway
PO Box 58185
Santa Clara, CA 95052-8185
(800) PRO-NTWK
Fax: (408) 988-5525

Boca Research
6413 Congress Ave.
Boca Raton, FL 33487
(407) 997-6227
Fax: (407) 997-0918

C

Cabletron Systems
35 Industrial Way
Rochester, NH 03867
(603) 332-9400
Fax: (603) 337-2444

Cameo Communications
71 Spitbrook Road
Nashua, NH 03060
(800) 438-4827; (603) 888-8869
Fax: (603) 888-8906

Canary Communications
1851 Zanker Road
San Jose, CA 95112-4213
(800) 883-9201; (408) 453-9201
Fax: (408) 453-0940

Chipcom Corp.
118 Turnpike Road
Southborough, MA 01772
(800) 228-9930; (508) 460-8900
Fax: (508) 460-8950

CNet Technology Corp.
2199 Zanker Road
San Jose, CA 95131
(408) 954-8000
Fax: (408) 954-8866

Codenoll Technology Corp.
1086 N. Broadway
Yonkers, NY 10701
(914) 965-6300
Fax: (914) 965-9811

Cogent Data Technologies
175 West St., PO Box 926
Friday Harbor, WA 98250
(800) 426-4368; (208) 378-2929
Fax: (206) 378-2882

Compaq Computer Corp.
PO Box 692000
Houston, TX 77269-2000
(800) 345-1518

Compaq Internetworking Products Group (formerly Thomas-Conrad Corp.)
13300 Technology Blvd.
Austin, TX 78759
(512) 433-6000; (800) 332-8683

Compex
4051 E. La Palma
Anaheim, CA 92807
(800) 279-8891; (714) 830 7302
Fax: (714) 630-6521

D

D-Link Systems
5 Musick
Irvine, CA 92718
(800) 326-1688; (714) 455-1688
Fax: (714) 455-2521

Data Interface Corp.
11130 Jolleyville Road, Suite 300
Austin, TX 78759
(800) 351-4244; (512) 346-5641
Fax: (512) 346-4035

David Systems
615 Tasman Drive
Sunnyvale, CA 94088-3718
(800) 762-7848; (408) 541-6000
Fax: (408) 541-8985

Dayna Communications
Sorenson Research Park, 849 W. Levoy Drive
Salt Lake City, UT 84123
(801) 269-7200
Fax: (801) 269-7363

DFI
135 Main Ave.
Sacramento, CA 95838
(918) 568-1234
Fax: (916) 568-1233

Digi International
6400 Flying Cloud Drive
Eden Prairie, MN 55344
(612) 943-9020; (800) 344-4273
Fax: (612) 943-5398

Digital Equipment Corp.
550 King St, LKGl -3/J17
Littleton, MA 01460
(800) DIGITAL; (508) 486-6963
Fax: (508) 486-6311

E

Eagle Technology
2202 N. Forbes Blvd.
Tucson, AZ 85745
(800) 233-5564
Fax: (602) 670-7359

Eicon Technology
2196 32nd Ave. (Lachine)
Montreal, QUE H8T 3H7 Canada
(800) 80-EICON
Fax: (214) 239-3304

F

Fibermux Corp.
21415 Plummer St.
Chatsworth, CA 91311
(800) 800-4624
Fax: (818) 709-1556

FTP Software
2 High St.
North Andover, MA 01645
(800) 282-4FTP; (508) 685-3300
Fax: (508) 794-4477

G

Gandalf Technologies
Cherry Hill Industrial Center - 9
Cherry Hill, NJ 08003-1688
(800) GANDALF
Fax: (613) 226-1717

General Technology Corp.
415 Pineda Court
Melbourne, FL 32940
(800) 274-2733; (407) 242-2733
Fax: (407) 254-1407

GVC Technologies
376 Lafayette Road
Sparta, NJ 07871
(201) 579-3630
Fax: (201) 579-2702

H

Hayes Microcomputer Products
5835 Peachtree Corners East
Norcross, GA 30092
(404) 441-1617
Fax: (404) 449-0087

Hewlett-Packard Co., Roseville Networks Div.
8000 Foothills Blvd.
Roseville, CA 95747
(800) 533-1333
Fax: (800) 333-1917

Hummingbird Communications Ltd.
2900 John St.
Markham, ONT L3R 5G3 Canada
(905) 470-1203
Fax: (905) 470-1207

I

IBM Corp.
PO Box 12195, Department CO9/B060
Research Triangle Park, NC 27709
(800) IBM-CALL; (800) IBM-CARY
Fax: (800) 2-IBM or (800) IBM-4

IBM Corp., DatagLANce Network Analyzer Development
Dept. E67, Bldg. 660, PO Box 12195
Research Triangle Park, NC 27709
(919) 254-1364
Fax: (800) IBM-4

IMC Networks
16931 Millikan Ave.
Irvine. CA 92714
(714) 724-1070
Fax: (714) 724-1020

Intel Corp.
5200 NE Elam Young Parkway
Hillsboro, OR 97124
(800) 538-3373
Fax: (800) 525-3019

InterConnections
14711 NE 29th Place
Bellevue, WA 98007
(800) 950-5773; (206) 881-4023
Fax: (206) 867-5022

Interphase Corp.
13800 Senlac
Dallas, TX 75234-8823
(800) FASTNET; (214) 919-9111

Ipswitch
669 Main Street
Wakefield, MA 01880
(617) 246-1150
Fax: (617) 245-2975

J

James River Group
125 N. First St.
Minneapolis, MN 55401
(612) 339-2521

K

Katron Technologies
7400 Harwin Drive, Suite 120
Houston, TX 77036
(713) 266-3891
Fax: (713) 266-3893

Kingston Technology Corp.
17600 Newhope St.
Fountain Valley, CA 92708
(800) 435-2620; (714) 435-2600
Fax: (714) 435-2699

Klever Computers
1028 W. Maude Ave.
Sunnyvale, CA 94086
(800) 745-4660
Fax: (408) 735-7723

L

LANCAST
10 Northern Blvd., Unit 5
Amherst, NH 03031
(800) 752-2768
Fax: (603) 881-9888

Lantronix
15353 Barranca Parkway
Irvine, CA 92718
(800) 422-7055; (714) 453-3990
Fax: (714) 453-3995

M

Madge Networks
2310 N. First St.
San Jose, CA 95131
(800) 876-2343; (408) 955-0700
Fax: (408) 955-0970

Megahertz Corp., a division of U.S. Robotics
605 N. 5600 W., PO Box 16020
Salt Lake City, UT 84116
(800) LAPTOPS
Fax: (801) 320-6022

MICOM Communications Corp.
4100 Los Angeles Ave.
Simi Valley, CA 93063
(800) 642-6687; (805) 583-8600
Fax: (805) 583-1997

Microdyne Corp.
3601 Eisenhower Ave.
Alexandria, VA 22304
(800) 255-3967
Fax: (703) 683-8924

Microtest
4747 N. 22nd St.
Phoenix, AZ 85016-4708
(800) 526-9675
Fax: (802) 952-6401

MiLAN Technology Corp.
894 Ross Drive
Sunnyvale, CA 94089-1443
(800) G0-MiLAN; (408) 752-2770
Fax: (408) 752-2790

N

National Semiconductor Corp.
M/S D3-615, PO Box 58090, 2900 Semiconductor Drive
Santa Clara, CA 95052-8090
(800) 227-1817, ext. 100
Fax: (408) 721-7662

Net Manage
10725 North De Anza Blvd.
Cupertino, CA 95014
(408) 973-7171
Fax: (408) 257-6405

Network Equipment Technologies (NET)
800 Saginaw Drive
Redwood City, CA 94063-4740
(415) 366-4400
Fax: (415) 780-5160

Network General Corp.
4200 Bohannon St.
Menlo Park, CA 94025
(415) 473-2000

Network Peripherals
1371 McCarthy Blvd.
Milpitas, CA 95035
(800) NPI-8855
Fax: (408) 321-9218

NetWorth (Compaq Internetworking Products Group)
8404 Esters Blvd.
Irving, TX 75063
(800) 544-5255; (214) 929-1700
Fax: (214) 929-1720

Newbridge Networks
594 Herndon Parkway
Herndon, VA 22070
(800) DO-VIVID; (703) 834-3600
Fax: (703) 708-5959

Novell
122 E. 1700 S
Provo, UT 84606
(800) NETWARE; (801) 429-5588

O

Olicom USA
900 W. Park Blvd., Suite 180
Plano, TX 75074
(800) 2-OLICOM
Fax: (214) 423-7261

P

Plustek USA
1362 Bordeau Drive
Sunnyvale, CA 94089
(408) 745-7111
Fax: (408) 745-7562

Proteon
9 Technology Drive
Westborough, MA 01581
(415) 960-1630
Fax: (415) 964-5181

R

Racal InterLan
155 Swanson Road
Boxborough, MA 01719
(800) LAN-TALK
Fax: (508) 263-8655

Racore Computer Products
170 Knowles Drive, Suite 204
Los Gatos, CA 95030
(800) 635-1274; (408) 374-8290
Fax: (408) 374-8290

Rockwell Network Systems
7402 Hollister Ave.
Santa Barbara, CA 93117
(800) 262-8023
Fax: (805) 968-6478

Rose Electronics
10850 Wilcrest, 900
Houston, TX 77092
(800) 333-9343; (713) 933-7673
Fax: (713) 933-0044

S

SilCom Manufacturing Technology
4854 Old National Highway, Suite 110
Atlanta, GA 30337
(800) 388-3807; (404) 767-0706
Fax: (404) 767-0709

Silicom Connectivity Solutions
15311 NE 90th St.
Redmond, WA 98052
(800) 474-5426; (206) 882-7995
Fax: (206) 882-4775

Solectek Corp.
6370 Nancy Ridge Drive, Suite 109
San Diego, CA 92121-3212
(800) 437-1518
Fax: (619) 457-2681

Spry
316 Occidental Ave. S, Suite 200
Seattle, WA 98104
(800) 777-9638; (208) 447-0300
Fax: (208) 447-9008

Standard Microsystems Corp.
80 Arkay Drive
Hauppauge, NY 11788
(800) SMC-4-YOU; (516) 435-6900
Fax: (516) 273-1803

SysKonnect
1922 Zanker Road
San Jose, CA 95112
(800) SK2-FDDI; (408) 725-4650
Fax: (408) 725-4654

T

T3plus Networking
3393 Octavius Drive
Santa Clara, CA 95054
(408) 727-5151; (800) 477-7585
Fax: (408) 727-5151

Top Microsystems Corp.
3320 Victor Court
Santa Clara, CA 95054
(800) 827-8721; (408) 980-9813
Fax: (408) 980-8626

X

Xinetron
2302 Walsh Ave.
Santa Clara, CA 95051
(800) 345-4415; (408) 727-5509
Fax: (408) 727-6499

Xircom
26025 Mureau Road
Calabasas, CA 91302
(800) 874-7875; (818) 878-7600
Fax: (818) 878-7830; (818) 878-7175

Z

ZERO ONE Networking
4920 E. La Palma Ave.
Anaheim, CA 92807
(714) 693-0804
Fax: (714) 693-0705

INDEX